6o Beautiful Bat Facts

Facts

A Handy Guide for Writers & the Bat Curious

Jess Schira

CONTENTS

Acknowledgements

Blurb Written by: Em Taylor

Editing/Proofreading by: BZ Hercules

Introduction

If you stopped a group of random people on the street and asked them to share their bat knowledge, expect the answers to include:

- "Not much."
- "They're horrible, dirty animals that carry all kinds of diseases that make humans and pets sick, which is why all bats should be killed."
- "I hate bats."
- "Batman!"
- "Bats are dirty."
- "Witches and Satanists are the only people who like bats."
- "Dracula turned into a bat."
- "Bats destroy homes."
- "Bats have rabies."

The interesting thing about these answers is that, while people are quick to share their feelings about bats, most of what they share has little to do with reality and is actually based on thousands of years' worth of superstition and hysteria.

Look at any point in history and you'll find examples of humans reacting badly to bats, particularly to microbats.

1

Folklore from numerous cultures contains countless examples of bats being accused of malicious acts, including consorting with witches, serving as minions for the devil, or being the reincarnation of someone who was filled with evil and hate during their human existence. Even today, when most societies have put superstition behind them, bats continue to get a bad rap. A surprising number of people aren't willing or able to forget about centuries-old beliefs.

Times are slowly changing.

During the past thirty to forty years, scientific interest in bats has kicked off. Every year, field studies and lab tests involving bats improve our knowledge of the tiny mammals. The studies reveal that instead of being terrifying harbingers of death, bats are passive animals who have sweet natures, fascinating social lives, and some remarkable skill sets. Most importantly, all bats, from the Kitti's hog-nosed bat to the Malaysian flying fox bat, play a vital role in our delicate ecosystem.

Despite all that's been learned, science has only begun unraveling the mysterious lives of bats. Despite all the time, energy, and money that's been dedicated to bat research, hundreds of species remain unexplored. The imagination races at the thought of all the different things each of those species might teach us, assuming they don't become extinct before science has an opportunity to observe them.

The great thing about bats is that the more you get to know about them, the less scary and the more amazing they become, until you suddenly fall in love with these marvelous creatures.

One quick note, I arranged the chapters of this book so that if a species is mentioned in a chapter, the following chapter is packed full of information about that species, provided I was able to find a chapter's worth of information.

Bats in Flight

Figure 1 ©art8MB
Acquired via Photo Deposit

10 Fast Bat Facts

- Bats aren't rodents or birds. They make up their own genus, which is called Chiroptera, a Latin word that means "hand wing."
- More than 6 million U.S. and Canadian bats have lost their lives to White-Nose Syndrome.
- There are one-thousand-plus different species of bats, which equals 20% of the Earth's mammal population.
- Bats were once a popular ingredient in love potions and "medicines."
- Bats account for approximately 50% of rain-forest-dwelling mammals.
- Apart from Antarctica and some extreme desert regions, bats live in every part of the world.
- White-Nose Syndrome research might unlock the key to curing AIDS.
- Carl Linnaeus believed bats and humans shared a common ancestor.
- Some plants rely exclusively on bats for pollination.
- Bat guano was a discussion point during President Fillmore's first State of the Union Address.

Spectacled Flying Fox

Figure 2 ©Beth Baisch
Acquired via Dreamstime.com

Beautiful Bat Fact #1
People Fear Bats

Do you screech and duck when a bat swoops down from a tree and glides over your head? Does the sight of a bat in your kitchen cause you to cover your head with a towel before running from the room? If so, you're not alone. Lots of people, myself included, have the same response. It's called the startle reaction.

Spooking at a bat isn't something to be ashamed of. In fact, studies indicate that a strong startle reaction is a good thing.

Unraveling the Startle Response

All mammals are born with a startle reaction, which is connected to the sympathetic nervous system. Experts believe it's nature's way of providing a natural defense against sudden attacks. It's an important component in our intuitive flight or fight reasoning.

In 1951, Frank Pierce Jones created an experiment that allowed him to "see" exactly how the startle response travels through the body. He watched the neck muscles contract, causing the head to jerk while the muscles around their eyes tightened. The participant's nervous system sent electrical pulses to their abdominal muscles, which tightened in preparation for a possible blow while the chest flattened. At nearly the same time, the individual's arms and shoulders stiffened, lifting into a defensive position while the knees flexed. At the same time, the heart rate, blood pressure, and respiration rates increased. Time and again, Jones watched this happen. Jones noted that while it took less than a split second for the participant's entire body to react to the perceived threat, it took a great deal longer for them to calm down once they realized they were safe.

So, instead of being embarrassed the next time you duck and swerve when a bat flies too close to your head, take comfort from the knowledge that your sympathetic nervous system is in perfect working order and prepared to handle any unexpected challenge that comes your way.

Once you've gotten over the initial surprise of seeing a bat, your blood pressure should return to normal and you'll remember that the bat means you no harm.

If you don't relax, or if just the thought of encountering a bat triggers a panic attack, you have chiroptophobia.

Symptoms of chiroptophobia include:

- Heart palpitations
- Uncontrollable screaming/crying
- Hysteria
- Hyperventilating
- Intense anxiety
- Nausea

What Triggers Chiroptophobia?

Phobias such as chiroptophobia are irritating and baffling. Few understand why they react so strongly to the mere sight of a bat and are often ashamed of their behavior, especially when they can't overcome the problem, despite telling themselves there's nothing to worry about.

There are different hypotheses about why phobias develop. One research team gathered data that indicated 45% of people who experience an intense fear reaction when they encounter an animal inherited the phobia. Even if the phobia wasn't passed genetically from parent to offspring, the potential to develop a phobia was.

The research team revealed that in the case of siblings, one can be bitten by a dog and never develop any fear, yet their sibling who wasn't bitten, and who might not have even witnessed the event, becomes fearful of all dogs simply because they inherited slightly different genetic material.

Some experts believe learned behavior also plays a role in the development of phobias such as chiroptophobia. If a child spends a great deal of time with someone who reacts badly whenever they see a bat, there's a strong possibility that the child will eventually become equally fearful.

In the case of bats, it's likely that most people don't develop chiroptophobia because of an incident, but rather in response to the symbolism and mythology connected to bats.

As a rule, humans and bats generally only see one another during twilight, a time of day when many of us are on edge and hyperaware of perceived threats, partly because the dimming light sharpens our flight instincts and partly because starting at an early age, we're told dreadful things come out after the sun sets. This creates an instinctive wariness of bats that's compounded by the fact that bats play a key role in many old vampire stories and Halloween tales.

The biggest reason people provided when asked about chiroptophobia is that the person is afraid that getting close to a bat will result in them contracting a horrible disease, like rabies.

It's true that bats are carriers for a number of zoonotic diseases, but the odds of them passing the disease on to you are slim. In the case of rabies, a disease that's passed from animal to human via saliva, only 5% of the bat population is infected, and most of those live in remote areas where they never encounter humans. Personally, I think that 5% is an extremely high estimate, and that it's based on a huge bat population, not individual colonies. The number doesn't mean that 5% of the bat colony that roosts in the tree on the edge of your property are rabid.

Another thing to keep in mind is that unlike dogs, who become aggressive once the disease matures in their system, rabid bats don't attack humans. They simply die. The only time they bite is when handled by a human or threatened by another animal.

The best way to avoid catching a disease from a bat is wearing heavy gloves when handling a downed bat. If you do receive a bat bite, immediately visit your doctor and get a rabies vaccine.

These concerns fester in the mind until even the thought of encountering a bat becomes unbearable. As a result, people who suffer from chiroptophobia do everything they can to ensure that they don't see a bat. If a bat is unfortunate enough to make its way into a house where a person with chiroptophobia lives, it's likely the first thing that person does is call a lethal exterminator.

It's Possible to Overcome Chiroptophobia

For the most part, it's possible to avoid bats, so most people don't seek treatment for their chiroptophobia; however, if you do want help, doctors who specialize in treating phobias use exposure therapy to help patients overcome their fears. Treatments begin with looking at pictures or videos of bats, and end with getting as up close and personal with a bat as possible.

Most people find that simply learning about how beautiful and good bats really are goes a long way towards easing their chiroptophobia symptoms, making it possible for them to explore ways that they can live in harmony with bats.

Resting Fruit Bat

Figure 3 ©Farinosa
Acquired via Deposit Photo

Beautiful Bat Fact #2
What Are Bats?

When you ask someone what a bat is, the answer you're most likely to receive is that they're a flying mouse/rat.

It's the wrong answer.

Not only are bats NOT flying mice/rats, they're not even rodents. They're no more closely related to mice, squirrels, rats, muskrats, or capybaras than humans are. Bats make up their very own classification of animals, called chiropterans, a word that translates to "hand-wing."

There's some debate about exactly how many different bat species exist. Depending on the source, the number ranges from about 900 to 1,000. Either way, it's a lot of bats. The sheer number of bat species found scattered around the world adds up to approximately 20% of the Earth's classified mammals. Every few years or so, another species is identified. Rodents are the only classification of mammal that contains more individual species than bats.

Because of the sheer number of different bat species, scientists use multiple things such as size, diet, and location to classify each individual species.

Big Bats, Little Bats, and Everything In-between

Bats are grouped into two size categories. There are

microbats and megabats.

These terms make classifying bats seem like an easy task, but once you start looking at a few different types of bats, you realize that knowing what classification a particular species falls into is much harder than anyone would expect. For example, it's easy to see how the enormous golden-crowned and Malayan flying fox bats with their six-foot wing spans are megabats and how the two-gram Kitti's hog-nosed bat is a microbat. Where things get more complicated is when you're looking at species such as the big brown bat, the Samoan flying fox bat, and the hundreds of other bat species that fall into the middle of the spectrum. Are they megabats or microbats?

Chiroptera experts discovered some me specific characteristics to make the classification process easier.

Characteristics of microbats include:

- They're nocturnal
- Sophisticated echolocation system
- They have tails
- You won't see a claw on the tip of their second finger
- Their bodies are between 4 and 16 cm (1.5 and 6.29 in) long
- Their eyes are quite small
- Their inner ears are protected by a tiny flap of skin called a "tragus"

Characteristics of megabats include:

- They're fruit/nectar eaters
- They have a claw on their second finger
- Their eyes are huge
- No tail
- Excellent sense of smell

Insects, Flowers, Fruit, and Sometimes Blood

Diet determines which sub-category a bat species is placed into.

Approximately 70% of all bats species are insectivores and they consume an astonishing number of bugs each night. A single little brown bat can consume six hundred to one thousand mosquitos in a single hour. One experiment revealed that bats eat enough earworms to save the global corn industry $1 billion every single year.

The remaining 30% of bats can be broken down into nectar feeders, who are important in the fertilization of flowers, and fruit eaters, who help reseed forests, and vampire bats that exist on a diet that consists of nothing but blood. There are also a few bat species that eat fish and snack on frogs.

Learning about bats not only helps you gain a better appreciation for these marvelous creatures, but also allows you to decide which ones best suit the unique ecology of your backyard and explore ways to both attract and preserve that particular species.

The Many Faces of Bats

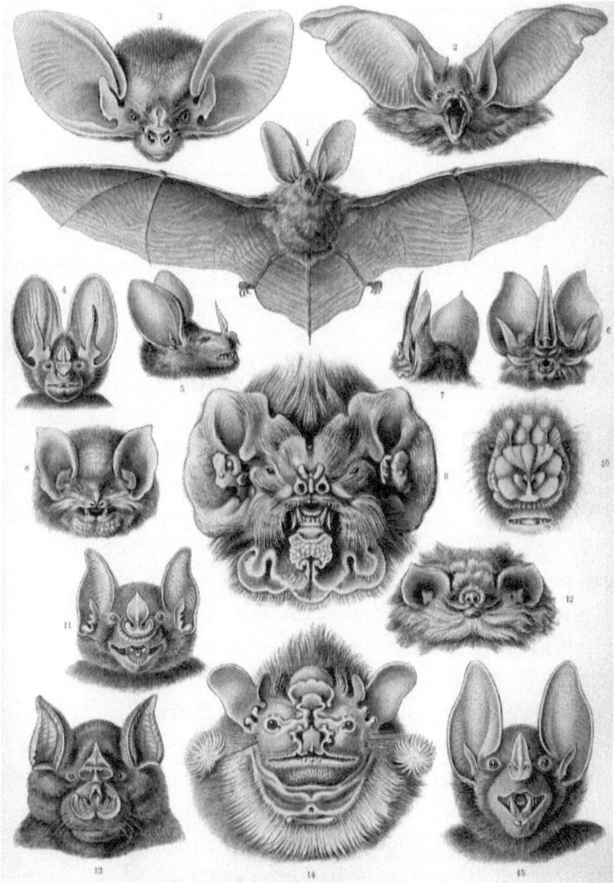

Figure 4 ©Ernst Haeckel

Beautiful Bat Fact #3
Giant Golden-Crowned and Malayan Flying Fox Bats: Sky Giants

Giant Golden-Crowned Flying Fox Bats

The sun is just starting to rise, indicating the end of your night fishing session on a reef near Mindanao Island. As you gather up your supplies, a movement in the sky catches your eye. Glancing up, you expect to see a large sea bird, perhaps even a critically endangered Philippine eagle, but the animal silhouetted against the rising sun isn't a Philippine eagle or even a bird for that matter. Not only is the flight pattern different, but the general shape of this massive winged creature is also off. A quick peek with a pair of binoculars reveals that it's not a bird at all, but rather an enormous bat with a nearly black body and long wings. Almost as if it knows you're watching, the bat tips its head to the side, just far enough for you to spy the patch of yellow on top of its narrow skull.

You're watching a giant golden-crowned flying fox bat (*Acerodon jubatus*) make its way home after spending the night picking fruit.

Outside of a zoo or sanctuary, the only place you'll find representatives of the species is in the Philippines, where they spend their days in the rain forest's canopy. At night, they leave their roost and take to the sky, sometimes flying for 40 km (25 miles) while looking for something to eat.

While searching for food, they follow the path of waterways. It's unknown if they have always used the rivers to guide their flight, or if they developed the habit in response to fruit farmers setting up farms on the rich shores and the bats simply learned to go where the pickings were the easiest. This species is particularly fond of figs, but they'll happily eat other types of native fruits as well.

The role the giant golden-crowned flying foxes play in the Philippine's ecosystem is seed distribution.

While silhouetted against the sun, this megabat seems monster-sized. Their body is an impressive 290 mm (22 in) long and their 1.5 – 1.7 meter (4.92-5.57 foot) wingspan dwarfs many of the birds that share the sky with the bat. However, at a mere 1.2 kg (2 lbs.), the bat is quite a bit smaller than most laying hens. For example, the average adult Rhode Island Red hen weighs a hefty 2.72 kg (6 lbs.)

While the golden-crowned flying fox is a lightweight in comparison to the average hen, its size does make it one of the world's biggest bat species.

In addition to being big, the species is quite striking. The crown of bright gold fur for which it is named stretches down the back of its neck, striking a delightful contrast to its russet fur. It has one of the prettiest faces. The combination of sharply pointed features, pronounced cheekbones, expressive eyes, and triangle-shaped ears bears a remarkable resemblance to foxes. But don't be fooled by the foxy face. Scientists and genetic experts have spent a great deal of time comparing the genetic markers of both flying fox bats and four-legged foxes, and there's no proof that the two species share a common ancestor. The only thing they have in common beyond their pretty faces is that they're both mammals.

During the day, members of the giant golden-crowned family like to hang out in large colonies and snooze in the tree canopy where their coloring and upside-down sleeping position makes it very difficult for predators to spot the bats. They look like dried, curled up leaves.

Having a naturally social personality, the giant golden-crowned bat prefers to roost in colonies, and the more bats in a colony, the happier everyone is. Before hunting and habitat destruction started taking a toll on these gentle giants, the colonies sometimes exceeded 100,000 bats, and the species isn't picky about who it hangs out with. They're happy to share their roosting spots and are often spotted hanging out with Malayan flying fox bats.

In addition to sleeping, giant golden-crowned fox bats adore personal grooming sessions. They'll spend large chunks of their time hanging out near a safe water source, scooping up large amounts of the water with their wings, and pouring it over their heads.

There have been instances of cave explorers, hikers, and spelunkers getting startled when they entered a cave and found a small colony of giant golden-crowned flying foxes. For reasons no one understands, sometimes a group of the bats choose to roost within deep caves, providing that the cave has multiple exit options and a source of water.

The giant golden-crowned fox bat is highly prized by hunters who sell both its luxurious pelt and sweet meat. The way that the species roosts in large batches makes it easy for the hunters to capture and hunt a large number of the bats in a very short period of time.

In an attempt to preserve this gorgeous bat, 57 km (14,000 acres) in the Subic Bay region has been set aside as a refuge for the animals. In addition to being a place that protects the magnificent bats from hunters, the area is also used by researchers who are interested in the species.

The overall population of the giant golden-crowned flying fox bats has significantly declined over the past three generations. The IUCN has classified the species as endangered and states that the current decline is approximately 10-15% every single year.

Malayan Flying Foxes

The giant golden-crowned flying fox is big, but with adult males often tipping the scales between 645 g and 100 g (about 2-3 lbs.) and developing a 1.7-meter (6 ft.) wingspan, Malayan flying foxes (*Pteropus vampyrus*), which some people call large flying foes, are a bit bigger.

Adult Malayan flying foxes have a thick, dark coat and a ruff of lighter hair that ranges from reddish black to deep russet around their neck. During the breeding season, it's not uncommon for the neck fur to brighten. If you are at an educational exhibit that features representatives of the species, you'll notice that in addition to being slightly smaller than the males, the females also have softer, thinner fur.

Unlike many flying fox bat species that stick to a very limited range, there are lots of places you can go where you stand a good chance of spotting these magnificent creatures. Their range includes:

- Parts of Australia
- Madagascar
- Mainland Asia
- Southern Vietnam
- Timor
- East Philippines

As a rule, this species prefers to roost in swampy, tropical areas, and generally choose secondary forest roost sites. It's not at all uncommon for a tree that's been selected as a roost site to contain over a thousand bats. In Australia, Malayan flying foxes and giant golden-crowned flying foxes are frequently found roosting together. The species spends its day roosting and catching up on sleep.

At night, their appetites get the better of them and they leave the safety of their roost and go in search of food.

When they leave the roost to forage for fruit, they frequently head towards large agricultural plantations, where they are the most likely to find a nice selection of fruit. This species favors feeding grounds that are between 0.4 and 12 km away from their roost, though it's not unheard of for the adults to fly as far as 60 km (37 miles) when searching for something to eat.

When the Malayan flying foxes leave the roost and begin foraging, they fracture into smaller family groups. It's possible for one of these family units to fly just a few feet over your head without you hearing them since their echolocation pulses are higher pitched than your ears are designed to detect. That changes once the bats find something to eat. At that point, they go into a full-fledged feeding frenzy that includes cries, growls, wing beating, and even screaming. The noise can be quite unbearable.

Although the species prefers to eat fruit, they're also active pollinators. The average Malayan flying fox is particularly fond of mangroves.

When it comes to reforestation efforts, the Malayan flying fox bat is worth its weight in gold. The animal's large size allows it to easily carry even large seeds away with it. The fact that they range so far means the seeds get dispersed a long way from the parent tree, improving genetic diversification and the overall health of that particular type of fruit tree species.

The way people feel about Malayan flying foxes varies. Tourists love them and frequently spend quite a bit of time trying to get a nice picture of one of these massive bats while it's roosting or flying.

On the other hand, farmers are less impressed by the bats. They consider them pests and work hard to discourage the bat from feeding on their fruit crop.

Preferred methods used to drive the bats from fruit plantations include:

- Nets
- Whirling devices
- Bright lights

Since many believe that the Malayan flying fox may have been the species that introduced the Nipah virus to Malaysia, India, and Bangladesh, people who live in close contact with the species are wary of the bat and try to keep their distance.

Like a vast majority of bat species, Malayan flying foxes engage in polygynous behavior. Experts believe that a healthy male that exhibits good genetic characteristics will mate with approximately ten females during a single breeding season. A female resists fertilizing the egg until she's satisfied that the conditions are ideal for her to be able to maintain both her health and the health of her pup. Gestation takes six months and after its birth, she carries the pup with her wherever she goes until the young bat is old enough to stay at the roost with the offspring of its mother's harem mates. The mother doesn't fully wean the pup until it's two or three months old.

Although Malayan flying foxes typically roost in large groups that often include more than a thousand bats, experts have noted that within the huge colony, there are smaller, harem-style groups that include a handful of females and a single male. Males are diligent about protecting their harem, especially against the intrusion of bachelor males.

ICUN currently has the Malayan flying fox listed as Near Threatened. While the overall population is in a state of decline, it's decreasing at a rate that's currently less than 30% per ten years. The two main threats to the species are habitat destruction and hunting. ICUN believes that if something doesn't change soon, the species status will be changed to vulnerable.

Giant Golden Crowned Flying Fox Bat
(*Acerodon jubatus*)

Figure 5 ©Latorilla
CC-BY-SA-3.0 via Wikimedia Commons

Malayan Flying Fox Bat
(*Pteropus vampyrus*)

Figure 6 © mazzzur
Acquired via Deposit Photo

Flying Fox Colony Roosting

Figure 7 © Vassiliy Kochetkov
Acquired via Dreamstime.com

Beautiful Bat Fact #4
Kitti's Hog-Nosed Bat: Littlest Member of the Bat World

Prior to his death, Kitti Thonglongya worked as both a zoologist and an author. He co-authored a book, <u>Bats from Thailand and Cambodia</u>. He was also responsible for starting a taxonomic study of Thai bats.

Kitti Thonglongya loved searching for new species and that was exactly what he was doing when he suffered a sudden and fatal heart attack. His partner, John E. Hill, claims that when he found Thonglongya's body, he also discovered another body, this one a small bat that he'd never seen before. After confirming that this teeny-tiny bat was unclassified, Hill named the species after his fallen friend. Today, it's formally called the Kitti's hog-nosed bat (*Craseonycteris thonglongyai*) but is more commonly known as the bumblebee bat.

The original Kitti's hog-nosed bat was discovered in a part of Thailand that's now called the Sai Yok National Park and as far as anyone can tell, that area makes up the bulk of its range, though they have been spotted in some of Thailand's western sections and also in the southeastern part of Myanmar (formally Burma.)

The bat is small. Really small. So small it would have been easy for Hill to have overlooked the tiny animal when he discovered his fallen friend. Fully grown adults are only about an inch long and weigh about one-fourth of an ounce; that's less than a penny weighs! The good news is that thanks to its incredibly long wings, it's easier to spot the Kitti's hog-nosed bat while it's in flight. The average wing span is about 6.7 inches.

If you're lucky to get up close and personal with a Kitti's hog-nosed bat, you'll notice that while it does have a tail, a characteristic all microbats share, it's so tiny you can barely see it. The animal's most distinguishing feature is its nose, which looks just like the snout you'd see on the market hogs at your county fair. Its silky fur ranges from a pale red to an attractive shade of grey, which makes the bat.

The shape and size of the Kitti's hog-nosed bat has puzzled many experts. Its measurements are so odd that they can't figure out how it's able to fly, and yet it is a very athletic and beautiful flier. The combination of tiny body and long wings means that the species bears an uncanny resemblance the golden snitch that Harry Potter chased whenever he played a game of Quidditch. The species is equipped with extra webbing between their hind legs, which allows them to execute elaborate and technical aerial routines while the shape of their wings allows them to hover in mid-air.

In Myanmar, the entire Kitti's hog-nosed bat population is restricted to just eight limestone caves. With thirty-five limestone caves, Thailand provides the species with a few more roosting options.

The species lives and hunts near slow-moving bodies of water, indicating that soft-bodied water insects make up a large portion of its diet. They also love to eat any spiders they can find. Experts believe that while the bat most likely catches most of the insects it consumes in mid-air, it's also possible that they grab unsuspecting bugs off leaves and tree branches. While some bat species carry their food to a safe location to eat it, the Kitti's hog-nosed bat will often consume its prey while it's still in flight.

The species prefers to hunt at dusk and dawn and typically spends about half an hour foraging for food before they return to their roots. It appears that when their numbers were strong, they roosted in colonies of one hundred to five hundred bats, but now it's not uncommon to find colonies of just ten bats. They generally roost in limestone caves and seldom travel more than 1 km from their roost site when foraging for insects.

Like most bats, the Kitti's hog-nosed bat gives birth to a single pup each year and likely cares for the offspring until it's nearly the same size as her. It's believed that the species mates late in the winter and that the pups are birthed during the mid to late spring.

In 2007, the Zoological Society of London's Edge of Existence Programme announced that the Kitti's hog-nosed bat was one of ten different species they were investigating.

While natural predators are a problem, bigger issues include the destruction of natural habitat. Tourism has been hard on these little bats, who find the presence of humans extremely stressful. The species is so sensitive to human distruption, that a group of monks who used one of the limestone caves for meditation inadvertently drove an entire colony of Kitti's hog-nosed bats from the cave.

The IUCN Red List of Threatened Species lists Kitti's hog-nosed bats as vulnerable. They estimated that in Thailand, the 2008 population consisted of about 10,000 bats and predicted a yearly population decrease of 10% over a ten-year period. The Myanmar population was estimated at 1,500 individuals.

Beautiful Bat Fact #5
Big Brown Bat: Beetle-Eating Machines

The summer sky turns a dark indigo as the sun slides closer to the horizon, in a blaze of brilliant reds, pinks, and oranges, a silent signal that sends most North American animals heading towards their beds, where they'll spend the rest of the night.

Time seems to slow, to settle into a sense of peacefulness that's shattered when a high-pitched chattering erupts from the inside of a half dead tree. Startled, a squirrel perched on a nearby tree limb spins and runs the other way. A second later, a steady stream of heavy-bodied, large, dark brown bats flow out of what seems like an impossibly small gap in a tree.

Once they're free of the tree, some angle their bodies upwards, disappearing into the tree canopy, while others aim lower until they're swallowed up by the lengthening shadows.

One of the last bats to exit the tree flies upwards before suddenly changing her mind and wheels towards a nearby ash tree, flying so close to the trunk, it seems like she's going to crash into it, but at the last possible second, she sails directly past the tree and catches the large green body of an adult emerald ash borer in her sharp teeth. A small week-old pup clings tightly to her chest the entire time.

This clever female is a big brown bat (*Eptesicus fuscus*). She and the rest of her maternity roost represent the most plentiful bats in the United States.

Thick brown fur covers a body that ranges from 9.9-12.9 cm (3.9–5.1 in) long and weighs anywhere from 0.49-0.56 oz. Although the medium brown fur is a nice uniform shade, it often has an oily appearance. Belly hair is a shade or two lighter than the back hair.

Although the short, broad wings aren't equipped for super high speeds or amazing aerobatics, they serve the big brown bat well. The wings provide the bat with just enough speed to chase the snout beetles and ground beetles they love consuming, and provide the bat with enough maneuverability to easily hunt in vegetable/flower gardens, over farm fields, and in dense forests.

Big brown bats have a voracious appetite. Before the female who ate the emerald ash borer returns to the roost, she'll spend the night consuming her weight in insects. Her powerful jaws and needle-sharp teeth allow her to efficiently crunch through the hard shell of many different types of beetles. Big brown bats are particularly fond of:

- Cucumber Beetles
- Ground Beetles
- Scarab Beetles
- Snout Beetles
- Stink Bugs

If the bat is unable to locate any of these insects, they're willing to adapt their hunting style and will consume leaf hoppers, large moths, and multiple types of borers.

The sheer number of insects the female big brown bat and her roostmates eat in a single night make the big brown bats a valuable asset to U.S. farmers. As we become more knowledgeable about the feeding habits of the big brown bat, many farmers have started exploring how they can encourage the species to roost on their land. Since the females like to roost in groups that range from twenty to three hundred related bats, a single colony can significantly reduce the amount of expensive pesticides a farmer uses to protect their crops. A single maternity colony of 150 big brown bats can prevent cucumber beetles from laying 33 million eggs.

Like so many vesper bats, male big brown bats prefer to live a solitary life and find small protected spaces where they spend their days. The males and females ignore one another until the leaves start to turn color, signaling the start of autumn. At this point, the males seek out the females and start their courtship routines, generally mating with several females. Egg fertilization doesn't take place for several more months, and she finally gives birth to her pup between May and July. The female's gestation period is two months and she'll care for her pup for 2.5 months. As a rule, big brown bats only have a single pup each spring, but twins do occasionally happen.

When both sexes are mixed together, it's easy to see that the females are a bit larger than the males. There have been instances of big brown bats deciding to hibernate on their own rather than joining a colony, though no one fully understands why.

It's not unheard of for big brown bats who have been hunting in far northern regions to start flying south in the fall, seeking out a hibernaculum in a slightly warmer climate. Preferred hibernaculums are well protected spaces with an internal temperature that range between 32 and 41 degrees Fahrenheit.

It's not unusual to spot big brown bats hunting late in the fall, long after other types of bats have started hibernating. During mild winters, there have even been cases where a big brown bat wakes from its hibernation and moves to a completely different hibernaculum in the middle of the winter. The working theory is that the longer hair and larger body size allow the big brown bat to better tolerate colder temperatures.

There are eleven big brown bat subspecies.

Big brown bats who avoid predation/funguses and who consistently store enough fat to get through the winter can live about twenty years.

Big brown bats have adapted well to human encroachment and don't appear to mind hunting and roosting in backyards, gardens, and active barns.

In 2016, ICUN listed the big brown bat as Least Concern, stating that between their wide distribution, number of colonies that reside in protected areas, and tolerance for habitat as the reason they don't believe this species will rapidly descend into the threatened category. That being said, it's likely that in certain regions, the big brown bat could be decreasing, in which case it's up to locals to do whatever they can to preserve the colonies in those areas.

Big Brown Bat
(Eptesicus fuscus)

Figure 8 ©U.S. Fish and Wildlife Service Headquarters
2.0)

Beautiful Bat Fact #6
Samoan Flying Fox Bat: A Keystone Species

High above the brilliant green forested volcanic hills of the Samoan National Park, a medium-sized black bat wings its way across the cloudless sky. Its wings beat a rapid tempo as it searches for wild grown fruit. Suddenly, as it sails over a ridge, a second bat joins it. This one flies without the first bat's lazy purpose, its course taking it directly to the first bat, who, upon seeing it, wheels and hastily flies out over the ocean, where it changes course and starts looking for fruit in an area that isn't already protected by another.

The second bat lands on a tree, hanging upside down, its huge eyes scanning the area for more unwanted guests while it makes elaborate gestures with its wings, warning anyone in the vicinity that the tree and the surrounding three kilometers belong to him and his mate. Still angry about the intrusion, the male scuttles about the tree, rubbing his neck on the branches and trunk, coating the bark with his scent. Finally, satisfied that the intruder is well and truly gone, the male releases his grip on the tree and takes flight, returning to the place where he left his mate and their young pup, stopping along the way to grab a quick snack.

Native to America Samoa, Polynesia, Fiji, and Samoa, the Samoan flying fox bat (*Pteropus samoensis*) is small by flying fox standards, the average weight is a mere one pound and its wing span is about three feet across. When in flight, the bat appears to be black in color, but if you're lucky enough to get close to one while it's roosting, you'll see that its body is actually covered in a thick pelt of stunning russet-colored fur while light brown or grey hair covers its head. The facial basal ridges are more developed than other types of flying foxes, making the Samoan flying fox bat look a little less like a canine than other flying fox species.

Like its cousins, the Samoan flying fox bat enjoys a diet that consists primarily of wild grown fruit, though when it's unable to find enough fruit to sustain its speedy metabolism, it alters its diet and chooses to chew on the leaves of its favorite fruit tree, or to sip the sweet nectar from the blooms. Both the drinking of the nectar and eating the fruit make this species crucial to the rainforest it calls home. The species has been observed feeding on thirty-three different types of native fruit.

Archeological evidence suggests that thousands of years ago, the Samoan flying fox bat was pivotal for creating the forests that attract today's tourist to the region. The evidence suggests that the Samoan flying fox, as well as two other species of bats, are keystone mammals to the region.

The fact that the Samoan flying foxes have been a part of the region for so long may explain why, instead of fearing the bats like so many American and European cultures, native Samoans have always prized the flying fox bat. While many cultures scorn bats and often use them as a symbol for darkness and evil, there are some exceptions. The native Samoans is one such culture. They have a long history of praising bats in their folk culture and mythology. One of their most famous stories is of a young queen who depended on bats for her survival.

In addition to peppering their folk tales and mythology with positive stories about the Samoan flying fox bat, the natives also depended on the species for food. The meat from the species is sweet, tender, and highly prized. It's often served at special events, such as birthday parties, traditional ceremonies, and other social gatherings.

It's worth noting that in the native language, the Samoan flying fox bat is called *pe'a*, which is also the name of the traditional Samoan male tattoo.

Scientists have had a difficult time getting an accurate reading on the population of the Samoan flying fox bat. What they do know is that in the late 1980's and early 1990's, the population declined rapidly, in large part to severe natural disasters. Since then, habitat destruction and hunting have led to a further decline in the population.

The species' territorial nature described at the start of this chapter is behavior that not only sets the Samoan flying fox apart from its cousins, but also most other bats. It's likely that the behavior developed because the species is one of just a handful of bat species that practices monogamous relationships. Not only do the males and females stick to one mate, it's likely that the males also help with the care of the pup.

Though little is known about the mating practices and courtship rituals of the Samoan flying fox, it's likely that the pair breeds sometime between August and December, possibly even while the pair is still caring for their current pup. Once the egg is fertilized, the gestation period lasts for approximately five months. Females typically give birth in May and June. The female carries her young pup around with her while feeding until it's about half her size, at which point, it's ready to start flying on its own. Mothers have been observed nursing pups that are three-quarters her size.

As concern over the dwindling population and understanding of the importance the Samoan flying fox plays in the local ecology increases, conservation measures are being put into place. The once thriving export business that oversaw the exportation of flying fox bat meat to Guam and a few other areas in the early 1980's has been shut down and steps have been taken to place additional restrictions on the hunting of these bats.

The U.S. Endangered Species Act has categorized the Samoan flying fox bat as a Category 2 Candidate Endangered Species.

The IUCN Red List has Samoan flying foxes classified as near threatened, but makes note that as a result of a number of events that took place from the 1980's through the 1990's, the species is quite close to being labeled as threatened.

Samoan Flying Fox Bat
(*Pteropus samoensis*)

Figure 9 Photo Acquired via National Park Services
https://www.nps.gov/media/photo/gallery.htm?id=EE40
7690-155D-4519-3EBCD6903FA6E056

Beautiful Bat Fact #7
Bat Origins Baffle Scientists

In the past, there have been a few naturalists and biologists, such as Carl Linnaeus and Lazzaro Spallanzani, who dedicated time to the study of bats, but these people have been few and far between. It's only been in the last thirty to fifty years that bat-related research has kicked into high gear, marking the first time in history that many resources have been dedicated to learning about these small winged mammals. Every day, bat biologists, conservationists, and researchers learn something new and exciting about bats.

One issue remains a mystery.

Where did bats come from?

While there are a few different ideas about the evolution of bats, at this point, it's little more than theory.

The best guess is that several million years ago, there was a small insect-eating shrew that made some change in its lifestyle that caused its descendants to slowly develop wings, echolocation, and in some cases, completely different digestive systems.

But that's just a hypothesis.

There was a point when paleontologists thought bats shared a common ancestor with flying squirrels, though they couldn't explain why one developed wings and the other grew a flap of skin. This theory sounds reasonable, but so far, genetic tests show zero evidence that bats/flying squirrels/flying lemurs share an ancestor.

When scientists get together and discuss the evolution of bats, there are some species that constantly get mentioned as possible ancestors, including:

- ***Chriacus***-omnivores that lived in trees. Developing wings would have allowed them to travel more safely while searching for food.
- ***Nandinia***-another omnivore that preferred living in trees. Scientists believe it frequently dropped to the ground for food, during which times it would have been vulnerable to predation.
- ***Protictus***-the skull shape and mandible design of these ancient animals was quite similar to modern bats.
- ***Ptilocercus***-Flying lemurs descended from this animal. It had several skeletal features such as flattened ribs, rotation carpus/metatarsal/phalanx, wide cervicals, and high-floating scapula that are found on today's bats.

In the grand scheme of things, knowing the type of animal bats evolved from might not seem important, but it really is. Understanding how bats evolved may provide us with important genetic clues that make saving them from genetic and biological threats (such as White-Nose Syndrome that's currently killing millions of bats) possible.

There's even a possibility that understanding the origins of bats may help save your life. A perfect example of how understanding evolution has saved human lives can be seen by looking at Pacific Yew trees.

Yew trees are important to human health because they produce the compounds needed to create Taxol, an important medication that aids with the treatment of several different cancers, including lung, ovarian, and breast cancer. The problem is that not only is the Pacific Yew a slow growing tree, it's also endangered, making harvesting the much-needed chemical compounds difficult. Evolution provided the solution. Scientists back-traced the yew's history, comparing its chemical compound to other trees in the same family, a process that eventually led them to find the needed compound in other more common, faster growing trees.

Similar examples of how a knowledge of evolution led to amazing scientific breakthroughs can be found in agriculture, medicine, bio-engineering, and more.

There's no telling how much our society will advance as our knowledge of the place bats fill on the evolutionary scale increases.

Why There's So Much Confusion

There are two main reasons why the origin of bats continues to baffle experts.

Bats are the only members of the Chiroptera order, which makes it difficult to backlink them to other mammals. The lack of known common ancestor with other mammals makes it difficult to speculate what species would have evolved into contemporary bats, lending credence to the idea that bats evolved independently.

Size poses another problem in tracing bat linage back to the beginning of time.

Large animals leave behind bits of skeletal remains, which serve as clues that help scientists piece together how contemporary animals came to be. But small skeletons break down fast and more completely. They were also more likely to be consumed, leaving precious little behind. The good news is that occasionally, someone gets lucky and stumbles across something unexpected that brings science one step closer to understanding where bats came from and how they evolved.

Wyoming has revealed to important clues, not necessarily the origins of bats, but to how some of their most amazing features developed.

Key Pieces to the Evolution of Bats Unearthed in Wyoming

In 2008, near Wyoming's Green River formation, a fossil was unearthed. Eventually, this fossil, or rather the animal that turned into the fossil, was named *Onychonycteris finneyi*. It represents the most primitive bat fossil ever discovered, and has yielded some important clues as to how early bats lived.

Tests indicate that the bat was alive and well 52.5 million years ago, making it the oldest bat fossil ever found. Examining *Onychonycteris finneyi* forced some researchers to reevaluate some theories they'd formed regarding the evolution of bats.

Based on the remains, experts feel that the living animal would have been about 25 centimeters (9.84 inches) long with a wing span of about 52 centimeters (20.42 inches). The wingspan isn't very long for that size body, so *Onychonycteris finneyi* wasn't a match for the speed and agility current bats possess, but researchers believe the wings were a big part of its life. The early bat would have managed to flap its wings and stay airborne for short bursts of true flight.

The claws on the *Onychonycteris finneyi's* toes and fingers provide important clues about its lifestyle. Its toe claws simply weren't designed in a way that would have allowed the primitive bat to cling to tiny grooves and cracks in cave ceilings. The shape and strength of the claws suggest that while this particular bat species flourished, it roosted in trees. The combination of a long, strong claw at the end of each finger and long, heavily muscled legs suggests that this bat was a climbing machine, easily able to scoot up a tree like a squirrel or even shimmy up rock faces as it pursued an insect.

It was the examination of the *Onychonycteris finneyi's* ears that really caught the scientific community off guard. This species lacked the ability to use echolocation to navigate while it flew, disproving the scientific community's hypothesis that echolocation and flight ability developed simultaneously. Based on this, the hypothesis is that bats started out as daytime hunters and possibly switched to nighttime hunting as a means of avoiding predation.

Technically, *Onychonycteris finneyi* is the oldest fossilized bat specimen ever found, but it would have lived at about the same time as *Icaronycteris*. While alive, the adult *Icaronycteris* was approximately 14 centimeters long with a 37-centimeter wingspan.

While the bats are two different species, they not only lived at about the same time, but they even lived in the same region and had a similar diet. Comparing the *Onychonycteris finneyi* fossil with the *Icaronycteris* fossil shows clear signs of evolving into an animal that's close to modern bats, the most important being that it did have the ability to echolocate, indicating that it was a nocturnal hunter.

In addition to the ability to echolocate, the *Icaronycteris's* ankles faced backwards, which would enable it to hang upside down. The differences between it and modern bats include a less rigid skeleton, less specialized dentition, and no tail membrane (something modern megabats still lack.) Stomach contents showed that the early bat was an insectivore with a fondness for moths.

The differences between the *Onychonycteris finneyi* and the *Icaronycteris* lead paleontologists to believe that *Onychonycteris finneyi* may be a bridge bat species that connects early bats to today's bats.

Archeologist Uncover Massive Prehistoric Bat in New Zealand

Bats are designed to fly – they're not designed to walk, or even crawl around on the ground – which is why most bat rescuers are quick to say that any bat on the ground is a bat that's in serious trouble. However, there are exceptions to every rule, and New Zealand's lesser-tailed bat species is a perfect example. While this species is a lovely flier, their skeletal and muscle structure also allows them to walk on the ground.

Some researchers believed that walking was a skill set the lesser-tailed bat developed in the past few centuries, possibly as a response to a decrease in flying insects or other environmental factors, but a recent discovery has blown that hypothesis out of the water.

The remains, which are believed to be about 16 million years old, were found when archeologists were digging near the site of the prehistoric Lake Manuherikia. The fossil was declared a member of the mystacina family, just like the lesser-tailed bat.

The fossil's limbs are quite different from most bats'. The reason for this was because the ancient bat spent a great deal of time walking around on the ground, the same way modern members of the mystacina family do today.

Contemporary scientists believe that New Zealand is home to two different mystacina species, though specimens of one haven't been seen since the sixties.

The current representative of the mystacina group is unique in that it not only hunts flying insects, but also forages on the ground. Strong wrists and feet that look like they've been put on backwards enable the bat to walk almost as well as it flies.

The recently unearthed fossil bears the same skeletal features as the contemporary bats, but has one noticeable and noteworthy difference: it's three times their size. By microbat standards, it's a monster-sized bat. The question is, why did the size decrease so drastically?

Bat Wings? On Dinosaurs?

There's speculation of a possible dinosaur/modern bat connection.

Since bats are mammals, few people stopped to consider whether or not they might trace their lineage all the way back to dinosaurs, but the discovery of a pigeon-sized fossil has some people wondering.

A farmer uncovered the remains in the Tiaojishan Formation, which is in China's Hebei Province. Studies indicate that the small winged animal was a member of the Scansoriopterygidae family. Its name is Yi qi.

Based on the remains, paleontologists have created computer generated image of what Yi qi looked like. The dinosaur was about the size and shape of a contemporary pigeon. It had a long neck and a bird-like head and teeth. It also had wings, which are what is generating the most interest in this particular species.

Fossilized remains of a winged dinosaur are nothing new. It's widely accepted that birds evolved from the members of the Scansoriopterygidae family, the same family Yi qi belongs to. What is surprising is that Yi qi's wings don't look much like bird wings, but bear a strong resemblance to bat wings; it's almost like they're an early prototype of what today's bats use to zip through the night sky.

The wings were devoid of feathers and appeared leathery, like bat wings. They were constructed around a gently curved, rod-like, anomalous bone that was distally tapered. This bone isn't like anything paleontologists have ever seen before in any of the theropod dinosaurs they've studied. Yi qi also has an extremely long third finger. The strange and surprising wing structure is how the name Yi qi was selected. In Mandarin Chinese, it means "strange wing."

It is also the first-time paleontologists have found evidence of a dinosaur that had both wings constructed out of a leathery membrane and a body covered in feathers.

After entering the data into a computer, researchers were able to run a program that indicates Yi qi would have been able to sustain true flight, though the periods of such would most likely have been very short. Based on what the computer program revealed, researchers believe Yi qi probably used its wings to fly from one tree top to another, or to even fly down to the ground from the tree canopy.

Yi qi is believed to have lived during the Callovian and/or Oxfordian periods.

There's no evidence suggesting that bats descended from Yi qi, but it's fun to wonder if maybe there isn't some unexpected evolutionary link.

Comparison of different wings more than 100 years Before Yi Qi was Discovered

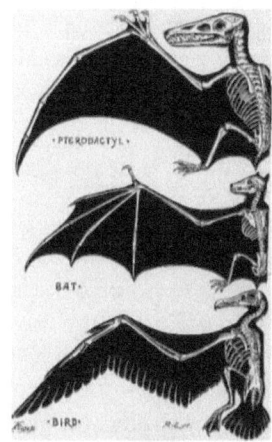

Figure 10 By John Romanes (1892): Darwin and after Darwin

Flying Primates

Back when Carl Linnaeus was a student, most of his teachers didn't have high expectations for him. Although he wasn't a bad student, his mediocre grades didn't make him stand out from the crowd. Yet there was one subject that captured his attention: botany, a class that wasn't available to all students. The only reason young Linnaeus managed to study it was private tutelage.

His teachers were more impressed with Linnaeus's natural fluency for Latin, a language he started speaking at approximately the same time he began walking.

As his secondary schooling drew to an end, his teachers told the young man to give up any hopes he had for continuing his education, that based on his academic performance up to that point, he lacked both the brains and the focus needed to attend the university.

Luckily, one teacher looked past Linnaeus's grades and saw the untapped potential within the boy. This teacher urged Lund University to accept the Swedish botany student. Linnaeus performed well at Lund, but he soon made a transfer to Uppsala University, where he'd been told he'd enjoy a stronger botany program. It didn't take Linnaeus long to discover that the botany program was underwhelming. He'd already acquired more knowledge of plants than the Uppsala professors who were supposed to be teaching him.

Soon Linnaeus started teaching the classes.

During this time, Linnaeus became frustrated and obsessed with the current form of classifying plants and animals. This frustration and the drive it triggered transformed Linnaeus from a lackluster student into one of the most respected scientific minds of his time. When he wasn't teaching or writing, he was outdoors, traveling all over the place, and observing nature. He used his knowledge to create a more efficient system for biological classification until he eventually earned the title "Father of Taxonomy."

You can thank Carl Linnaeus for the fancy scientific names currently given to all known living things.

Linnaeus spent a great deal of time studying bats. He was the first person to realize that, contrary to what everyone had always thought, bats weren't rodents and made up their very own genera. He also became interested in the evolution of bats.

In 1758, Linnaeus shocked the world with an interesting theory. He hypothesized that megabats, especially flying foxes, were actually flying primates. Linnaeus believed millions of years ago, humans, monkeys, and flying foxes shared a common ancestor.

Cool, right? And just a little shocking.

It's easy to see how Linnaeus came up with his flying primate idea. Bat wings and human hands are quite similar. Bats are very intelligent, and the female bat's breasts bear a strong resemblance to human breasts. The more you look at these features, the more plausible the flying primate hypothesis becomes.

Although interesting, Linnaeus's theory was ultimately rejected by other scientific minds of the era. The basis of the rejection was that Linnaeus believed that the Flying Primate Theory only applied to flying foxes, not to microbats. For the Flying Primate Theory to work, two different, but extremely similar, hand-winged creatures had to have evolved separately. The idea simply defied logic.

Eventually, the scientific debate died down. For about two centuries, no one really thought about it much until 1986, when Australian neuroscientist, Jack Pettigrew, breathed new life into Linnaeus's theory. Pettigrew had some very interesting data that appeared to do what had always been assumed impossible. He'd found scientific data that confirmed Linnaeus's two-hundred-plus-year-old hypothesis. Or did it?

Pettigrew pointed out that the bat's brain's superior colliculus and the eye's retina connected in a manner that had only been observed in primates.

Additional studies conducted in 1989 found additional similarities. Support of Pettigrew's flying primate theory grew.

While Pettigrew had many believers, eventually, a DNA comparison revealed nothing that would indicate that bats and primates shared a common ancestor.

While no one knows exactly how bats evolved or why they did, the one thing no one can deny is that for as long as humans and bats have co-existed, bats have been horribly mistreated.

Bat Skeleton

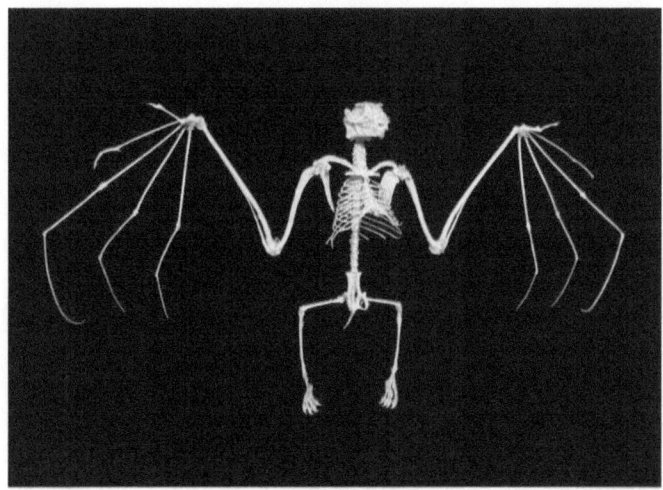

Figure 11 ©Rose Waddell
Acquired via Dreamstime.com

Beautiful Bat Fact #8
Bats have a Bad Reputation

Finding positive examples of bats in history, mythology, and folklore isn't easy. Traditionally, bats are used to symbolize darkness and evil manifestations.

Dracula's Metamorphosis

Ever since Dracula famously transformed himself into a bat so he could spy on Mina Murray Harker, it's difficult to separate thoughts of bats from thoughts of vampires. In our minds, they belong together, and even though it's a fictional connection, the association hasn't done much to alleviate the suspicion people have always harbored against bats.

Bram Stoker never actively discussed his decision to have Dracula take the form of a bat during the story, but most historians feel it wasn't a spontaneous or random idea. They feel the transformation was in line with various superstitions that had been sweeping through Europe and the United States for centuries.

Many mistakenly believe that the Stoker was the first person to suggest a connection between bats and vampires. He wasn't. Not by a long shot.

Since the dawn of time, humans have distrusted bats. The situation wasn't helped in 1526 when famed explorer, F. De Oviedo y Valdes, wrote an account of his recent trip to Costa Rica, which included a brief description of bats consuming blood. A few years later, in 1565, another explorer, M.G. Benzoni, provided a graphic description of how bats bit his toes and drank his blood while he slept.

These tales of blood-sucking bats likely gave birth to the idea of bats and vampires being one and the same. Stoker simply capitalized on the concept.

Stoker wasn't even the first author to explore a relationship between bats and vampires. Years before Dracula hit bookstores, two other popular stories played on the link many believed bats and vampires shared.

Varney the Vampire was a Penny Dreadful serial story. While the vampire in the story didn't transform into a bat the way Dracula did, in some illustrations, Varney has a distinctly bat-like appearance. Many literary scholars believe Varney helped inspire Stoker's Dracula.

There's no denying the influence a later story, Vikram and the Vampire, had on Stoker. The story was penned by Sir Richard Burton, who described the vampire character as "like a flying fox." Not only was Stoker friends with Burton, it's rumored that he "borrowed" certain aspects of Burton's physical appearance for Dracula.

Stoker also kept a clipping of an article that ran in the *New York World* newspaper on February 2, 1896. The article discussed the Vampire Phenomenon that held New England in its thrall. Near the end of the article, the story addressed a tale of a man who swore his horse's blood had been drained by vampire bats. Current knowledge of the feeding habits of vampire bats is enough to prove this story was as fictional as Stoker's Dracula, but at the time people believed it, and it clearly was a source of inspiration for the famous Irish author.

Personally, I suspect the connection to vampires and bats goes all the way back to Ancient Mayan folklore and their vengeful and frightening god, Camazotz.

I believe that as more people explored the world and encountered exotic bats, the stories they brought back about flying fox bats with their six-foot wing spans and sharp canine teeth, the stories became entangled with the tales explorers told about real vampire bats, and mixed with ancient folklore. Once this happened, it didn't take long for people to buy into the idea of a link between vampires and bats.

Aesop's Bats

Aesop was a slave who became famous for the stories he told. The stories involved familiar animals who were used to explain either the world or to teach a lesson.

In two of his tales, Aesop used bats to represent duality of nature in both stories.

In the first bat-themed Aesop tale, a bat tells a bird-hating weasel that wishes to kill it that it's really a mouse. The same bat later escapes death a second time by telling a mouse-hating weasel that it's a bird and not a mouse at all.

In another story, Aesop uses the bat to explain how refusing to take a side can result in one being shunned. In this tale, during a great battle, the bat flops back and forth, constantly siding with whichever side it believes is about to win. When the battle ends, both sides refuse to accept the bat, driving it away from the daylight and forcing it to spend eternity alone and surrounded by darkness.

The Romans had a similar story, though in their version, it's Mars, God of War, who banishes the bat.

Aesop's stories laid the groundwork for the bat to be connected to:

- Mixed signals
- Negative/dark thoughts or influences
- Duality of nature
- Black bats in dreams often indicate a pending disaster
- A white bat symbolized a loved one's pending death

Aztec/Mayan Culture

It's a bit difficult to decide exactly how the Aztecs and Mayans felt about bats. Some of their stories honor bats, while others don't. They did assign bats with supernatural traits and claimed that they had deadly powers. What is known is that both cultures were fascinated by bats. Archeologists have found thousands of pieces of art that depict images of bats, many of them "bat masks" that bear a striking resemblance to Bob Kane's Batman character.

Camazotz

The Mayans believed that Camazotz, God of Xibalba, was bat-like in shape and may have helped stoke the concept that vampires had the ability to turn into bats. Although he stood like a human and had human arms, images of Camazotz depict long claws, bat wings, and blood dripping from some wicked-looking fangs. His bizarrely shaped nose bears a striking resemblance to that of native leaf-nosed bats.

The Mayans believed that he lived in a cave with his minions, native vampire bats, and was responsible for ruling the death realms.

Camazotz wasn't a benevolent god. He was accused of decapitating one of the Hero Twins. According to legend, the head was saved and used as a ball whenever the gods got together to play games. The Mayans also believed that he had no qualms about destroying entire populations after they'd sinned.

Bats Continuously Maligned in Folklore/Mythology

At some point, individuals of the Christian faith started connecting the bat to the devil, a point that's illustrated in a painting that dates back to 1475 and depicts the devil with a pair of leathery wings that bear a striking resemblance to bat wings. Some early Christian stories suggest that when bored, the devil turned into a bat and whiled away the time by harassing people.

Scotland

In Scotland, many believed bats provided a type of courier service and carried messages from witches to the devil. The exact nature of the message the bats were rumored to have carried is vague, but the idea that the bats could be telling the devil about their sins was enough to ensure that any bat that found its way into a Scottish home was promptly murdered.

It's possible that it's this Scottish belief that caused many to accuse women of being witches simply because bats were noticed on their property or near the woman's house. While the connection between bats and witches dates all the way back to ancient Samhain ceremonies, the first time the presence of bats was formally used as proof of witchcraft was in 1332.

Germany

In Germany, there's an old myth warning against allowing any bats into the home, as the animal's presence is a sign that the devil is gunning for your soul. This folk tale bears a strong resemblance to one Jewish, German, and Slovenian immigrants shared that suggested the presence of a bat in a person's attic foreshadowed the death of someone living in that same house.

Finland

In days long past, Finnish people believed that bats were a physical manifestation of human souls. This doesn't sound like a terrible thing until you dig a little deeper into the belief, at which point you learn that the reason the soul morphed into a bat was the result of a violent death and the human's soul was doomed to spend eternity on earth in bat form.

Greece

While bats aren't often mentioned in Greek mythology, it's easy to see they weren't one of the culture's favorite animals.

Ancient Greeks felt that due to the bat's nocturnal nature and preference for inhabiting caves, they must be some sort of demonic being that was born in Hades. They were connected to Hades by the Furies, who are depicted with leathery wings and distinctly bat-like features.

Africa

The folklore surrounding bats changes from one province to another, but it's rare for a positive light to shine on bats. Those who call the Ivory Coast home still believe that bats represent the spirits of people who passed away. Meanwhile, in Madagascar, bats are thought to be the reincarnation of both vicious criminals and the unburied dead. Some believe bats represented dark sorcerers.

Mother Cuddling her Young Pup

Figure 12 ©arievdwolde
Acquired via Deposit Photo

Beautiful Bat Fact #9
Bats Don't Collude with Witches

There've been times during both European and early American history when accusations of witchcraft were bandied about with alarming regularity. It didn't take much for someone to accuse a foe, friend, or neighbor of practicing the dark arts.

During these periods, few women, particularly single women, were safe. It didn't take much to be accused of being a witch and, in most cases, the only way the accused could prove her innocence was to die a horrible death.

While it's unclear just when this happened, at some point, someone decided that bats and witches were working together. We do know that by the time Shakespeare got around to writing <u>Macbeth</u>, the connection between witches and bats was so strong, he used "wool of bat" as a key ingredient in the potion the three witches worked on. In <u>The Tempest</u>, Shakespeare once again turned to bats when he needed ingredients for a curse.

The Appearance of Bats was Enough for an Accusation of Witchcraft to Stand

According to an article published in *BATS Magazine*, the connection between bats and witches can be traced all the way back to 14TH century France, when locals noted a group of bats near the home of Lady Jacaume of Bayonne. Based on the presence of the small animals, Lady Jacaume was found guilty of witchcraft and burned.

This was not an isolated occurrence. Throughout the following centuries, there are scattered reports of bat sightings being used as grounds to accuse women of being witches. Living near a hollow tree, cave, or simply having a few bats living in their attic would have been very bad news for many women.

Witchcraft and Bats Blood Connected to Impotence

During the 14th Century, Villanova was home to a physician named Arnold who strongly opposed witchcraft and magic of any kind. He wrote a treatise called *On Bewitchments* that not only provided a great deal of information about the negative impact magic had on the human body, but also possible cures.

Arnold was convinced that the reason some local men struggled with impotency issues was because their wives had visited a local witch who used bat's blood to write a powerful inscription on a piece of wood that was placed beneath the husband's bed. Arnold believed that the only way to break the curse was to get rid of the bloody inscription before performing an exorcism.

Bat's Blood Remains Powerful

While fear about witchcraft has faded, there are those that still practice, and they continue to seek out bats.

In the late 1950's, a taxidermist in California sold bat blood to customers, who most likely used it for spells or charms. There have also been scattered reports in Mexico, Ohio, Illinois, and Georgia of bat blood being used for a variety of interesting purposes, which includes being placed in conjure bags and to call up evil spirits. There's currently a rash of "mummified" bats being offered for sale via the internet, and while it's impossible to know what all of these mummies are being used for, it's not outside the realm of possibility that some are finding their way into spells and charm bags.

While it might be impossible to convince those who enjoy witchcraft and like to try their hand at casting spells and creating various charms to stop using bats, it's important to remember that the bats don't actually choose to be involved in these activities and therefore should never be blamed.

The good news is that while some cultures truly believed that bats represented witchcraft and a wide assortment of other evils, there have been some cultures that revered bats.

Orphaned Flying Fox Bat Wrapped in a Towel

Figure 13 ©Beth Baisch
Acquired via Dreamstime.com

Beautiful Bat Fact #10
Some Cultures Prized Bats

While history and folklore contain plenty of examples of bats getting the short end of the stick, there are also examples of bats being treated with the respect they deserve.

Bats in Cherokee Mythology

In an ancient Cherokee story, the ground-dwelling animals and the birds took separate sides during a ball game. Two small mice begged to be allowed to play with the birds. Wishing to include the mice, the eagles fashioned a pair of wings for one of the mice out of some spare pieces of leather. The new wings made the bat a valuable member of the team. The eagles lacked enough spare leather to fashion a matching set of wings for the second mouse, so they helped stretch its skin and it became the first flying squirrel.

Bats in Chinese Culture

You'll be hard pressed to find a culture with more

respect for bats than early China. While people all over the world treated bats with suspicion, the Chinese celebrated their existence.

Several thousand years before Europe embraced Christianity and started to fear bats, members of the Oriental world were developing a great deal of respect and admiration for the tiny mammals. When a person spotted a bat hanging around their house, they didn't assume it had been sent by a vengeful or evil being; instead, they treated the bat as a sign of joy and great happiness.

Romance and the Chinese Bat

Antique artwork depicts bats drawn near or entwined with peaches, which were considered a symbol of female fertility. Historians believe that the combination of the bats and peach fruit/flowers represented the active and passive forces that exist between men and women. The bat symbolized the male while the fruit/flower represented the female.

Wealth and the Chinese Bat

The bat symbolizes many different things in China, including wealth. In fact, the Chinese word for bat is "fook," which shares the exact same pronunciation as the Chinese word for "prosperity." It's important to note that in China, words like wealth and prosperity don't necessarily imply money. The appearance of a bat signifies happiness and longevity in Feng Shui applications.

Five Little Bats

Seeing five bats at the same time is an excellent omen. For centuries, Chinese artists have used five bats to symbolize the five Chinese blessings:
- A long life

- Good health
- A virtuous life
- Prosperity
- A natural death

The five little bats motif remains popular and is often printed on the red envelopes Chinese children receive during the New Year's feasts.

Bats in Japanese Culture

Many Japanese beliefs closely mirror beliefs found in China, so it's no surprise to learn that while bats might not have been quite as highly prized in Japan, they were respected and viewed as symbols of good luck and fortune. Images of bats have been found adorning swords, prized pieces of pottery, and kimonos.

Sadly, in recent years, people living in Japan have lost interest in bats. It's unusual for artists to incorporate bats into their work and on the rare occasion someone does feature a bat, it's more of a Western-style bat with fangs, glowing eyes, and other dark tones. The good news is that thanks to some high-quality documentaries, summertime bat festivals, and books, Japan is working to once again shine a positive light on their native bats, which are called Koumori.

Bats and Early Native Mexican Cultures

Even though the Mayan god Camazotz was connected to bats, not all Native Mexican lore involving bats was negative. In one story that dealt with how the earth's topography was created, an elderly bat is credited with creating the valleys and slopes needed to drain the land so corn could grow.

Bats and the Samoan Culture

The Samoans have a lovely folk tale about a native princess, Leutogi. According to the story, Leutogi married the king of the neighboring Tonga Island as part of a peace agreement between the two islands. One day, Leutogi discovered an ailing baby bat. Before returning the young bat to its family, she nursed it back to health. Her husband's people objected to her actions and ridiculed the Samoan princess.

Later, when the native Tongans fell on hard times, they turned on Leutogi, blaming her for everything that had gone wrong on the island since her marriage. She was tried, found guilty of witchcraft, and sentenced to die.

Upon learning of her fate, the bat she saved convinced its colony to fly over the burning pyre, using their urine to douse the flames and save the princess.

Furious that she'd been rescued, the Tongans exiled the princess, forcing her to live on a barren island where they assumed she'd die of starvation or exposure. They failed to consider the loyalty of the bats, who not only kept the exiled princess company, but also provided her with fish and nuts.

Eventually, Leutogi became a goddess and took it upon herself to protect all bats, which the Samoans worshipped.

Bats for Protection

Even though most Europeans and Americans have traditionally harbored a deep mistrust of bats, they often turned to the animal when they wanted an extra layer of protection or a they sought to develop a special skill. Archeological digs have unearthed shields and lances that were adorned with the images of bats, which historians believe were used as both a symbol of protection and as an image that the knight hoped would scare his foes.

German gamblers frequently used a bit of bright red

thread to sew a bat's heart to their arms. The reason for doing this was because it was believed that the tiny heart brought luck, especially during card games.

In Austria's Tyrol regions, many men clung to the belief that keeping the left eye of a bat tucked into their pocket or sewn into their clothing rendered the bearer invisible.

Bats as Symbols of Hope

Examples of bats being used for positive symbolism include:

- Learning to love our enemies
- Touching base with inner demons and learning from the experience
- Exploring low-points/underworlds/depths of humanity
- Thought renewal
- Tapping into resources that help lead us out of darkness
- Rebirth
- Seeing through illusions
- Improved communication

Contemporary Authors Take a Pro-Bat Stance

Perhaps the most shining example of using bats to symbolize goodness (of sorts) was when Bob Kane and Bill Finger used the mammals to inspire the legendary character, Bruce Wayne, to don the superhero's mantle and become Batman. In the comic books, Bruce Wayne chose the bat as his symbol because the animal showed itself to him at a crucial point in his life. The Batman movie franchise chose to have the character overcome his chiroptophobia, an act he felt gave him the strength to overcome his enemies.

Neither Bob Kane nor Bill Finger ever stated why they decided to go with bats, though on at least one occasion, Kane mentioned that an old movie, the *Bat Whisperer*, was one of his sources of inspiration. It's unlikely that either artist realized that the character would slowly help alter the general perception of the bats. Kids who fell in love with Batman came to see the symbol of the bat as something that was good, and this in turn made them less likely to react badly to bats in the real world. After all, if Batman is a superhero, doesn't it stand to reason that bats also are?

The link between Batman and bats is so strong, that Ben Affleck, who currently plays the character, released a public service announcement that was designed to raise awareness of bats and white-nose syndrome, a fungal condition that has resulted in more than 6.5 million bat fatalities.

Batman isn't the only example of contemporary art that shines a positive light on bats. There are a few different children book series that have bats as main characters. Hopefully, this trend continues and helps change the way the world feels about these amazing animals.

Books that star bats include:

- The Box of Bats Book Gift Set by Brian Lies (individual books also available)
- Nightsong by Ari Berk
- Stellaluna by Janelle Cannon
- Bat Jamboree by Kathi Appelt
- The Little Vampires are Confused About Bats by Rebecca Hicks

Wahlberg's Epauletted Fruit Bats
(*Epomophorus wahlbergi*)

Figure 14 ©Charles Sichel-outcalt
Acquired via Dreamstime.com

Beautiful Bat Fact #11
Looking for Love? Bats May Help.

Finding love has never been easy.

Before things like Match.com, the Tinder app, and cheesy barroom pickup lines, the lovelorn often turned to love potions and spells whenever they needed a little help in the romance department. Some of these potions/spells/charms required a bat.

Bats, Beer, and Conjugal Relations!

When most people think of famed Roman scholar and naturalist, Pliny the Elder, they picture large mugs full of foamy beer, not bats. It's perfectly natural, after all; Pliny was the person who realized that the wild plants growing near his home was a type of hops, which he named lupus Salictarius. This act was so important, today many beer drinkers enjoy Pliny the Elder beer.

But Pliny enjoyed many things, including sitting up late at night, possibly while enjoying a nice beer, and watching bats and talking to his friends about their love lives.

Pliny must have spent a great deal of time worrying about how his buddies fared with the ladies, because a night came when something he saw a bat do made him go, "Ah ha!" He called his friends to him and told them that if they really wanted to improve their conjugal relations with their wives, they needed to catch a few bats. After accomplishing this task, they were to take a single drop of clotted bat blood and slide it under their lady love's pillow while she slept. Upon waking, the woman would be so overcome with passion, she wouldn't be able to keep her hands off her man.

Despite my best efforts, I wasn't able to determine if this was a long-term solution to problems in the marital bed, or if the guy needed to procure a fresh drop of bat blood whenever he wanted to get lucky.

Tired of Dating Apps? Go Old School. Grind up a Bat.

Pliny wasn't alone in his belief that there was a link between bats and romance.

According to legend, a lonely young Texan had his eye on a special young lady. He wasn't having any luck convincing her to return his attention. After watching the lad moon around town for a few weeks, one of the locals urged him to catch a bat and tie it to an anthill.

After the ants stripped the tiny body bare, the lovelorn young man hung the bat's wishbone from his own neck, wearing it as a pendant while he beat the remaining bones with a rock. When the bones were nothing more than a very finely ground powder, the young Texan mixed them in some vodka and urged his crush to join him for a drink. She was the one who ingested the bat bone cocktail.

This wasn't a random practical joke.

European records indicate that the macabre potion was often used when young men were looking for wives. The biggest variation seems to be that instead of vodka, the guys mixed the powdered bones into beer and ale. Apparently, the type of drink wasn't nearly as important as the bat bones.

Attract Hordes of Potential Mates

Men weren't the only ones who turned to bats when they needed assistance in the romance department. Women also had a few bat-related tricks up their sleeves.

While translating a Greco-Egyptian papyrus, scholars discovered that single women of the era who wanted to attract the attention of a potential mate were advised to remove the eyes from a still-living bat, after which they were to release the bat back into the wild. The young woman placed the eyes into a homemade dog statue (fashioned out of wax or uncooked flour). She then used a needle to manipulate the eyes before the entire dog was placed into a vase and tossed at a crossroad. According to the papyrus, this would attract the man the woman sought and might even bring a few into town for her girlfriends as well.

Before you grab a net and embark on a wild bat hunt, I must point out that I've been unable to find any data indicating how successful these attempts at romance really were.

Spectacled Flying Fox Bat Eating Wild Figs

Figure 15 ©Beth Baisch
Acquired via Dreamstime.com

Beautiful Bat Fact #12
Doctors of Yesteryear Loved Bats

Humans might have considered bats to be the night time harbingers of a great many evils, but that didn't stop them from turning to bats whenever they needed a little medical care.

Throughout history, there are many accounts of bats, or rather parts of bats, being used in the treatment of specific medical conditions, including:

- Hair Loss
- Sexual frustration
- Hypochondria
- Tumors
- Gout
- Vision Problems
- And more

Reversing Poor Vision

The first record of bats being used for medicinal purposes was written in the *Papyrus Ebers*, which historians believe dates back to 1550 BC. The papyrus is full of ancient medical cures, including one that used bats to help those who were suffering from trachoma, a disease that causes the inside of the eyelids to become rough, which in turn irritates the eye. To help reverse the effects, the doctors created an ointment that was equal parts bat blood, honey, frankincense, potsherd, and lizard's blood.

Ibu al-Beithar, an Arabic physician, incorporated bats and various bat parts into his treatments. When a patient had leucoma, they were advised to take a boiled bat brain and mix it with onion juice and, after using the mixture, their cataract would disappear.

Relief from Gout

Bats were particularly popular amongst doctors with patients suffering from gout, a painful health issue that's plagued many people throughout history, including King Henry the Eighth. Even as they suffered from the painful condition, people took a kind of pride in developing gout, even going so far as to say it came from an excess of good living.

Since the patients had both a great deal of wealth and influence, and in the case of King Henry, the ability to remove an unsuccessful doctor's head if it was believed that the physician wasn't doing enough to cure the condition, doctors were desperate to try anything, including bits and pieces of bats, if it meant providing their patients with some relief.

One doctor didn't go out hunting bats, but he did provide each of his gout patients with a recipe that described how to "properly prepare" a bat and use it to ease their suffering. Once the patient finished preparing the bat and ate it, the doctor assured them that they would be cured. The same doctor used this cure when patients came to him for help with alopecia.

Aelius Galenus is thought to be the single greatest physician the Roman Empire produced. During his lifetime, he created several ground-breaking medical treatments and saved many lives.

His patients included the very powerful, many of

whom developed gout. He urged each of his gout patients to catch and boil three bats. After boiling the bats, the patient cut or ground up the bats and mixed them with three raw eggs, a dash of flaxseed, some ox dung, a full cup of oil, and some wax. Once the mixture was prepared, the patient rubbed it on their feet and any other part of their body that was painful.

There aren't any records indicating whether the cure worked to ease the gout, but I'm willing to be that Galenus's cure took a toll in their social life.

Prevent Baldness

While it's unclear where the rumor that a bat would entangle itself into a woman's long hair started, there's no denying that several cultures have a long history of using bats to help with various hair issues.

In India, women were instructed to remove the wings from dead bats and crush them up. The powdered wings were mixed with some other ingredients, including coconut oil, and stored for three months before being used as a shampoo. The women believed the bat shampoo kept their hair shiny and thick, and that it helped prevent them from going grey.

Ancient Arabic doctors advised mothers to rub their children's thighs with a liberal amount of bat blood to prevent hair from growing on the child's legs. Meanwhile, in other parts of the world, bat blood and bat brains were mixed together and either consumed or used as a shampoo with the hopes of preventing baldness.

Treating Tumors

Bits and pieces of actual bats weren't the only place doctors of yesteryear looked when they needed a cure. Guano was also a popular choice. Swedish explorer Peter Forsskål was amazed to discover that Egyptians used bats to treat tumors. When someone developed a tumor, their family went to work gathering as much bat guano as they could find, which they mixed with vinegar. The resulting paste was then smeared over the tumor.

Curing Hypochondria

When the average contemporary individual hears about a doctor using a recipe that calls for balsam of bat, adders, suckling whelps, deer marrow, ox bones, earthworms, and hogs' grease, most of us assume the doctor was some unqualified hack. But in the 15th century, Sir Theodore Mayerne, a highly educated physician whose resume included providing medical care to five different kings, used that recipe to "cure" hypochondriacs.

Mayerne referred to this cure as "Bat Balsam."

Resolving Pica

In the United States, bats were used to cure children who had developed Pica from eating enormous quantities of dirt. The doctor advised parents to place a bat on a skewer and roast it. After removing the bat's skin, it should be fed to the child. Reports indicate that after eating the roasted bat, the child would never feel compelled to consume dirt again.

By no means were bats the only creature physicians reached for when they needed a cure. Researchers estimate that over the years, more than 1,500 different members of the animal kingdom have been used for medicinal purposes, but I find it interesting that given how worried many people were about the possibility of bats being evil, that they were willing to use the animal to resurrect their health.

Egyptian Fruit Bats
(*Rousettus aegyptiacus*)

Figure 16 © Digistockpix
Acquired via **Dreamstime.com**

Beautiful Bat Fact #13
The Odds of a Bat Making You Sick are Slim

One of the reasons so many people have an adverse reaction to bats is because they're convinced all bats have rabies.

This isn't true!

Yes, bats can be infected by the rabies virus, and yes, if the infected bat bites a human or a pet, the bitten party can contract the disease.

What's not true is that all bats are rabid; far from it.

When the Center for Disease Control (CDC) originally determined that bats carried rabies, it caused widespread panic and resulted in people who saw bats on their property destroying natural habitats as they waged war on the tiny flying mammals, most of whom were perfectly healthy and a valuable part of the ecosystem.

What the CDC didn't make clear is that bats aren't the only animals that can pass rabies on to you and your pet via a bite. Foxes, raccoons, rats, possums, mice, skunks, dogs, and feral cats can also be infected.

The best way to make sure your pet doesn't become rabid is staying on top of their rabies vaccination.

The best way to prevent yourself from contracting rabies is to not touch any dead or grounded bat with your bare skin. If you do get bitten by a bat, the first thing you need to do is stop in at the nearest hospital and tell them what happened. Don't let them blow you off. Insist that they vaccinate you for the disease right away. As long as you're immediately vaccinated, you should remain healthy.

Remember, **all mammals, including humans, can contract and pass on the rabies virus**. In no way, shape, or form are bats the only carriers.

The Truth About Bats and Rabies

It's estimated that less than 5% of all the bats in the world are rabid and they die shortly after contracting the disease, resulting in very few bats actually passing it on to humans or beloved family pets. Most of the cases of humans contracting rabies from bats stem from the person picking up and handling the bat.

There are lots of interesting facts about rabies, including:

- All mammals can contract rabies
- All mammals can pass rabies on to another animal via saliva

While bites are the most common method for passing the rabies virus from one mammal to the next, many suspect that the virus can be passed on if saliva enters the body through the eyes, mouth, or an open wound.

- The rabies virus outlives its victim by a considerable period
- Freezing temperatures don't kill the virus; only heat causes the viral cells to die
- The rabies virus travels through the body via the nervous system and takes over the brain
- Humans who work with wildlife should get routine rabies vaccinations

There's no known cure for rabies once the symptoms start, which is why it's so important to get vaccinated as soon as you've been bitten.

Rabies is an old virus. Historians have found evidence that the disease concerned both the ancient Mesopotamians and ancient Egyptians. Both cultures used hieroglyphics to keep records of the disease.

Many believe that rabies was introduced to North America via European sled dogs.

Pay attention to the news and listen for reports of rabies outbreaks in your area. It's believed that rabies is introduced when animals relocate.

If there's been one reported case of rabies in the area, take extra efforts to keep your pets and yourself away from local wildlife. When it comes to diseases like rabies, it's better to be safe than sorry. The best way to make sure your pets (and livestock) don't contract rabies is by remaining diligent about getting them vaccinated.

If you find a dead bat, or even a living one that's behaving strangely, you should have it tested for rabies, which will tell you if the local bat population is in the middle of an outbreak.

Whether the animal is dead or alive, don't touch it with your bare hands! Remember, the virus outlives its victims, so if the dead bat was infected, it could still pass it on to you. Use a shovel or a scoop to transfer it into a Ziploc bag. If you absolutely must touch it, wear very heavy rubber gloves.

Take the bat's body to the nearest medical center or veterinarian office, where the staff will help you contact the CDC and arrange for the animal to be tested.

If the bat is still alive, use heavy gloves to gently transport it into a safe container that has air holes so it can breathe, and bring the bat to either a veterinarian's office or contact a local bat rescue. The staff is trained to recognize whether the animal is sick or injured and will take the appropriate action. In most cases, if the bat is merely tired or hurt, it can be rehabilitated and released into the wild.

Rather than teaching your children to fear bats because they've been known to carry rabies, teach your children how to determine when an animal is sick, and warn them that they should never touch an animal that's sick or dead. This keeps your child safe and healthy without making them afraid of bats.

Bats, Humans, and Histoplasmosis

While rabies is the disease most humans fear when they think about bats, there are other health problems that link bats and humans. In this case, the bats aren't directly responsible for the humans' health problems, but their guano is to blame.

Individuals who live in the Eastern or Central United States, as well as in part of Central America, South America, Australia, Africa, and Asia, and notice a large bat population, are at risk of developing histoplasmosis, a medical condition caused by inhaling bits of fungal spores. The fungal spores are commonly found in areas that contain a large concentration of bat droppings.

The fungus isn't found in newer bat droppings, but rather droppings that are a few years old.

Most people can inhale the spores and don't experience any problems; however, if your immune system has already been compromised, the mold spores can trigger a severe infection that requires medical treatment. Young infants, the elderly, and individuals who already have a compromised immune system are the most at risk for developing severe histoplasmosis.

Symptoms usually appear three to seventeen days after inhaling the spores.

Early symptoms include:

- Fever
- Cough
- Fatigue (extreme tiredness)
- Chills
- Headache
- Chest pain
- Body aches

In most cases, the symptoms disappear within a month, assuming you stop inhaling the mold spores; however, in some cases, a long-term lung infection can develop and doctors are unable to prevent the infection from spreading to other parts of the patient's body, including their central nervous system.

The best way to prevent yourself from developing histoplasmosis is to make sure bat guano doesn't build up near your home. If you have a large bat population, set aside time each month to clean up the mess. Make sure you wear gloves and a dust mask while you perform the chore.

Remember, histoplasmosis isn't directly caused by bats, but rather mold that forms in large amounts of bat guano.

The Link Between the Ebola Virus and Bats

Ebola is a deadly virus that has plagued West Africa since the mid-1970's. Since the first case garnered medical attention, doctors and researchers alike have searched for where the virus came from.

There's no denying that bats are reservoir hosts for an assortment of diseases that impact humans, but it wasn't until a research team traveled to Guinea, where approximately twenty thousand different cases of Ebola have been reported, that a possible connection between the winged mammals and humans was investigated.

The first thing the research team observed was that many of the animals locals often use for food, such as monkeys and duikers, showed no evidence of the virus, indicating that the reservoir host wasn't a species that the locals hunted, but rather one that lives in close contact with humans. The team captured and tested 169 bats with representatives of thirteen different local species. None tested positive for Ebola.

As the researchers continued collecting data, they made an interesting discovery. Méliandou, the village the team was investigating, was home to a number of insectivorous bats, called *lolibelo* (bat experts call them Angolan free-tailed bats). The adults mostly ignore these fairly small, insect-feeding bats, but many of the village children loved hunting them, and would frequently consume what they caught since the bats proved to be a good source of protein.

Angolian free-tailed bats are often mistaken for little free-tailed bats and vice versa. The two species bear a remarkable resemblance to one another. Both species have short, charcoal colored fur and pale colored bellies. When representatives of both species are place side by side, the Angolian bat is a bit bigger and has a much broader mouth. The Angolian free-tailed bat's most distinctive features are it's forward facing ears and large wrinkly lips. The species is designed for fast flight. Their jaws are powerful enough to easily crush a beetle's armored exoskeleton.

Villagers directed the Bat Pack to a large, recently burned tree that had not only once served as home to a large colony of Angolan free-tailed bats, but had also been one of the favorite play spots of the first child to die from Ebola in that village. Since the tree had been burned and the bats killed prior to the team reaching Méliandou, there was no way to positively determine if the bats carried Ebola. While it's possible that the child who originally contracted the virus may have contracted the disease by inhaling bat guano, it's also possible that they caught and played with an infected bat.

When left to their own devices, these small bats prefer to live in hollow trees and avoid contact with humans. However, as more of their natural habit gets destroyed, the Angolan free-tailed bats have been forced to look for alternate roosts and now frequently find themselves settling under eaves and in small, dark building nooks.

Based on their findings, Fabian Leendertz, the wildlife epidemiologist involved in the study, feels that given the size of the local Angolan free-tailed bat population and how many bats live in the area and how heavily hunted they are compared to how many people have contract Ebola from bats, the number of bats carrying the Ebola virus must be quite tiny.

Researchers agree that while Ebola is a problem, culling all bats, such as what the Méliandou villagers attempted to do, isn't the answer. Bats such as the Angolan free-tailed bats are an important part of the ecosystem. A significant decrease in their numbers would result in an increase in other insect-borne diseases, including malaria.

One of the steps Guinean officials have taken in an attempt to decrease the number of Ebola cases is actually good news for bats. They've banned local restaurants from making and selling bat soup to customers. The lack of sales means hunters won't have a reason to hunt and kill local fruit bats, giving the bat population an opportunity to grow.

While a number of zoonotic diseases have been linked to bats, there's also scientific evidence that they could hold the key to helping humans extend both the length and quality of our own lives.

Angolan Free-Tailed Bat
(Mops condylura)

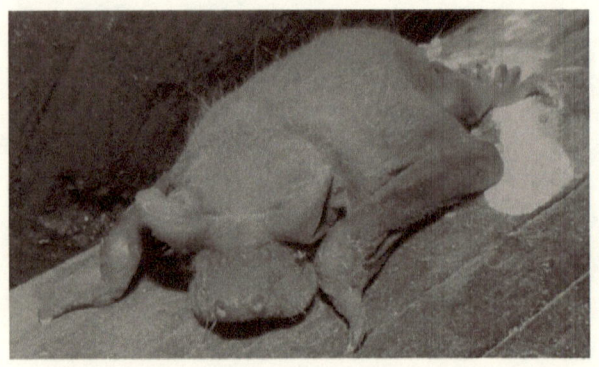

Figure 17 © Bernard DUPONT
[CC BY-SA 2.0], via Wikimedia Commons

Beautiful Bat Fact #14
Want to Live Longer? Consult a Bat

There was a time, when if pressed to answer a trivia question about the average life span of a bat, I'd probably have said five years or some such figure. It seems like a reasonable length of time given how small bats are.

I would have been wrong. Very wrong.

Bats live exceptionally long lives. Instead of living a few years, they can survive for decades.

While the exact life span varies from one species to another, all bats enjoy long lives. Some live about twenty years. Others, like the little brown bat, can celebrate their fortieth birthday provided they're able to avoid predators, flying accidents, starvation, and white-nose syndrome. The bat with the most impressive life span is the Brandt's bat. Members of this species might weigh in at a paltry 4-8 grams, but they don't let their small size stop them from living a long, long time. They're capable of living up to forty-one years, making it the longest living mammal per its body size.

Missing: One Gene Sequence

A group of researchers who has been dubbed the "Bat Pack" has dedicated long hours exploring exactly why bats live so long. For the purposes of their experiment, they used one megabat species, the black flying fox bat, and one microbat species, the David's myotis, and conducted an analysis on the bats' genes.

The results of a gene analysis stunned the Bat Pack. It revealed that bats' immune systems work like no other mammal's in the world. Because of an AWOL gene sequence, the immune system of bats never experiences a cytokine storm, a potentially fatal condition that affects other mammals, including humans.

When attacked by a virus, the immune system produces compounds called cytokines. These are good things. In a perfect situation, the freshly produced cytokines help the body fight the infection.

The best way to explain cytokines is that they operate as couriers, transferring messages from one group of cells to another. Their purpose is to help any area of the body that's fighting a virus respond in the best possible fashion, preventing the infection or disease from growing even worse, or moving to another part of the body, such as from the stomach to the intestines or from the lungs to the heart.

Cytokines also play an important role in controlling inflammation and are a key component in managing arthritis pain.

But sometimes things go tragically wrong and a cytokine storm rips through the body. When this happens, cytokine production has gone into overdrive, and instead of helping cure the infection, the cytokines cause the various systems to overreact, often with fatal consequences.

The inflammation caused by the presence of the cytokines uses systemic circulation to spread from the localized site where the infection exists and takes over the body. This leads to an increase in extravascular pressure while the body's tissue perfusion decreases. When the process works properly, the inflammation triggered by the cytokines aids in healing the tissue, but during a cytokine storm, the organs can't cope with the inflammation and start malfunctioning.

An example of a cytokine storm is seen in someone who is fighting a lung infection. When the immune system responds correctly, the cytokines help the various tissues respond to the infection and fight it off. However, if a cytokine storm takes place, the compounds tell the tissues to overrespond, which leads to the air passageways swelling shut, and causes the person to develop a condition called acute respiratory distress syndrome (ARDS) and go into multisystem organ failure. If the individual doesn't seek medical care right away, they'll die.

This is a relatively new area of study. Prior to the early 1990's, few people had any idea that the immune system could attack itself and turn even more deadly than the original infection.

Armed with this new knowledge of how the human immune system works, historians and medical experts reviewed famous events, such as the 1918 Spanish Flu. The illness started in Europe and quickly became a global problem. Between 1918 and 1919, the virus infected more than 500 million people and claimed between 20 million to 50 million lives. Many victims died within days of developing the first symptom, some only lived a few hours. After investigating the historical files, it's now believed that cytokine storms were responsible for most of the deaths.

Approximately half of the patients who contracted the avian flu and received medical care died because of cytokine storms.

A missing genome sequence prevents bats from developing cytokine storms, provided they're not hibernating. Many members of the medical community hope the continued exploration of bat genes and immune systems will uncover ways that the medical community can prevent humans from perishing because of cytokine storms.

Possible Cure for Ebola?

There's no denying that bats serve as a reservoir host for a series of zoonotic diseases, including Ebola. What has baffled the scientific community is that while some bats carry Ebola, they never seem to develop any ill effects from the condition. Bats with Ebola are just as healthy and happy as those that don't have it. Researchers would like to know why.

Many believe that unlocking why bats are immune to Ebola will lead to important advances in treating humans who have contracted the virus, and even more importantly, developing a vaccine that will eradicate the disease once and for all.

When researchers delved into this mystery, the first thing they learned is that while the bats are active (not hibernating) their immune systems never shut down. This is the exact opposite of how human immune systems work. Ours go dormant whenever we're healthy, only kicking into gear after we contract an infection, bacteria, or virus.

The constantly functioning immune system enables bats to fight off diseases and infections before they do any real damage to the bat's system. The bat doesn't even know that they have contracted something.

Bats' immune systems function with just three interferons, which are types of proteins designed to prevent viral cells from replicating. They're only released when the immune system detects an infection. Humans have a significantly higher number, but so far, researchers aren't clear as to how the diverse levels of interferons impact overall health or how having fewer allows bat to enjoy such long lives.

Scientists hope to use the information they've gathered about bats and how they fight off the Ebola virus and use it to alter the way the human immune system responds to Ebola and other zoonotic viruses.

Bats Aren't Immune to Everything

When compared to other mammals, bats are remarkably healthy, but that doesn't mean they fly around in a state of perpetual good health. Despite the super effective immune system, there are things the bat simply can't battle. As any bat conservationist in the North America will tell you that fungal infections, particularly white-nose syndrome, hit the bat population hard.

Winging Their Way to Cancer-Free Lives

Another aspect of bat health that's caught the attention of the medical community is cancer. Bats don't develop cancerous cells, something all other types of mammals are prone to.

The current hypothesis is that the incredible amount of energy bats spend whenever they fly prevents them from creating extra energy stores that lead to the development of cancer causing free radicals.

Bats also have a gene that's been named P53 that's responsible for repairing damaged DNA. The scientific community believes bats developed this gene to stay in good condition for flight, and that this gene boosts their metabolism and removes free radicals from the bat's system, allowing it to enjoy a long, cancer-free life.

Hopefully, by learning more about how P53 and how it works, the information might lead to better diabetes treatments and possibly even a cure.

The amount of energy used to fly is also why you never see fat bats.

Hope for Those with AIDS

Since making its way to the United States and Canada somewhere around 2006, white-nose syndrome (WNS) has decimated the bat population. In the past ten years, more than 6.7 million bats have fallen victim to the fungus. Given how slowly bats reproduce, it will take a long time for the population to recover from the loss, if it ever does.

In situations like this, it's important to look for a silver lining, for some sign that things aren't as hopeless as they appear.

In this case, WNS could mean good things for those currently fighting AIDS.

While looking at bat carcasses to determine how their bodies respond to WNS, wildlife pathologists obtained information about the immune system that doctors treating AIDS patients found useful.

Bats are hibernating when they develop WNS; their bodies have geared down their immune system. The slowed down immune system allows them to conserve additional energy during the winter, but it also means that they're susceptible to things that wouldn't bother them while their immune system is fully functional.

The sudden resurgence of the immune system not only causes the bats to use too much energy to make it through the rest of the winter, but they also develop immune reconstitution inflammatory syndrome (IRIS), which leads to the destruction of perfectly healthy cells and tissues.

This is the exact same thing that happens to humans when they contract AIDS. The medical community hopes that as scientists continue to look for a way to help bats fight WNS, they'll manage to use the information to come up with a way to prevent or reverse the tissue damage connected to AIDS.

Orphaned Spectacled Flying Fox Bat Pup

Figure 18 © **Beth Baisch**
Acquired via Dreamstime.com

Beautiful Bat Facts #15
The Brandt's Bat: Practically Immortal

The setting sun causes the Welsh woods you're hiking beside to darken. The song birds you heard when you first started your hike have quieted, replaced by the sound of a few late-night toads calling to one another and the buzz of night-time insects. You brush a limb to the side, startling a moth who had been hiding under a leaf. Panicked, it flies towards your face. Instinctively, you start to raise your hand to bat it aside, but before you complete the gesture, a small bat with large wings and shaggy, light brown fur that seems to be touched with gold swoops past your shoulder and grabs the moth. Startled, you blink, only to open your eyes to find both the bat and the moth gone.

You've just experienced a close encounter with a Brandt's bat. You should count yourself lucky. Lots of people who have lived in Wales their whole life have never seen this shy member of the vesper bat family.

Wales is just one of the places where you might get lucky and encounter the Brandt's bat *(Myotis brandtii)*. They're also native to the northern and western sections of England, southern Scotland, Austria, and even in some sections of Germany, though the farther you roam from Wales, the smaller your odds of encountering this particular species becomes.

The Brandt's bat was officially discovered in 1845 but during the 1970's, researchers made a shocking discovery. It turns out that some of what they thought were Brandt's bats were an entirely different species, which were named whiskered bats.

You really can't blame anyone for making such a mistake. Even those who are familiar with both species often get them mixed up. The problem is that it's nearly impossible to see the characteristics that separate the two species as they fly past you. Identification requires a closer look. When identifying the females, biologists look at the dentition. When dealing with the males, the fastest way to know which is a Brandt's bat and which is a whiskered bat is taking a look at the animal's penis. The male Brandt's bat has a bulbous penis, whereas the whiskered bat's penis is, well, it's a whiskered penis. Other minor differentiating characteristics include the shape of the bat's ear tragus. And, if you're lucky enough to get a representative of both species side by side, you'll notice that with a body length of between 35 and 50 mm long and 210 mm – 240 mm wingspan, the Brandt's bat is just a shade bigger.

If you pay attention to the way a bat is flying, you can also tell if your night time companion is a Brandt's bat. The species' wing load is a shade lower than the whiskered bat's, providing it with better maneuverability, a handy feature, considering that it likes hanging out and hunting in heavily wooded areas. As a rule, Brandt's bats stick to woodlands while the whiskered bats tend to favor slightly more open areas that are close to wetlands, such as a pond at the edge of a forest.

During the summer, the females gather in colonies of twenty to sixty bats and form a maternity roost. The species favors roosts where they'll experience minimal disturbance and seem to prefer trees and old buildings, favoring smaller, crevice-types roosts, though some roosting colonies have been discovered making use of the underside of bridges and underpasses. They give birth to a single pup between June and July, which they care for until the youngster reaches its six-week birthday, at which point it's time for the little one to fend for itself. The young bats have grey fur for the first year of their life.

Baby Brandt's bats cling to their mother for the first three weeks of their life. At the third week mark, most of the pups are strong enough to begin flying. Pups who survive the first few months have the ability to live for a long time. Members of this species can live to the ripe old age of forty-one years. The oldest known living Brandt's bat was discovered in 2005. A research team was catching bats in a Siberian cave and were shocked to capture a male Brandt's bat who was wearing a tag that indicated he'd been caught before, in 1964. Forty-one years had passed since researchers first encountered this bat., making him the longest living small mammal in the world. Ounce-per-ounce, the Brandt's bat has the longest life span of any mammal.

While the females like to form small maternity colonies, male Brandt's bats prefer a more solitary existence, though I was unable to find any evidence that they're territorial.

As the days grow cooler and shorter, Brandt's bats move out of their summertime roosts and into the underground hibernaculums. When searching for a place to spend the long winter months, this species looks for caves and mine shafts that are relatively dry. This species tends to stay in their hibernaculum until about May.

The University of Bristol considers the risk of world-wide extinction for the Brandt's bat to be low.

Brandt's Bat
(Myotis brandtii)

Figure 19 © N.Vėlavičienė,
[GFDL or CC-BY-SA-3.0], via Wikimedia Commons

Beautiful Bat Fact #16
Black Flying Fox Bat: Spreading Seeds One Meal at a Time

If you find yourself walking through one of Australia's wooded areas, take a moment to look up at the tree canopy. Chances are good you'll spot large black things hanging from the boughs that look like giant seed pods. Peer just a little closer and you'll realize that what you're really seeing isn't seeds, they aren't even vegetation, but rather the black flying fox bats (*Pteropus alecto*) that call Australia home.

Weighing between 1 and 2.5 lbs., they have a wingspan of 4-5 feet, making them significantly larger than the birds that share the woods. From a distance, they appear completely black, but on closer inspection, you'll notice silver hair mixed with the black. A collar of reddish-brown fur adorns their neck and more reddish fur forms raccoon-like rings around their enormous eyes.

Like most flying fox bats, this is a very social species, not only do they roost in large colonies, they're also happy to share their roosts with other bat species. It's not uncommon to see little red flying fox bats and grey-headed flying foxes mingling with black flying foxes.

Day roosts (which are sometimes called camps) can contain as many as 30,000 individual bats, though these days, it's rare to find that many bats in one place.

Maintaining a comfortable body temperature is a constant struggle for this species. When it's cold, they'll wrap their wings tightly around their torsos, holding in as much body heat as they can. When it's hot, they spread their wings and start slowly flapping them, using them as fans to generate some air flow.

While not the fastest animal in the sky, the black flying fox isn't a slouch in the speed department. It has been clocked at speeds of twenty to twenty-five miles per hour. It's not unusual for them to travel as far as thirty miles from their roost to find food.

Black flying foxes form large colonies that roost in the tree canopies. Their favorite food is overripe mangos, though they'll settle for other types of fruit as well. The best places to catch a glimpse of these winged sky giants are in northern and eastern Australia's river estuaries, eucalyptus forests, rainforests, and paperback forests where they deposit seeds. The bat is mostly interested in extracting as much juice from the fruit as possible. They chew the fruit, using their teeth to mash it into a sticky pulp, extracting as much juice as possible before spitting the skin, pulp, and seed out.

While the mating season does vary from one region to another, as a rule, black flying foxes breed between February and April. When they decide it's time to catch a female's eye, the males select a small section of a branch and claim it as their own, defending it against any males who come to close. When not defending their branch, the males spend the bulk of the breeding season carefully grooming their soft fur and showing off their genitals.

Female black flying foxes plan their pregnancy around the times when food is most abundant. In the northern part of Australia, they give birth to a single pup in July and August, while mothers in the southern part of the country give birth between October and March. She'll spend the first month following the pup's birth carrying it with her at all times, not leaving it at the roost until it's about four weeks old. Pups start flying and joining their mothers on foraging adventures between two and three months old.

The IUCN Red List currently has black flying foxes listed as least concern. While there's some concern that the changing climate could lead to an increase in heat related deaths, on the whole, it's felt that between the species wide range and the overall size of its population, the species will be around for a long time to come.

The biggest threat the black flying fox population currently faces is the fruit bat hunting that takes place in Sualwesi. It's estimated that the hunting is responsible for a 20-25% decrease in the region's population.

Black Flying Fox Bat
(Pteropus alecto)

Figure 20 ©EcoPic
Acquired via Deposit Photos

Beautiful Bat Fact #17
Your Life Could Rest in a Vampire Bat's Winged Hands

You'll have a difficult time finding a mammal that generates more fear than the vampire bat. Just the saying the words "vampire bat" is enough to make most people squirm. The three types of vampire bats represent the most misunderstood of all the bats, which is saying a lot, considering how little the average person knows about bats, which is a pity. If people would just set aside their fear long enough, they'd discover that all three types of vampire bats are amazing, genuine scientific marvels. And who knows, the day may even come when you owe your life to one.

Three Distinct Species of Vampire Bats

There are only three documented species of vampire bats in the world. All three types of vampire bats range includes Central and South America.

One of the many interesting things about these blood-drinkers is that while they all feed off blood, each species seeks out a different type of prey.

The Common Vampire Bat

The vampire bat that researchers have gathered the

most knowledge of goes by the name common vampire bat (*Desmodus rotundus.*) This bat feeds on other animals, preferring livestock.

While they generally leave people alone, if they come across you while you're asleep, they may bite your toe. What a healthy common vampire bat won't do is suddenly swoop down and attack you just so that it can help itself to your blood. Researchers who study the common vampire bat say that despite having the word "vampire" in their name, members of the species are quite gentle and easy to work with.

Aside from the fact that it lives off blood, the most interesting thing about the common vampire bat is that unlike other bat species, including other vampire bats, it frequently walks around on the ground. In fact, it crawls while it feeds. The common vampire bat's anatomy is uniquely suited for moving on the ground. Its hind legs are strong enough to support most of its weight, and it has unusually long thumbs that not only help it maneuver, but also push against the ground, allowing it to make impressive three-foot leaps.

While common vampire bats prefer a colony size of approximately one hundred bats, larger colonies of one thousand common vampire bats have been observed.

The White-Winged Vampire Bat

The white-winged vampire bat (*Diaemus youngi*) is the only vampire bat that feeds on both livestock and birds, though it seems to prefer to cuddle up to birds as opposed to facing the possibility of getting stepped on while feeding on cattle. They like to hang upside down off branches while they feed on sleeping birds.

White-winged vampire bats will feed on chickens. Their favorite place to feed is under the chicken's breast, where the feathers can be easily nudged aside, and the blood flow is quite heavy in that area. Normally, the hen never wakes. If it does, it assumes the bat is one of their chicks. In other cases, the bat climbs onto a hen's back, convincing her it's a mating rooster, and bites the back of the neck. The hen stays docile until the bat finishes eating and flies away.

In addition to the white marks that outline its wings, the other identifying feature of the white-winged vampire bat is its teeth. It's the only known bat with twenty-two teeth as opposed to twenty. When its mouth is open, two distinctive oral glands are visible.

The Hairy-Legged Vampire Bat

While there was a female hairy-legged vampire bat found in Texas, she's an anomaly. The species prefers to stay further south in more tropical climates.

The hairy-legged vampire bat's identifying characteristics include:

- Small rounded ears
- A cute pug nose
- A soft brown coat
- No tail
- Large middle upper incisors

The hairy-legged vampire bat's most interesting feature is its calcar. This is a bony growth on the bat's ankle bone that is quite similar to a rooster's spur. The hairy-legged vampire is the only bat that has such a dominate calcar. It uses the spur to help it cling to birds while it feeds.

People who work closely with vampire bats report that while quite docile once caught, the hairy-legged vampire bat is quite shy, easily spooked by humans. They prefer nesting in smaller colonies and can be frequently found in hollow trees, caves, and mines. They are quite content to share their roosting grounds with other bat species.

The hairy-legged vampire bat is particularly fond of free-range chickens.

With the help of heat sensors in their noses, the hairy-legged bat identifies the part of the chicken that has the best blood flow, preferring the cloacal area. After gently removing the feathers, the bat makes a small incision and begins to drink. The bat remains upright while feeding. It takes approximately half an hour for the bat to consume the amount of blood it needs to survive. By this time, it's swallowed half its body weight in blood.

The hairy-legged vampire bat is the rarest of the three vampire bats.

What Makes Vampire Bats Unique

The detail that makes vampire bats so unique is that they're the only mammal in the world that can survive on a diet that consists entirely of blood. While no one knows for sure how such a mammal managed to evolve, many scientists believe that vampires bats may have become blood drinkers as a direct response to a decrease in a previous food supply.

What's amazing is how much the vampire bat's anatomy differs from, say, the little brown bat.

They Detect Body Heat with Their Faces

Whenever you touch something really hot and jump back, you've activated your heat-sensitive channels. Ours aren't very sensitive and only exist as a source of a protection from hot items, such as curling irons and stove tops.

Vampire bats also have heat-sensitive channels that are significantly more finely tuned than our own. The tiny bats use these highly specialized nerves that are located in their faces to determine the exact location of the vein they need to bite into to get dinner. Only three types of snakes are known to possess similar temperature-sensitive channels.

Memorizing Breathing Patterns

Vampire bats take good listening skills to a whole new level. It turns out that they have brain cells that are only activated by the sound of breathing, which the bat uses to determine which animal will provide its dinner.

Not only do the bats use the sound of breathing to locate dinner, researchers involved in the study also report that bats can identify and remember up to three distinct types of breathing sounds. So if a common vampire bat feeds on a certain cow one night and encounters that same cow a few nights later, it's believed that bats use this information so they can return to an animal that proved to be a good feeding source.

They Have Amazing Mouths

Fictional vampires suck blood. Vampire bats make a small incision and then lap up the blood that oozes out of the wound. Doing this requires a mouth that's just a little different from their bug-eating cousins.

Once a vampire bat gets close to the animal it's selected as its dinner, it uses its teeth to gently remove the hair/feathers from the area where it senses a good, strong vein. Once a small area is cleared, it nicks the vein with almost surgical precision. The bat's saliva contains a natural plasminogen activator that prevents the blood from clotting before the bat has finished eating. The resulting wound is quite small. The bat doesn't have to suck the blood from the animal because the circulatory system does all the work. Grooves in the lips and tongue make it easy for the bat to get every single drop.

Internal Organs Specially Adapted to Efficiently Handle an All-Blood Diet

All three vampire bat species need to consume a large (given their size) amount of blood in a very brief period (twenty to thirty minutes). The less time they're feeding, the less likely they are to be attacked by an angry chicken or stomped to death by a cow. Their survival depends on the bat consuming half its body weight, which takes half an hour.

After eating half its weight at every meal, the vampire bat still must fly back to their roost.

It turns out that accomplishing all this requires some extra special internal organs. Vampire bats have a stomach lining that separates the water from the other stuff in the blood that the bats require, and sends it directly to the kidneys, which promptly excrete it. This means that the entire time the bat is eating, it's also urinating, keeping its water weight down so it can safely return to its roost.

Vampire Bats Have Big Brains

Researchers have noticed something interesting about the vampire bat's brain. It's quite large in comparison to the tiny bodies and when compared to the brain size of other bat species. What really interested scientists is that the part that appears to be the most different from other bats is the larger neocortex, a section that's primarily responsible for complex social behavior and connections.

How Much Blood Do Vampire Bats Need

To survive, all three types of vampire bats must feed at least every other night. When they feed, it takes them approximately thirty minutes to consume their body weight in blood. This sounds like a lot until you remember that these bats only weigh two ounces. The couple of ounces of blood the bat consumes doesn't have a negative impact on the animal they feed on.

Bat researchers were stunned to learn that when vampire bats are unable to feed, they turn to their colony mates for help. Vampire bats regurgitate their food and share it with friends who haven't been able to feed. This behavior is commonly seen amongst female vampire bats. When one female gives birth, the other females share their food, allowing the new mother to stay in the cave and tend to her pup.

Female vampire bats share food with both direct relations and non-relations. It's believed that this act is designed to help "buy" favors from other bats, helping ensure the colony's survival.

How They'll Save Your Life

The medical community has started to sit up and take notice of vampire bats. They're particularly interested in the protein found in the bat's saliva that prevents clotting while the little animal helps itself to dinner.

Every single year, 795,000 Americans suffer from a stroke. Approximately 87% of the strokes are categorized as ischemic strokes, which means that a blood clot blocked a vessel, making it impossible for a part of the brain to receive enough oxygen-rich blood and, as a result, some of the brain tissue dies. This leads to long term and often permanent issues such as paralysis, slurring speech, and a decrease in cognitive functions. Doctors currently have a cocktail of drugs they can use to break down the clot, but the success of the treatment depends on how long it takes for the patient to seek medical help. Most patients fail to make it to the hospital on time.

Researchers are just starting to understand that the vampire bat saliva contains active components that work together to not only prevent blood from clotting while the bat feeds, but that also helps dilate the veins and arteries. The enzyme contained within the saliva that's of the most interest to the medical community is called desmoteplase, or DSPA.

It also turns out that the components alter themselves so that they counteract any natural defensive antibodies the prey's body has created, which is why vampire bats can keep feeding on the same victim for several nights in a row.

Based on early tests, doctors were optimistic that the medication they're testing made from vampire bat saliva, called Draculin, will buy more time for the patients, increasing the odds of a full recovery.

There's hope that Draculin will also help lower and break up blood clots that form in other parts of the body.

Draculin made it through Phase 1 testing.

Common Vampire Bat
(*Desmodus rotundus*)

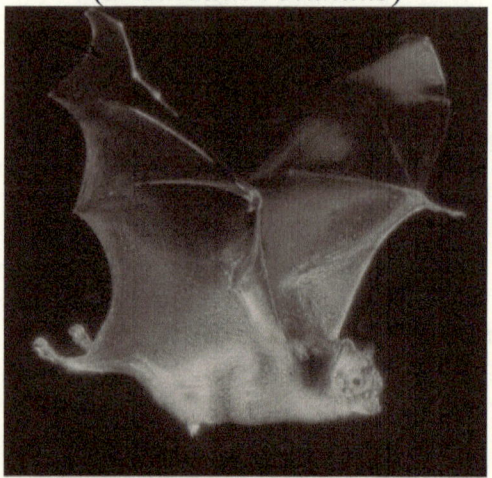

Figure 21 ©Uwe Schmidt (File:Desmo-Flug-01.tif)
[CC BY-SA 4.0], via Wikimedia Commons

Figure 22 ©Uwe Schmidt
[CC BY-SA 4.0], via Wikimedia Commons

White-Winged Vampire Bat
(*Diaemus youngi*)

Figure 23 ©Gcarter2
[CC BY-SA 2.5], via Wikimedia Commons

Hairy-Legged Vampire Bat
(*Diphylla ecaudata*)

Figure 24 ©Gerry Carter
[CC BY-SA 4.0] via Wikimedia Commons

Beautiful Bat Fact #18
Imposters!

Approximately 1% of all bat species are carnivorous. This doesn't mean that they're vampire bats; those are completely unique and limited to the three species already mentioned.

Because rumors of vampire bats consuming blood and killing both animals and people (not to mention, turning into Dracula-style vampires) many people didn't know the actual difference between a real vampire bat and a carnivorous bat.

Stories of vicious vampire bats date back as far as the 16th century. There was a period of approximately two hundred years where many bats were saddled with a vampire label simply because they happened to have large canine teeth, even though they'd never be able to survive a single day on an all-blood diet. These are now called false vampire bats. There are even some fruit bats, who have been given common names that have the word "vamp" in them.

Examples of carnivorous bats that aren't vampire bats even though someone once thought they must be include:

- Greater false vampire bat (*Megaderma lyra*)
- Peter's woolly false vampire bat *(Chrotopterus auritus)*

- African false vampire bat (*Cardioderma cor*)
- Linnaeus's false vampire bat (*Vampyrum spectrum*)
- Australian giant false vampire bat (*Macroderma gigas*)

These bats tend to be on the larger side and have long canine teeth, which they use to both kill and consume their prey. Some species favor small rodents while others prefer hunting small lizards. According to bat experts who have worked with different false vampire bats, they're all very intelligent and quite friendly and that as long as they're healthy and not threatened, they won't harm humans.

The Linnaeus's false vampire bat is particularly fascinating. Not only have certain members of this particular species become very fond of humans (in a good way) but it's one of the few bat species where the male offers assistance in raising the pup.

One captive male was observed wrapping his wings around both mother and pup during rest periods and remained attentive until the pup was reached weaning age. The male also delivered food to the growing pup.

Linnaeus's false vampire bats are sometimes called spectral bats. IUCN has the Linnaeus's false vampire bat classified as near threatened but includes a note that the species is close to qualifying for threatened.

Linnaeus's False Vampire Bat
(*Vampyrum spectrum*)

Figure 25 ©Ryan Somma
[CC BY-SA 2.0], via Wikimedia Commons

Beautiful Bat Fact #19
Bats and Dolphins Share Convergent Genetics

One of the few things everyone knows about bats is that they use echolocation (though most people call it sonar) to help them fly at night. Few understand just how complex and cool the process really is.

When bats go out for the night, they constantly emit a series of ultrasonic pulses. These sounds emerge from either the bat's nose or mouth, depending on the species. The pulses bounce off objects and the bats use the return sound to draw a mental map of their surroundings. The entire process happens so quickly, bats can track a mosquito's flight pattern.

When You Blindfold a Bat ...

No one spent too much time thinking about how bats managed to fly so well during the night time until 18th Century Italian Catholic priest and biologist Lazzaro Spallanzani turned his attention to the flying mammals. He suspected that bats used sound to navigate. To prove his hypothesis, he caught several bats and put tiny blindfolds on them and observed how they flew while their eyes were covered. As technology improved, more contemporary scientists took his initial visual observations and added to them.

The next big breakthrough in how bat's echolocation worked occurred during the 1930's when Donald Griffin, a graduate of Harvard University, put bats in a soundproof room and used an electroacoustical meter, which allowed him to hear the echolocation pulses for the first time. This knowledge was enough to fully grasp how the sounds bounced off objects and aided with navigation, information that was vital when developing the sonar equipment the U.S. Navy used during WWII.

Producing the Pulses

Different bat species use different methods for producing the echolocation pulses that enable them to smoothly navigate the world after the sun sets. Some species, like the big brown bat, create the pulses with their mouths, while others like the greater horseshoe bat have a specially adapted nose that generates the sound.

The process bats use when generating echolocation pulses isn't different from the way you make sounds that are used for communicating. Air is pushed over the vocal chords, which creates a specific sound wave.

What makes bats special is that not only can they produce a high-pitched sound, but they're also equipped to hear its echo and use the echo to glean all sorts of information about their current surroundings.

What has fascinated researchers ever since they decided to get serious about bat research is how quickly the bats produce the pulses. The echolocation pulses are generated at a speed of 190 times per second.

To learn more about how physiology made it possible for bats to be so noisy, researchers selected members of the Daubenton's bat and placed them in a flight cage. The cage was equipped with several highly sensitive microphones.

As the bats explored their new surroundings, the researchers collected data that included how frequently they called, how often they could call before the sound overlapped, and how long it took the echo to return to the bat.

The team discovered that the bats heard the echo approximately one millisecond after making the call.

When the team tested how quickly the muscles that make up the larynx contracted, they learned that 190 times per second was the fastest contraction speed, making the larynx approximately 100 times faster contracting than human leg muscles. The speed of the contractions inspired the researchers to call the bat's vocal muscles superfast muscles. Other examples of superfast muscles include those that allow rattlesnakes to rattle and the toadfish's swim bladder to generate sound.

Superfast muscles don't work like regular muscles. They have special needs. The speed they're operating means they require additional energy, which they get in the form of both calcium-shuttling proteins and mitochondria. The protein, called myosin, that's responsible for forcing the muscle to contract is also different from the myosin found in regular muscles. Researchers are currently exploring the exact nature of this myosin.

Wiggly Ears

Human ears contain four muscles that exist for the sole purpose of keeping our ears attached to our skulls. As a result, our ears don't do anything interesting beside hear. Useful, but pretty boring, especially when compared to bat ears, which have more than twenty, that's right TWENTY, separate muscles that allow each ear to perform an impressive array of precise maneuvers.

Do you know what's even more remarkable than the enormous range of motion bat ears have? The speed at which they move. According to a Virginia Tech associate professor, Rolf Mueller, bats can change the shape of their ear three times faster than you can blink.

Everyone assumed that the amazing ear mobility was connected to echolocation, but researchers have only begun to fully understand how the process works.

When bats use echolocation, they receive two different incoming signals. One for each ear, allowing the bats to create a detailed, three-dimensional map of their surroundings. In addition to filtering the two signals, the bat can also distinguish different, subtle sounds, helping them identify falling leaves from a potential dinner.

While conducting his research, Rolf Mueller discovered that the mobility of the bat's ears not only help them better detect the returning echolocation signal, but also allows the bat to shape the pulses, increasing the amount of information the bat receives from each pulse.

Objects in the Brain May Be Smaller Than They Appear

Life as a nocturnal mammal has equipped bats with a few interesting tools, including a brain that carries a spatial map of everything their echolocation pulses bounce off of. Research conducted by a team at Technische Universität München (TUM) surprised many bat lovers when they revealed that the internal spatial map changes in less time than it takes to blink an eye in order to accommodate a variety of external factors.

When a bat receives the ping back from their initial echolocation burst, they process an incredible amount of information that allows them to create a detailed map in their mind. They swiftly process a large amount of information. In addition to identifying the size and distance of an item that's directly ahead of them, they also calculate the lateral distance between themselves and objects.

Researchers describe the mental map as being quite

similar to the one vehicle navigation systems provide. In order to make the map as accurate as it can be, bats quickly calculate a variety of factors, including:

- How long it took for the original ping to return
- The angle of the reflected echo
- The echo's wave spectrum

One of the most surprising things the research team discovered is that the mental map isn't always to scale. The closer a bat is to an object, the larger that object becomes when placed on their mental map, probably to ensure the bat doesn't accidentally crash into one of the edges.

What About Noise?

As a rule, bats avoid venturing out of their roosts during rainy conditions. It was assumed that the reason for this was because echolocation didn't work in rainy and windy conditions.

You know how difficult it is to hear anything when we're in a noisy environment. All the sounds blend together until they turn into white noise. It's irritating and disorienting; it must be worse for bats that rely on echolocation for, well, for everything.

And rain to bats has to be about the same as standing in a room full of talking people is to us. Right?

It turns out that this isn't the case at all.

Rain and wind makes things more challenging, but not impossible for night-time-loving bats.

Norwegian University of Science and Technology's Department of Chemical Engineering's associate professor, Nadav Bar, studied how bats handle a variety of situations, including flying during noisy weather conditions. He discovered that bats are equipped with a kind of low-pass filtration system, which allows the bats to remove the ambient sounds that should disrupt their flight.

It's likely that the real reason bats don't like rainy and windy conditions is because the insects they hunt are harder to find.

Navigating Crowds

If you've ever had an opportunity to visit a bat-friendly site such as Bracken Cave in Texas or another area where bats fly in and out in numbers that climb into the thousands, you must have marveled at how so many animals can maneuver and perform complicated aerial feats and seemingly never crash. After all, every single one of them is sending out echolocation pulses which has to make navigating nearly impossible. Yet every single night, they manage to pull off the same routine.

Scientists are just starting to understand how the process works.

Using special equipment, researchers discovered that the bats don't stop echolocating while flying in crowds, but they do decrease the number of pulses they send out. It's a phenomenon scientists call mutual suppression.

By using a robotic bat, scientists learned that when the bats saw the robobat, they called more, but when the robotic bat started emitting echolocation pulses, the real bats toned their pulses down, decreasing the odds of interference.

Researchers hope that by learning as much as they can about how bats' echolocation works while in a crowd, they'll hone better technology for wireless signals, improving wi-fi and cell phone signals.

As a rule, bats emit echolocation pulses the entire time they're flying, but just like with all good rules, there's an exception. In the case of bats and echolocation, that exception happens when they're flying with a group of other bats

Studies indicate that when there's a group of bats flying together, they'll take turns echolocating.

The research was done by University of Maryland representatives, Wei Xian, Chen Chiu, and Cynthia Moss. Based on echolocation sounds they'd recorded of a group of big brown bats sailing around a lab situation, they determined that when bats were in a group, 76% of the time there was at least one bat that remained silent for at least 0.2 seconds. That might not seem like much time for you and me, but considering how much information a bat collects during that span, it's a long, long time to be quiet.

The study showed that the closer the bats drew to one another, the quieter they became.

It hasn't been proven yet, but the working theory for the silence while in a crowd is so that the bats don't get their echolocation signals crossed. By remaining silent, there's less chance of getting signals jammed or taking another bat's signal as their own and making a navigation error.

Since bat behavior and traits vary so much from one species to another, it's possible that other bat species don't turn off their echolocation, even while they're surrounded by other bats.

Getting an Edge on the Competition

University of Maryland in College Park researcher Aaron Corcoran and Wake Forest University biologist William Conner joined forces to study how Mexican free-tailed bats dealt with competition while hunting insects. They caught some bats and fitted them with bat-sized microphones and infrared cameras.

They observed that when one of the bats homed in on a tiger moth, their echolocation sound changed. They only heard this particular sound when there was another bat in the same area.

Bats use this signal in exactly the same way that Navy engineers use a particular signal to jam the sonar abilities of enemy ships. In the bats' case, the pitch of the sound blocks the competing bat's echolocation just enough that it can't hone in on the same moth. And they're effective; the research team reports that 86% of the time, the other bat was stymied by the signal and forced to look elsewhere for its dinner.

Old-World Fruit Bats Do It with Their Wings

For the longest time, it was assumed that old-world fruit bats didn't have echolocation. Since they rarely flew at night, they wouldn't need it.

Then a study that involved putting a group of fruit bats in a room, turning out the lights, and recording revealed that yes, the bats did use echolocation. The difference was that instead of using their mouths and noses to emit the high-frequency pulses, the fruit bats use their wings to create echolocation pulses. At this point, no one knows exactly how the wings form the clicks, but the scientists did find that when they altered the wing's movement just a little bit, the clicking stopped.

The echolocation the old-world fruit bats use isn't nearly as sophisticated or accurate as what the smaller bats use when hunting insects, but it's enough to enable the bat to safely fly back to their roost after the sun sets.

Bats, Dolphins, and Convergent Evolution

At first, bats and dolphins don't appear to have anything in common, but when you stop and think about it, they're both extremally intelligent. Both are capable of amazing agility. And both use echolocation to help them maneuver. Science recently revealed that they also share a genetic connection.

This doesn't mean that bats and dolphins share a

common ancestor; they don't. They're connected through convergent evolution, a term used to describe two completely different animals who happen to share similar traits. Sharks and dolphins are also connected through convergent evolution, even though one is a mammal and the other a fish.

Scientist recently learned that convergent evolution appears at the genetic level.

Echolocation is a natural wonder. It's amazing to think that nature devised the tools needed for some animals to easily move through their environment. In order to work, nature had to come up with a series of complex physical traits that not only allowed bats and dolphins to send and receive audio signals, but to also process the information gleaned from the returning signals.

When the genes of both dolphins and echolocating bats were examined, researchers saw examples of convergence in approximately two hundred genome regions. That's a lot of similarities. Prior to examining the genomic regions, scientists anticipated finding anywhere from ten to thirty converged genes.

Another shock was that in addition to sharing genes connected to echolocation, there was also evidence of genetic similarity in the eyes of both animals.

It will be interesting to learn what other areas the animals experience convergence and if that helps scientists come up with ideas about how bats originated.

Good News for the Blind

The better scientists understand exactly how bat echolocation works, the easier it becomes for them to devise ways of using that information to help improve the quality of human lives. Many believe that what's already been learned about bat's echolocation methods can be taken and used to help the blind gain more independence.

People who work with the blind noticed that some individuals instinctively develop ways to use echolocation to help them navigate crowded rooms without the use of the cane. Different people have different systems, which can include snapping fingers, whistling, and clickers. Others haven't been able to develop this extra sense.

There's a company, NeuroPop, that's taking what they've learned from bats and current technology and are working to develop a tool that would do the echolocating for those who struggle to hone natural echolocation skills.

It will be interesting to see how the continued study of echolocation improves human quality of life.

Grey Long-Eared Bat Uses its Long Ears to Hear Bugs Walking Across the Ground

Figure 26 ©lifeonwhite
Acquired via Deposit Photo

Beautiful Bat Fact #20
The Stealthy Barbastelle Bat

A pretty, narrow foot bridge spans a small lake in Great Britain, beckoning you to cross it. Unable to resist, you use the bridge to walk across the lake, enjoying the soft music provided by crickets and frogs. Starlight sparkles on the dark, calm water.

A soft splash catches your attention and you look over and down just in time to see a tiny, dark bat angle up from the dark surface. Peering more intently into the night, you see that there are, in fact, several tiny bats all around you.

Based on the location, it's likely that you're in walking across the preferred hunting ground of a barbastelle bat colony. You should consider yourself very lucky. Spotting one of these bats is very rare. Not only are they a very shy and elusive species, they are also growing quite rare with only a few suspected roosting sites remaining in England.

Barbastelle bats (*Barbastella barbastellus*) were named for the small patch of white hair that surrounds their mouth. The name translates to "star beard." They have small mouths and weak teeth, which limits their diet to smaller, more delicate insects like moths and flies.

During the warmer months, the barbastelle bat, who has a reputation for being elusive, stays in the woods, hunting an assortment of forest bugs. At some point in the autumn, they conceive a pup that's not born until late in the spring.

During the winter, the barbastelle bats seeks shelter underground and hibernates. Females enjoy living in a large colony environment, with the colony often taking over several trees. The males prefer smaller groups and avoid raising the pups.

It's unusual for anyone who isn't actively looking for them to glimpse any barbastelle bats. These native British bats prefer woodlands where crevices and half rotted trunks to serve as roosts.

The best time to catch a glimpse of a barbastelle bat is at dusk when they take to the sky. Their preferred hunting style is swooping low to slow-moving water, like ponds, ditches, and small lakes. They also like to hunt at tree-top level, where they put on a surprisingly agile performance while they chase after bugs. Looking for barbastelle bats is strongly discouraged since this species is shy and easily disturbed.

While they prefer hunting airborne insects, if the opportunity presents itself, a barbastelle bat will grab an unsuspecting bug off a leaf or pluck one out of a spider web.

The way barbastelle bats hunt, especially when pursuing long-eared moths is fascinating. The hunting style inspired a group of researchers from University of Tübingen, Germany and headed up by Anna-Maria Seibert to take a closer look. The team quickly realized that barbastelle bats have a unique way of using their echolocation skills and it helps them catch the long-eared moths that they love eating.

When there are moths about, a barbastelle bat emits an echolocation pulse that's quite different from the rest of their bursts. It's anywhere from ten to one hundred times weaker. The research team discovered that the moths can't hear this weak pulse, even when they're close to the bat, allowing the bat to swoop in and grab the moth. It happens so quickly, the moth can't make any lifesaving evasive maneuvers.

In addition to being quieter than a regular echolocation pulse, the soft pulse is also aimed upwards.

The bats rotate between the weak pulse, officially called a Type 2 pulse, and a normal-sounding echolocation pulse. At first, this behavior baffled the research team until they realized that doing this allowed them to pinpoint the exact location of the moth and catch it without exerting much effort, which is why the research team dubbed the soft echolocation pulse "stealth mode."

The bat uses its mouth to emit a Type 1 echolocation pulse, while its nose creates the Type 2 signal, which is sent straight up into the air. The Type 2 pulse doesn't travel as far as Type 1.

The IUCN Red List has the barbastelle bat classified as near threatened and predicts that over the next fifteen years, the population will decrease by thirty percent.

Barbastelle Bat

(*Barbastella barbastellus*)

Figure 27 ©C. Robiller / Naturlichter.de
[CC BY-SA 3.0], via Wikimedia Commons

Beautiful Bat Fact #21
Greater Bulldog Bats: Fishing Pros

One moment, you're sitting beside a calm pond, watching the sun slip below the horizon, and the next you are watching several large bats flying over the calm water. They make a few loops around the flat surface, when suddenly one swoops low, sinking its feet deep into the water, much like an eagle. As it angles back into the night sky, you see the silver flash of a minnow that's securely wrapped in the bat's toes.

The bats you're watching are greater bulldog bats and they're using their echolocation skills for an interesting purpose.

When it comes to classifying bats by diet, there are three main categories:

- Bats that eat bugs
- Bats that consume nectar
- Bats that consume fruit

However, once in a while, you'll run across a species, like the greater bulldog bat, that refuses to conform to standard dietary rules and opts to dine on something completely different. Their primary food source is small fish.

One glance at the greater bulldog bat and it's easy to

see that it's built differently from its cousins. To begin with, weighing in at 50–90 grams and with a body length of 4.3-5.0 in, and with a wingspan of three feet, it's significantly larger. The bat's third digit is noticeably longer than the rest of their "fingers." In comparison to other species, their hind legs and feet are quite powerful.

The greater bulldog bat gets its name for its interesting-looking face, which is a bit smashed looking. A skinfold bisects its lips, giving it an uncanny resemblance to English bulldogs. It also has cheek pouches that allow the bat to carry food, which are visible even when the bat's mouth is empty.

Identifying the boys and girls is easy. This is one of the few bat species with gender specific colors. The males are a lovely rusty orange color while females are soft grey. Both sexes have a white line that runs down the length of their spine.

This is a social species. Females hunt in groups of up to fifteen adult females while the males prefer solo hunting expeditions. When they return to their roost, the colonies include hundreds of bats, each made up of several small groups of close friends. The small harem-style groups feature a handful of females and one male.

Harem-less males sometimes choose to roost by themselves, but most prefer sharing a bachelor pad with other unattached guys. The females stick together for a long time, but they replace their male consort approximately every two years. The harem will return to the same roost for several years in a row provided it's not destroyed.

While hunting, the greater bulldog bat slowly flies a few feet above the water. While the bat swoops and soars above the water, it sends echolocation pulses downward and uses the return echo to gauge which water ripples are fish small enough for the bat to consume.

When the bat identifies its dinner, it rapidly descends, looking a great deal like an eagle or osprey while it fishes.

The bat uses its powerful hind legs and claws to snatch the fish out of the water. As soon as the fish is caught, the bat sweeps its tail membrane forward, under its body, and transfers the fish to its mouth. The bat chooses to eat its dinner while it's still flying, or sometimes carries it to a perch and enjoys a more leisurely meal.

During the course of a single night, a greater bulldog bat catches anywhere from thirty to forty fish, and the largest fish they can safely handle is about ten centimeters long. While fish are the greater bulldog bat's preferred food, when it's having a difficult night finding enough to eat, it turns to other food sources, including:

- Shrimp
- Water insects
- Scorpions
- Crabs

Although they prefer to stay above the water, if something happens and the bat ends up in the water, they're able to swim. They can also take flight while in the water.

The greater bulldog bat prefers fishing in upstream locations, probably because stronger currents make it difficult for the echolocation to function properly. Upstream areas also have fewer predators that either provide competition or will dine on the bats.

Why Do Bats Fish?

Why did greater bulldog bats start fishing? It's a question that has intrigued chiropterologists since they first observed the species' unique feeding habits. So a group of biologists decided it was time to figure out the answer once and for all.

A group of curious researchers from the University of Copenhagen and the University of the Basque Country

(Spain) came together and created an experiment that allowed them to explore what would happen if long-fingered bats weren't able to forage for insects.

The research team set up two field study bases. One in Valencia, Western Spain, a location selected specifically because the management team of a local golf course had reported that a colony of bats had been observed fishing in the course's pond. A second field study base was erected in Ròtova, Spain where the team identified a colony of bats that fed strictly on insects. The research team chose to observe the European long-fingered bat (*Myotis capaccinii*) for the duration of the field study.

Before starting the field study, the Ròtova team analyzed bat guano and confirmed that the colony they were about to observe had not been consuming fish.

The team observed that the Valencia European long-fingered bat colony had developed a very interesting fishing style. The bats appeared to look for bodies that stay stationary on or near the water's surface, a behavior common to water bugs. Once the bat starts approaching the insect, their echolocation signal changes: the bat lowers the call-end-frequency and widens the bandwidth while shortening the pulse interval. During the approach, the bats execute short dips.

Where things get interesting is if the bat's prey starts diving downward, the bat changes their flight pattern and begins using deep, long dips and captures the fish. They also adjust their echolocation to a *buzz I*-biased terminal phase.

The team determined that what they wanted to learn from their field study was if this method for adapting different hunting methods for fish and water bugs was something the colony had acquired via experience and observing their mother hunting, or if it was biologically programmed into the species, and therefore a hunting style a colony that didn't typically fish, such as the one in Ròtova, would easily pick up.

In the beginning, the team used stationary and temporary targets and observed for both the piscivorous (fish-consuming) bats and the insectivorous (insect-consuming bats) sought while foraging. Using high-speed cameras, the team observed both types of bats using the same type of hunting and echolocation strategy when homing in on the stationary targets. The field study was conducted for ten nights in a row.

By the study's conclusion, the team had observed that both the piscivorous and insectivorous bats did alter their hunting patterns when they encountered a temporary target that sank deeper into the water at the bat's approach. The temporary targets encouraged the bats to make deeper and longer dips into the water. The team also observed that even the insectivorous colony changed their echolocation pattern when seeking a temporary target.

The team did note that while both bat colonies adapted their hunting approach when seeking the temporary fish target, the approach that the insectivorous bats used was not an exact replica of the one the piscivorous colony had perfected.

However, the data doesn't support any of these assumptions, but suggest an intermediate scenario. Both piscivorous and insectivorous individuals use different techniques to capture insects and to catch fish, but the fishing technique of piscivorous individuals also differs from that of insectivorous individuals. Hence, there is a shared primary ability to react to a disappearing target, but unlike insectivorous individuals, piscivorous individuals have honed their attack technique for fishing. The Valencia colony exhibited a far greater difference when attacking the two different types of target, likely because during their time fishing in the golf course pond, the bats have figured out which method generates the best results, while the Ròtova colony was struggling with a learning curve. All the signs indicate that it wouldn't take much longer before the Ròtova bats mirrored the fishing practices of the Valencia colony.

The most interesting thing the team observed was how the bats from the different colonies behaved when they tried and failed to latch on to the temporary target. Bats from the Ròtova colony started the motion of sweeping their feet to their mouths even when they missed the target, whereas the Valencia colony didn't. Based on what they observed, the very fact that the Valencia bats didn't start this telltale movement, the team decided that the bats knew they were targeting a fish, something considerably heavier than a water bug, and that they needed to do everything possible to make the attack as cost-effective as possible. By conserving their energy during the hunt and not trying to bring their legs forward while still in the water, they ensured that they'd have the energy to make a capture the next time they homed in on a fish.

Based on their findings, the research team concluded that nature imbues the long-fingered bat with the ability to not only instinctively recognize fish as a reliable source of food, but to also hunt them, even though it may not have ever consumed fish before. Based on reports that the Daubenton's bat (*Myotis daubentonii,*) a trawling bat species, has been observed fishing, there's a strong possibility that most, if not all, of the larger microbat species have the instincts and ability to catch and consume fish in the event that the insect supply suddenly disappears.

The team hopes that this study and similar studies that will be conducted in the future will aid in our understanding of the learning process.

The study also indicates that while we don't know why greater bulldog bats prefer fishing to eating water bugs, it does provide us with some valuable information about how the habit was started.

IUCN Red List has both the greater bulldog bat and the Daubenton's bat listed as least concern.

Beautiful Bat Fact #22
Fringe-lipped Bats

A large fringe-lipped bat flies over a lowland rainforest, arcing back and forth over its favorite swampy hunting location. It calls out several times, its echolocation cries pinpointing several insects that would make a good meal, but it ignores those, preferring to keep its senses peeled for a very different sound.

Just as the bat's about to give up and take advantage of one of the nearby bugs, it hears what it's been waiting for: the hesitant croak of the týngara frog.

Fringe-Lipped Bats vs. Týngara Frogs

If you're in the Central or South America's lowland rain forests and find yourself looking at a medium-sized bat with coarse, brownish-grey fur, a leafed nose, and a chin that's covered in lumps, you've encountered a fringe-lipped bat.

This species' claim to fame is its eating habits.

The delicacy fringe-lipped bats (*Trachops cirrhosus*) most enjoy is the male týngara frog, which the bats actively hunt during the frog's breeding season. The male frog makes a very specific call that not only attracts interested females, but that also allows nearby bats to pinpoint the frog's location.

A recent research study indicates that the bats use two different sounds to help them identify the frogs.

This particular study focused on how noise impacted bats was conducted with the use of robotic frogs designed to mimic the mating calls of the týngara frog as well as the sound of the frog's vocal sacs filling with air. The experiment involved the research team setting the frogs in a flight cage with bats. When the team added sounds over top of the frog's call, they observed a marked increase in the bat's echolocation, and the bat became more aggressive about attacking the robotic frog that emitted both the mating call and that inflated its sac. When the ambient noise decreased, the bats hunted both frogs equally.

This ability to distinguish between the sounds may hold the secret to how bats can hunt and navigate while in a noisy environment. Based on what they observed, the research team hypothesized that the bats, and possibly other predators, have the ability to alter their preferred sensory mode and adapt to noisy environments in order to signal out a specific target.

How "Warts" Keep Bats Safe

Fringe-lipped bats take their name from the knobs that cover the lower half of its face. It turns out that these wart-like growths serve a very important purpose. They contain sensors that detect whether a frog is poisonous before the bat consumes it.

A research team made this discovery when they caught eight fringe-lipped bats and exposed them to several different frogs and toads. Some of the frogs were the týngara frog that the bats were very familiar with. Other potential meals included two types of poisonous toads.

The purpose of the experiment was to learn if the frogs' calls were the only things the bats used when hunting for their next meal.

Pre-recorded sounds of the týngara frog were used to direct the participating bats' attention to the unfamiliar toads. Upon hearing the familiar sound, the bats responded and went directly into hunting mode, swooping in low. For all intents and purposes, it looked like they were going to consume the dangerous toads. While the bats did snatch the toads up and look like they were prepared to drag them to a safe place for consumption, chemical cues released through the toad's skin and detected by the wart-like sensors prompted the bats to release the toad and fly to another section of the flight cage.

The toads that were much larger than what the bats typically prey on were left completely alone, indicating that bats don't waste their valuable energy hunting prey they'll never be able to manage.

Getting Turned on to New Frogs

One of the things that puzzled bat experts was just how the bats learn that frogs are edible. A study done by a University of Texas at Austin biology team discovered that the bats learn about dining on frogs by listening to other bats.

When a frog that a bat has never eaten before appears on the scene, the bat pays attention to other bats who are hunting to determine if any of them have encountered the frog before and swoop in to eat it. If a bat does, the fringe-lipped bat makes a mental note about the frog's sound and will eat it the next time it encounters one that sounds the same.

It doesn't take long for the information about the new type of frog to spread throughout an entire bat colony.

According to the researchers, the bats use their echolocation abilities to pin-point the location of other bat and then continue to listen while the bat chews. It takes about five times for the bat to make a firm impression about a frog's edibility.

Based on what they observed, the team hypothesis that the fringe-lipped bat's ability to listen to and learn from the eating behaviors of fellow bats allows them to quickly adjust to changing food supplies, ensuring the species' survival.

The fringe-lipped bat also eats insects and small lizards when they're unable to find frogs.

The IUCN Red List has fringe-lipped bats categorized as a species of least concern.

Fringe-Lipped Bat

Figure 28 ©Karin Schneeberger
[GFDL or CC BY 3.0], via Wikimedia Commons

Týngara Frog

Figure 29 ©Brian Gratwicke
[CC BY 2.0], via Wikimedia Commons

Beautiful Bat Fact #23
If It's Flat and Horizontal, Bats Think It's Water

Bats are surprisingly clever mammals and many species have shown a remarkable talent for adapting to the changes humans have made to the world, but it turns out that there's one thing bats just can't figure out. Nature hasn't equipped them with the tools needed to identify one type of flat surface from another.

As far as bats are concerned, if something is flat and horizontal, it must be water.

A group of scientists representing Max Planck Institute for Ornithology in Seewiesen were curious as to whether bats could identify the difference between different types of horizontal surfaces and devised an experiment.

The team found a large flight room and set up a number of flat, smooth, horizontal surfaces that included surfaces made out of:

- Wood
- Metal
- Plastic

The team rigged the flight cage with red light that wouldn't disturb the bats' behavior but which provided enough light for the scientists to see what the bats were up to. Each of the bats used for the experiment attempted to swoop down and drink from each of the plates. The team noted that during a ten-minute span, one poor bat made about a hundred different attempts to drink from the plates. It didn't matter that the surfaces didn't feel or smell like water, all the bats' instincts told them it was water and therefore drinkable. It was like the animals simply couldn't process any of the other clues.

When all was said and done, the team tested eleven different species and got the same types of results. The bats couldn't learn that the flat, horizontal surfaces weren't puddles of drinkable water. The one exception was wooden plates; the bats still tried to drink from the plates made of wood, but were less persistent about that surface than they were the metal and plastic surfaces.

Curious about whether this is learned or information bats are born with, the team collected some young, flightless juvenile bats along with their mothers and raised them in captivity until the juveniles were ready to start flying, at which point they were moved to the flight cage and exposed to the plates.

Even though it was the first time the young bats had flown independently, like their mothers, they treated each of the plates as a drinking surface, indicating that the recognition of how echolocation echoes off the flat surfaces is hardwired into bat DNA.

All eleven species of bats used for the experiment were insectivorous.

Based on what happened during the experiment, the team concluded that while bats do have plenty of other senses, and that it's likely these senses told the bats the plates weren't puddles, but that bats depend on and trust echolocation so much, the information provided by their other senses can't override what the echoes tell the bats. And the echoes indicate that flat horizontal surfaces represent water.

The team believes that in nature, the bats probably diligently test smooth, flat humanmade surfaces such as skylights several times before eventually giving up and moving to a completely different location. The experiment does show why bats often have a difficult time adapting to human encroachment. The more humans the bat encounters while foraging, the more manmade, non-liquid surfaces the bat encounters, which makes it harder for them to locate water when they need a drink.

Bat Flying Low Over Pool of Water

Figure 30 ©Rinus Baak
Acquired via Dreamstime.com

Beautiful Bat Facts #24
Bugs Fight Back

Bats are hunting machines. Once a bug is on a bat's radar, it doesn't have a chance of surviving the encounter. Or does it? One study revealed that when Mexican free-tailed bats detect both a tiger moth and another bat in the same area, the first bat to observe the moth uses a special jamming signal that causes the slower bat to miss the moth. The system is 86% effective.

Researchers now know that the bats aren't the only ones using jamming signals in this particular dog fight. The moths also have a few tricks up their wings.

Researchers had previously learned that the moths heard and recognized bats' echolocation pulses, giving the moths the opportunity to use evasive measures. Scientists now know that one of those evasive measures involves creating a pulse of their own that effectively surprises the bat, causing them to lose the moth.

To collect data, the researchers involved in the study relied on both high-speed infrared video and ultrasonic recordings. They used big brown bats for the experiment.

They learned that the moths had a couple of different approaches when the big brown bats were around.

One sound startled the bats, which has a limited degree of effectiveness. The moths also have an ultrasound pulse that temporarily jams the bat's echolocation signals, making it difficult for the bat to determine the exact location of the moth, and giving the moth a chance to safely slip away.

When researchers examined tiger moths, they learned that the moths had developed complex ultrasound emitters that generate 450 ultrasound clicks per tenth of a second. Tiger moths have a tymbal which they use to generate the clicks.

Researchers believe that bats learn to recognize the clicks of different types of insect species that consume toxic plants and actively avoid forging on those insects. What researchers haven't determined is if bats are equipped with this knowledge at birth, or if it's something they learn at a young age when their mothers are teaching them how to hunt.

It's also believed that since tiger moths consume a high amount of toxic plants, bats discover that the moths taste foul, and that they learn to avoid the badly flavored insects.

Some researchers feel that, based on this information, it's likely that some insects may use ultrasound pulses to warn bats that they're poisonous or taste extremely bad, the way that some brightly colored insects warn daytime hunting birds away.

Hawk moths take a different approach when it comes to dealing with bats. These moths use their genitals to generate sounds that actually scrambles the bat's echolocation signals.

Researchers have only just begun to explore the different ways that bugs fight back against bats. It's likely that as we learn more about the different methods insects use to ward off bats, the military will be able to use this information to help improve their stealth technology.

Beautiful Bat Fact #25
Bats Use Their Voices for More than
Echolocation

It's no secret that bats use echolocation to navigate and hunt at night. For years, that was about the only bat fact the average person was familiar with. One of the things the scientific community has discovered is that the bats use sound for more than creating a mental map of their surroundings. They also talk to one another. It's an aspect of bats scientists have just begun to explore.

There's a great deal to still learn about how bats use both verbal and nonverbal communication; the one thing we conclusively know is that it's extremely complex.

Different Species, Different Languages

It's difficult to determine whether bats from different species understand one another. While there are some definite similarities in their communications, there are also some differences that are clearly unique to specific species.

Communication Between the Sexes

Bats also have different forms of communication that they use for different situations. Bats that sing during the breeding season don't use the love songs the rest of the year. When the male of some bat species stakes out his territory, either as his personal hunting grounds or to use as his "love shack," their chirps and calls develop an aggressive tone, designed to let other males know that they're encroaching and that it's in their best interest to move on.

Researchers weren't surprised to learn that females use different tones and chirps when communicating with other females than they do when they connect with males. The degree of difference was startling. Researchers quickly learned to identify the sexes of both bats engaged in a conversation.

Bats Recognize the Sound of Their Friend's Voice

It turns out that just like you recognize the voices of cherished friends and family members without consulting caller ID, individual bats have distinctive voices and the ability to distinguish those they know from bats they're unfamiliar with. This may explain how some bats, like the greater horseshoe bat, identify and select previous mates.

Silke Voigt-Heucke of the Leibniz Institute for Zoo and Wildlife Research made this interesting discovery while working with lesser bulldog bats. The scientists recorded calls from bats the group they were testing knew and ones that were unfamiliar. When the team played the familiar calls, the bats exhibited friendly social body language. When pre-recorded echolocation calls of other lesser bulldog bats were played, the test bats responded with their own call, which included an acoustical signature that was totally unique to that bat.

The team concluded that bats have a complex language.

Humans Miss Out on Most Bat Communications

The echolocation bats use to navigate has always been done at a frequency that's too high for human ears to detect. The same is true for most forms of bat communication. Although some songs and vocal cues pitch to a low enough frequency for human ears to detect, such as the angry chatter of a little brown bat when they're disturbed, most of the communication requires special equipment.

Tent Making Bats Like These Use Their
Voices for Hunting, Navigation, and Even
Finding Their Colony's New Roosting Site

Figure 31 © Seadam
Acquired via Dreamstime.com

Beautiful Bat Fact #26
Size Matters

For bats, size matters … ear size, that is.

Bat ears come into two forms: tiny and adorable, or huge and magnificent. Those big ears aren't just for show. They're extremally sensitive, making it possible for large eared bats to detect insects shuffling across the ground. This trait allows the bats to hunt close to the ground. Some big eared species have even been known to simply rest in one spot, laying in wait for an unsuspecting insect to walk past. While this style isn't as elegant as catching bugs in mid-air, it does allows the bat to conserve a great deal of energy, which goes a long way towards ensuring the bat thrives even when the food supply is depleted.

So why don't all bat species have massive ears?

The answer is simple.

Nature doesn't give away anything.

Growing those long, beautiful, super-efficient ears, long ears meant making some sacrifices in the flight department. A Lund University research team took it upon themselves to find out just how much the massive ears cost the bats. The results caught everyone off guard.

The Assumption

Going into the research project, it was assumed that the sheer amount of drag created by the ears impacted the animal's flight mobility and also caused the bat to burn more energy while flying than the small-eared species. This wasn't a random hypothesis. It was based on three facts.

First, those long, proud ears don't look very aerodynamic.

Second, the hunting style of long-eared bat species, which is slow and close to the ground, indicates that the longer the ears, the more energy the bat must use to stay airborne.

Third, this isn't the first time scientists have explored how the size of a bat's ears impacts its ability to fly. Similar studies have been done, though in those instances, the researchers built models that were designed to represent specific bat species. The Lund University team took a different approach. They took live bats and placed them into a wind tunnel, which allowed them to closely observe how the bat responded to different wind conditions.

The Reality

To conduct the experiment, the team used two different bat species. Short-eared bat species were represented by the Pallas's long-tongued bat (*Glossophaga soricina*). The brown long-eared bat (*Plecotus auritus*) was used to showcase the flight abilities of long-eared bats.

The research team worked with each animal, patiently training it to fly through a wind tunnel to a piece of food the team had placed on a stick. Once the bats were ready, the researchers used a combination of different wind conditions, laser-illuminated smoke particles, and high-speed cameras to capture every single aspect of the animal's flying prowess.

The team discovered that the degree of body drag coefficient was higher than anticipated for the long-eared bats as was the measured aerodynamic power. Yes, the long ears do slow the bats down and cause them to burn energy, but by comparing the results of the Lund University wind tunnel experiment to the data collected by researchers who used models to determine the impact long ears have on flight, it's easy to see that as long-eared bats evolved, they developed a few tricks that allows them to actually use their ears to improve their ability to maneuver while airborne.

The smoke particles used to showcase exactly what happened while the brown long-eared bats used for the experiment navigated the wind tunnel indicate that when the bat flies, the air behind them angles downwards, showing that the bat has learned how to use both their body and extra-long ears to help them obtain lift. The research team also observed that to send themselves forward, the bats held their wings high and angled away from their body when they completed a wing stroke.

The wake the bats created while flying through the wind tunnel at what's considered a medium cruising speed (3–5 m/s) for the species showed that while the bat used both its ears and body to generate lift, doing so caused the ears to interfere with the wing root vortices, leading to a reduction in the inner wings' performance.

The Bonus

Even though the purpose of the experiment was to learn just how much of an adverse effect long ears have on a species' ability to fly, what really excited the scientific community was what the wind tunnel experiment taught them about how the wings of the long-eared bats work.

The team noted that while the ears impacted the performance of the inner wing, the animal compensated for this by adjusting their wing pitch mechanism after each upstroke, which improved pitch and yaw control.

As the long-eared bat begins its downstroke, it brings the wings forward in relation to its body position, until the wing is basically flipped upside down. When the bat completes the downstroke, it has created a start vortex that's connected to the root vortex.

At this point, the bat starts the upstroke by decreasing elbow flexion, generating another wake within the wake created by the downstroke. While the wing continues moving upwards, the bat adjusts it so the outer edge shifts slightly up and back. Near the middle of the wing, the bat creates a vortex that has an opposite spin to the tip vortex, establishing a spiraling tip vortex. During the next downstroke, the bat will connect the span-wise vortex to this spiraling tip vortex.

When the wing is at the exact transition point between upstroke and downstroke, the bat creates a reversed vortex structure that ranges from one to three different vortex loops.

The team was delighted to see the structure repeated each time they conducted a test flight, but they admit that the sheer complexity of the wakes the bats generated combined with differing wingbeats make getting an accurate analysis difficult. Now that the Lund team has discovered that large ears aren't nearly the hinderance everyone assumed, future research programs can be designed to take a closer look at exactly how the ears are used during flights.

What This Means for Humans

The data collected by the Lund University team has certain parts of the scientific community very excited. Obviously, chiropterologists are excited to have some new information about bats, but aero-engineers are equally excited. Why? Because they hope that by continuing to study exactly how long-eared bats use their ears to aid with flying, they'll be able to take the information and create new technology that will aid with the future development of drones.

Grey Long-Eared Bat Shows of Its Magnificent Ears

Figure 32 © lifeonwhite
Acquired via Deposit Photos

Hildegarde's Tomb Bats have Much Smaller Ears

Figure 33 © Ivkuzmin
Acquired via Dreamstime.com

Beautiful Bat Fact #27
Brown Long-Eared Bat

A medium-sized greyish-brown bat rests near the entrance of a small hole in the side of a tree, soaking up the heat provided from the setting sun. As the sun sinks lower, the bat slowly starts to stir, shaking off the deep sleep it enjoyed all day long. The ram-horn-like ears that had curled towards the back of its skull slowly unfurl until they seem nearly as big as the bat itself. Keeping its toes curled tightly into the wood, the bat spreads its broad wings, giving them an experimental flap or two, the movement sending the blood rushing through the complex circulatory system that lies just below the thin membrane.

With one more practice flap, the bat releases its grip on the tree and swiftly flies out of the hold, heading to a nearby park where it's confident it will find a nice assortment of insects who are just waiting to become the bat's next meal. Forty additional bats fly out after it.

This particular bat is the brown long-eared bat (*Plecotus auritus*), Great Britain's second most common bat. In addition to the long ears that have a delicate, finely shaped tragus, the species can be identified by its fluffy, long, grey-brown fur and lighter-colored belly. Young brown long-eared bats are pale grey and don't develop the deeper brown shading until they reach sexual maturity.

This species is one that has adapted well to human encroachment. In fact, it's so well adapted that the species often sets up maternity roosts in attics. They also roost in tree holes and any bat boxes they find. When it's time to choose a hibernaculum, they often settle into hollow walls, old mines, caves, and tunnels. Sometimes, they will hibernate in dead hollow trees. During the summer, the bat likes to roost with a colony that includes forty to fifty bats. What is unusual is that several males will sometimes roost with the females instead of seeking out a solitary roost.

Brown long-eared bats will hunt in open woodlands that have both deciduous and coniferous trees, but they also love foraging in parks and even people's yards. The number of insects they consume every night combined with how well they've adapted to humans makes them a valuable resource in both urban developments and farms.

The quietness of their echolocation has resulted in many scientists referring to brown long-eared bats as whispering bats. Most of their calls range in frequency from 25-50 kHz.

Like many long-eared bats, the brown long-eared bat flies quite slowly, sticking closer to the ground than the pipistrelles that often hunt in the same areas, and has exceptionally good hearing. Instead of using echolocation to pinpoint a bug, if it chooses, the brown long-eared bat can use the small sounds an insect makes as it eats or moves around to hone in on its exact location.

While the brown long-eared bat can grab insects out of mid-air when it wants, it favors a gleaning style of hunting and generally grabs moths, flies, and beetles off trees, structures, and the ground. Small kills get eaten on the go, but when the bat scores a particularly large bug, they settle on a favored perch and take their time eating it. The bats are very loyal to their perch, which is generally a tree branch. A small pile of dismembered insect remains indicates that a brown long-eared bat has been perched above the pile.

The brown long-eared bat breeding season takes place in the fall, with the female giving birth to a single pup (twins occasionally occur) near the middle of June. The pups start to fly at about three weeks old and are ready to fend for themselves at six weeks old.

A healthy brown long-eared bat can live for twenty-two years.

The ICUN Red List has the brown long-eared bat listed as least concern due to range and its ability to adapt to life with humans.

Brown Long-Eared Bat in Flight

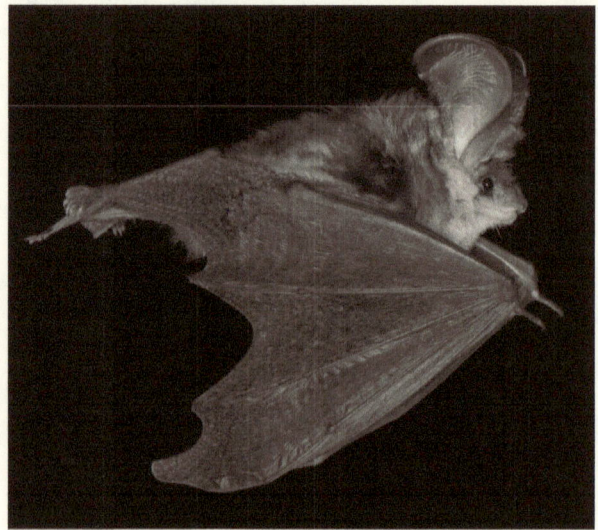

Figure 34 © gezafarkas
Acquired via Deposit Photos

Brown Long-Eared Bat

Figure 35 © gezafarkas
Acquired via Deposit Photos

Beautiful Bat Fact #28
Bat Wings: Complex Scientific Marvels

Bats get a lot of air time. According to one ScienceDaily article, during the span of a single night, a microbat flies approximately 600-700 km (372.8- 434.9 miles.) When the microbat locates an insect they think will make a nice meal, they can reach speeds of 40 meters (0,024 miles) per second. In order to accomplish these feats, the bat has to possess a healthy, specially designed wing.

To the average person, the bat wings seem simple. In this case, appearances really do deceive.

Look a little closer and you'll notice that the wing bears an amazing resemblance to your own hand (the literal translation of Chiroptera, the bat's classification, is hand-wing.) The wing doesn't just look like a hand, it also moves like a hand, allowing the bat to "swim" through the air instead of flapping like birds do. The "thumb" extends over the top of the wing, which allows the bat grasp prey. They also rely on their thumb when climbing trees and cave walls.

Study some high-resolution bat photographs or watch a group of bats hunt mosquitos above your backyard, and you will notice that their wings are significantly more complex than those of a bird. Bat wings are designed for improved range of motion. The flexibility and design of the bat wing enables the animal to instantly change direction, hover in mid-air, dive down on its prey, move at an incredible rate of speed, and travel long distances.

Over the years, several well-respected scientists have dedicated enormous amounts of research time to learning as much as they can about how bat wings work.

Beat-for-Beat, Bat Wings are More Efficient than Bird Wings

Over the years, numerous studies have focused on bat wings in comparison to bird wings, and in nearly every way, the bats have proven to be the more efficient flyer.

One study took small bats, hummingbirds, and large moths, and researchers compared the amount of oxygen each animal used while in flight. The results fascinated the scientific study, but for several years, no one really understood why the bats used less energy while in flight.

An article in a 2006 issue of *Bioinspiration and Biomimetics* shed light on how all those little joints in their wings allow bats to gracefully swoop through the air without burning the same amount of energy as their non-mammal counterparts.

To really "see" how bat wings differed from birds', researchers placed bats in a fog-filled wind tunnel. The researchers observed how the fog particles moved in the wake of the bat passing through them to collect data on each wing beat.

The study revealed that bat wings and bird wings perform quite differently. While birds flap their wings and separate individual feathers to aid in taking off and while flying, the bats move their wings in a backwards and sometimes upside-down motion to help them stay aloft and to help them obtain lift, the differences are particularly obvious when the animals fly at a slower pace.

The way birds and bats deal with turbulence also differs. Birds move their wings in a way that swirls the air around them while flying through a patch of turbulence, creating a single vortex that encompassed both wings. When exposed to the same turbulent conditions, the bats maneuvered their wings to create a single vortex, but a different vortex developed behind each wing. This double vortex provides the bat with greater flight control.

The research team feels that the fact that the Pallas's Long-Tongued bats used for the study create different vortex for each wing stems from the fact that unlike the birds, the bats lack a tail, which the birds use to connect their vortex and maneuver through the turbulence, allowing the bat to remain aerodynamically independent without sacrificing maneuverability or stability.

One University of Portland biologist believes that the wing's design provides the bat with more lift per stroke, making it a great deal more efficient during situations where slow flight is required, such as when gathering nectar.

Faster than a Speeding … Bird

Until recently, the common swift has enjoyed the distinction of being the fastest winged animal, but not anymore.

The common swift can reach speeds of approximately 112km/h (69.7 mph), which is quite impressive, but doesn't come anywhere near the speed of Brazilian free-tailed bats, which recently clocked in at 160 km/h (99.42 mph.)

The new speed champion was crowned after the University of Tennessee in Knoxville's Gary McCracken and the Institute for Ornithology's Max Planck devised a system that allowed them to fasten a bat-sized radio transmitter to the bats. The pair then used a small aircraft fitted with a receiver to collect data on how fast the bats were flying and the types of wind conditions the animals encountered.

It'll be interesting to see if the Brazilian free-tailed bats will be able to maintain their status, or if another bat will eventually prove to be faster yet.

Highly Specialized Design

A study conducted by John Hopkin's University and led by researcher Cynthia Moss revealed some interesting things about the anatomy of bat wings.

The "wing" we see when a bat flies over our head is a membrane that's supported by the bat's fingers. To accommodate the membrane and provide the strength needed for flight, the bat arm has a small radius when compared to the ulna and humerus bones. The pectoral girdle is a specialized design that helps the bat achieve the range of motion they need for their aerial acrobatics.

Take a closer look and you'll observe fine hairs on the wings. It turns out, these hairs are quite similar to a cat's whiskers and are important to the bat's survival.

Each of the hairs contain intricate sensory cells that play a key role in the animal's ability to fly smoothly.

When the tiny hairs were removed from the wings, scientists noticed a marked increase in the length of time it took the bat to slow and that the bat was no longer able to make incredibly tight turns. The researchers later confirmed that the sensory cells shared a direct link to the brain cells, providing vital information about environmental conditions the bat needed to hunt safely.

With the assistance of touch receptor expert Ellen Lumpkin, a Columbia University biologist, Moss discovered that the small hairs contained two types of sensory cells. The cells found close to the follicle are Merkel cells, while the ones closer to the tip are called lanceolate endings.

Prior to the study, it was assumed that the bat's wing sent signals in the same manner as a human hand or animal's forelimb. Researchers thought signals from the wings traveled to the cervical spine with only a few getting routed to the thoracic spine. In reality, the bat wing contains nerve pathways that go to both the animal's trunk and its neck. This discovery leads Moss to believe that the wing isn't an appendage, but rather a growth that forms during prenatal development and is formed out of trunk tissue.

Just below the membrane's outer layer are several visible blood vessels that make up a vascular system that's every bit as complicated and sophisticated as what lies beneath our own skin. It contains a complex map of veins, capillaries, and arterioles that work together to maintain the health of the animal's wings.

In the wings, the veins do more than transport blood. They also gently pulse. These contractions serve to not only keep the blood moving through the wing and towards the heart while the bat forages, but also help the bat maintain a safe blood pressure level while it's roosting. Without the complex circulatory system contained within the wings, it wouldn't be possible for bats to drop directly from the upside-down position they roost in and directly into flight.

While bats don't use their wings to breathe, the wings do play an important role in gas exchange. The wing's membrane is thin, so thin that in warm weather, CO_2 is released via the wing membrane. The amount of gas exchange that takes place via the wing membrane varies depending on a number of variables, but in some species, the total gas exchange through the wings was measured at 10% when the temps were between 33°C and 35°C. As the bat prepares to hibernate and is in the process of decreasing their metabolic rate, the total gas exchange slows, but it doesn't stop. Studies show that even while the wings are tightly folded around the bat's body as it hibernates, there's still a passive gas exchange taking place via the wing membrane. This passive gas exchange plays an important role in the bat's ability to survive the hibernation period. If something happens, such as the wing is attacked by *Pseudogymnoascus destructans*, the fungus that causes White-Nose Syndrome, the bat is forced to make up for the lack of passive gas exchange by increasing its lung usage, which in turn hastens water loss due to pulmonary evaporation.

No Two Bats Have the Same Wings

Sybill Amelon of the USDA Forest Service, along with researchers from the University of Missouri, Sarah Hooper and Kathryn Womack, recently shocked the scientific community when they announced that they'd learned that they can use the wings to accurately identify individual bats. It turns out that each wing contains a set of "wing prints" that work just like human fingerprints. Each set is completely unique to each bat.

Anyone lucky enough to get up close and personal with a bat will notice that the wing membrane is full of little lines which, despite what they look like, aren't creases or wrinkles but actually collagen-elastin bundles. Each of these bundles plays a key role in ensuring that the wing is both strong enough and flexible enough for flight. They also ensure that the wing heals quickly if the bat gets tangled in briars or thorns. It also turns out that the structure of the bundles is unique to every single bat.

Amelon's team examined the wings of four different bat species and discovered that the lines met the four requirements of scientific standards established for unique identification requirements, which are:

- Collectability
- Distinctiveness
- Permanence
- Universality

The bundles create such distinctive markings that all it took was basic training for others to be able to use the lines to earn a 96% success rate when they were asked to identify the a photograph of a bat.

Confirming that the wings are a reliable source of identification may enable chiropterologists and bat rehabbers to explore an alternative method of identifying bats that doesn't require the use of banding which has the potential to harm bats.

Why Science is So Obsessed with Bat Wings

The group of people most interested in learning how bats fly aren't biologists, but rather engineers and developers. They hope that as the scientific community steadily unravels the mystery surrounding exactly how bats fly as well as they do, that this information can be used to develop better man-made aerial devices.

Bat Shows Off Its Wings While Expertly Sipping Nectar

Figure 36 © Spackadet2
Acquired via Dreamstime.com

Beautiful Bat Fact #29
Bats Pay Dearly for Soggy Conditions

It's rare to see a bat out and about when it's raining. For a long time, it was assumed that the sound of rain hindered the bat's echolocation skills, but since they have a way to deal with that issue, another hypothesis was created: bugs rarely venture out when it's raining so why would the bats that feed on them? It makes sense.

Thanks to a study conducted by Germany's Leibniz Institute for Zoo and Wildlife Research, going out in wet conditions when there may not be many insects about costs insect-feeding bats in a big way. Not only aren't they able to find much to eat, each hunt takes a big toll on the bat.

Flying takes a great deal of energy. Each time they go out on a hunt, the bat uses approximately ten times more energy than they do when they're resting, and that's when the weather conditions are ideal. The amount of energy they burn through is why they eat more than half their body weight each night.

Research now indicates that getting wet and having to fly around in a soggy fur coat doubles the amount of energy the bat uses, energy that's going to be difficult to replace given the soggy weather conditions.

The interesting thing about the study was that when the soaking wet bats were weighed, they weren't any heavier than when they'd been dry. Based on this information, the research team determined that the reason for the increased energy usage was loss of body heat. They also wonder if the wet fur takes a toll on the bat's aerodynamic ability.

The team used bats they caught in Costa Rica for the research project. It will be interesting to see if further research reveals that the different bat species, such as the fishing and swimming greater bulldog bat, have the same reaction when their fur gets wet.

Beautiful Bat Fact #30
Blind as a Bat? You Should Be So Lucky!

Somewhere along the line, someone used the phrase "blind as a bat" and the saying stuck. The general assumption is that the origins of this rumor developed from the idea that because bats hunt at night and have small eyes, they must not see well. The person who started the rumor was wrong.

Bats have surprisingly good vision, especially in comparison to humans. The average bat sees three times better than the average human. So really, being blind as a bat would be a good thing.

Through the Eyes of a Bat

Bat have two spectral cone photoreceptor types within their eyes. One helps the bat see during daylight hours. The second cone helps the bat see colors, something nectar-loving bats use when choosing which plant to pollinate.

A series of tests conducted by a team of researchers at the Max Planck Institute for Brain Research in Frankfurt and the University of Oldenburg revealed that the double cones provides the bat with better vision at twilight when they're leaving their roost.

Don't be fooled by microbats' small eyes. The visual centers of their brains are highly developed.

Polarized Light Gives Bats an Edge

Humans struggle to cope with polarized light; it's one of the main reasons we always have a pair of sunglasses tucked into the center console, but bats love the intense light and use it as a kind of compass.

When the setting sun creates polarized light and the bats are fleeing their daytime roosts, they use the scattered polarized rays to create a mark on their mental map. The light then serves as a kind of compass, helping the bats head in the direction of the best hunting grounds.

While we only see polarized light rays when the sun is setting or rising, bat eyes are so well adapted that they continue to see the light on cloudy days and for a long time after the sun officially sets.

A Flying Fox Shows off its Gorgeous Eyes

Figure 37 © Sergey Taran
Acquired via Dreamstime.com

Beautiful Bat Fact #25
Why Sleep Upside Down?

If you walk into a cave where a group of bats is hibernating, you'll find all of them hanging upside down. This habit puzzled researchers for a long time, but after studying the wings and how bats fly, it was determined that the sleeping position wasn't selected because bats were trying to increase blood flow to their brain, but was actually a clever survival mechanism.

Tricking Predators

Bats instinctively seek out places that most predators don't like. Very few of the predators that feed on bats like to venture into the caves bats love and fewer still will climb up to the ceiling. In addition to roosting in an out of the way location, hanging upside down makes it difficult for most predators to see the bat, which often looks like a bit of dried leaf or clump of cobweb hanging from the ceiling.

Speedy Get-Aways

Avoiding predators represents one reason bats hang upside down while resting.

The main reason they prefer to sleep in such an awkward position stems from how they're wings are designed. Bird wings are designed to obtain lift upon take-off. Bats struggle to obtain lift, it's one of the only areas where birds wings best bat wings.

When a bat decides to leave their roost, it lets go of whatever it's clinging to and literally falls off the cave roof, tree branch, underside of a bridge, or rain gutter. As they fall, they spread their wings and let air pressure build up under the leathery skin until the pressure is strong enough for them to fly.

The entire process takes less than a moment.

While you and I would find hanging upside down a difficult sleeping position, researchers learned that bats find their preferred sleeping position to be quite relaxing, which is important, particularly to hibernating bats. Staying relaxed and in a deep sleep is the only way the bat can conserve enough energy to survive the cold months.

Despite Spending So Much Time Upside Down, They Don't Get Headaches

One of the reasons we humans spend a limited amount of time hanging upside down and standing on our heads stems from the fact that after just a few minutes, we develop colossal headaches.

Bats don't suffer from this problem.

The reason for this. Size.

On the average day, you should have approximately 2 gallons of blood flowing through your veins. When your head goes down, the blood surges to the area. That's why you're supposed to tuck your head between your knees whenever you feel faint. The problem is that we're only designed to tolerate that degree of pressure for very short periods of time.

Bats, even megabats like flying fox bats, are considerably smaller. They're small enough that gravity impacts them differently than it does you. The decreased gravitational pull means less blood pooling in their brains, allowing them to hang upside down for as long as they like.

Sleeping Bat

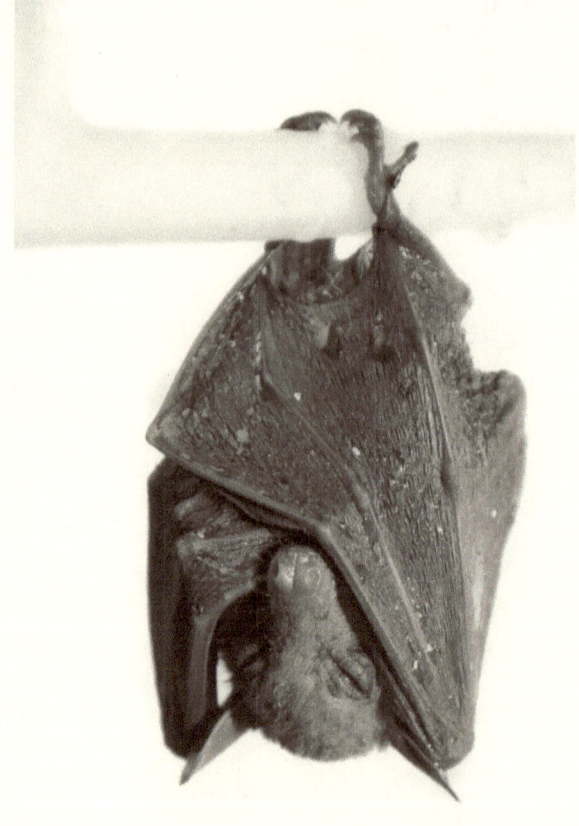

Figure 38 © Antoni Halim
Acquired via Dreamstime.com

Beautiful Bat Fact #32
Sucker-Footed Bats: There's an Exception
to Every Rule

The hot eastern Madagascar sun beats down on the dense forest. The intense heat sends most mammals deeper into the forest, desperate to find some relief in the dark shadows. At the edge of the forest stands one lone Ravenala tree with a secret. No one knows it, but hidden deep within the cones created by one of its tightly curled-up leaves, a colony of several tiny chocolate-colored bats called sucker-footed bats (*Myzopoda aurita*) are nestled together, taking advantage of the protection the leaf provides against both the sun and predators. They cling to the leaf's slippery surface as they sleep the day away, saving up all their strength for when the sun sets and they take to the evening sky for a night of feasting on moths and any other soft-bodied insects they encounter.

Sucker-footed bats are easily identified by their long, soft-looking ears, which have targus that prevents debris from falling into the ear canal and aids with echolocation. While lots of bat species have long ears and prominent targuses, sucker-footed bats are one of the few that also have a strange-looking, mushroom-shaped bump at the base of each ear. Look a little closer, and you'll notice something far more interesting than the ears that the bat takes its name from: they have pad attachments on both their wrists and ankles, which look like horseshoes and give the bats traction while they walk on slippery leaves.

These pads are why the species was named "sucker-footed" bats.

Sucker-footed bats are small. Small enough that they can fly quite close to a human and no one will ever see them. They weigh about a half ounce and once they're fully grown, they're only 5.08 cm (2 in.) long.

Since the discovery of the first sucker-footed bat in 1878, researchers have been fascinated by their feet, which are so different from all other bat species. While bat experts understood the pads help the tiny bat cling to the palm leaves, they weren't sure how the suction pads worked. They were also puzzled why this tiny bat species bucks bat convention and sleeps head up rather than hanging upside down.

Paul Racey, a biologist at Riskin and Brown, took it upon himself to learn the answers. Prior to starting his research, he hypothesized that the suction pads in the bat's feet worked in a manner that was quite similar to how gecko feet work. The results he collected surprised him.

Racey learned that the sucker-footed bat's suction pads were much stronger than anyone realized. They're designed to hold more than 8.6 times the bat's actual weight, allowing it to stay securely attached to the leaves during strong winds. Racey also learned that the suction pads only adhered to the leaf when the bat was head up. When the bat turned upside down, the sucker pads provided very little suction, allowing the bat to easily fall off the leaf and gain the lift needed to take flight.

The most interesting thing about the experiment was that the little bat's suction pads don't require suction to work. When the bat moves on a leaf, they exude a substance that's a great deal like sweat and holds them to the leaf. The effect is a great deal like the tacky section on a Post-It note.

A series of experiments revealed that the suction pad's design enables the little bats to easily walk up the leaves. Unlike some sucker-footed animals, they don't have to unstick their feet with each step, making it easier for them to move, avoid predation, and use less energy.

Racey and his team might have solved the twin mysteries of how the sucker-footed bats pads work and why they sleep right-side up, but one open mystery remains. No one knows anything about female sucker-footed bats. Despite years of research, despite netting (and releasing) more than 800 sucker-footed bats over the course of his career, Racey hasn't identified a single female sucker-footed bat. They're as baffling and nearly as rare Tolkein's Entwives. The researchers do know the females exist. The body of one was found and shipped to the Smithsonian more than thirty years ago, and the team found several juvenile males.

The IUCN Red List has the sucker-footed bat listed as least concern, siting the species' wide range and the fact that they seem to have actually benefited from some of the deforestation. The only real concern the organization has about this species is its dependency on the Ravenala tree. If Ravenala trees are struck by some sort of blight or invasive species, it's unclear how the sucker-footed bat would respond.

Beautiful Bat Fact #33
Bats in Love: Dating isn't Easy

Until recently, little was known about the mating practices of bats, mostly because it wasn't an area that had sparked much interest in the scientific community, and partly because people rarely stumble across a pair of mating bats.

Now that biologists have begun delving into the sex lives of bats, it's becoming obvious that when it comes to carnal matters, bats have more to teach us than we ever believed possible.

Courtship Rituals

If you think finding a human partner is tough, be thankful you're not a bat.

For most bat species, creating the perfect date is placed squarely on the male's shoulders. Each species has developed its own techniques for wooing a mate.

Mood Music

For some bats, the key to a successful date night is having just the right playlist.

Female lesser short-tailed bats don't use music to set

the scene, but they are attracted to guys with the best singing voices. And the length of the performance puts Pavarotti to shame. The male lesser short-tailed bat spends six to seven hours serenading their lady love. And the guys have a long playlist; they're capable of singing up to four hundred different songs per minute.

Before breaking out in song, the male sets the scene. He spends a nice chunk of time searching through the old-growth forest for an appealing crevice or branch, which they set up as their "love roost." When the female decides which guy has the sweetest voice, she enters the roost he's selected, they enjoy a moment of passion, and she departs. The next night, the process starts up all over again.

Researchers have observed that some males share mating roosts, which increases the odds of each of them getting some action.

The Mexican free-tailed bat is another species that sings about their quest for true love. Their courtship songs involve buzzes, trills, and chirps. The songs aren't random; the bats remember what patterns work and which don't attract the ideal mate.

Honking Competitions

Male hammer-head bats (*Hypsignathus monstrosus*) also like to vocalize their desire to find a mate; however, while the lesser short-tailed bats and Mexican free-tailed bats have pretty voices and a complex set of songs, the hammer-headed fellas like to keep things simple. When the urge to find a mate hits, the males line up and start honking. That's right. They use their impressive noses to honk their carnal desires. And female hammer-headed bats soak it up. As far as researchers can tell, the females use the tone of the honk, how loud the honk is, and whether a male manages to out honk his companions to determine who wins their affections.

Some Do It Orally

It's always been assumed that fellatio, or as it's more commonly called, oral sex, was a human obsession. Until now.

Researchers were shocked when they observed female greater short-nosed fruit bats engaging in oral sex prior to the actual copulation. While no one knows precisely why the females in this particular species behave this way, researchers have noted for that every second of fellatio, the actual copulation lasts an additional six seconds.

There's two possible reasons that the greater short-nosed fruit bats engage in fellatio behavior prior to copulation. The first is that by prolonging the sex act, there's a greater chance of conception. It's also possible that it could make sex safer, since it's possible bacteria in the female's saliva kills some STDs.

Cologne Only a Bat Can Love

While some bats, such as the minor epauletted fruit bats (*Epomophorus minor*) have tufts of hair that the females of their species find attractive, researchers believe that the females are less interested in what the tufts look like and are more concerned with the scent, which may relay information about the male's genetics, overall social position, and general health, allowing her to decide whether her current suitor is a good match, or if she should wait for someone better to come along.

The greater sac-winged bats fill the pouches on their wings with a mixture of secretions that drive the lady bats wild, and the Australian spectacled flying fox smears secretions on their neck while preparing for date nights.

Long-nosed bats also use scent to attract their mates, but in their case, the preferred perfume is sweat and it's produced by subcutaneous glands located in the male's dorsal patches.

Strong Construction Skills Required

Female short-nosed fruit bats want a house and they expect their guys to make that happen. As the breeding season approaches, the males go to work constructing tents out of stems. Once construction is complete, the male covers the opening in a layer of his own saliva, probably to warn other males away.

The tents aren't easy to create. The males start the construction process a full month ahead of the breeding season. It's in the male's best interest to put some real effort into the construction process, since deep, nicely designed tents attract an entire harem of willing females to his spit-coated door.

The white-throated round-eared bat *(Lophostoma silvicolum)* also provides a "home" for its mate, but instead of building one from scratch, it excavates a termite hill.

Love Doesn't Come Cheap

Female common vampire bats don't give away their affections. First, the male has to prove himself worthy by providing her a gift, which comes in the form of a shared blood dinner.

Size Matters

It turns out that when it comes to bats and reproduction, size really does matter.

Pound-for-pound, male bats are incredibly well endowed. Their testicles represent anywhere from between 0.12 percent and 8.5 percent of the bat's overall body mass. By comparison, the testicles make up just 0.02 to 0.75 percent of the body mass of primates, including humans.

After studying 334 different bat species, a Scott

Pitnick led research team rocked the world with the news that bats can have big brains or big balls, but they can't have both. It turns out that most species opted for big balls.

During their respective breeding seasons, most female bats enjoy the attention of multiple partners. It's believed that the reason male bats have such large testicles stems from the need for a power ejaculation. The stronger that is, the better the odds are that his sperm will be the one that makes it to the egg first, and that male's genetic legacy passes on to the next generation.

While most bat species have more balls than brains, there are exceptions. Researchers report that the bat species who are believed to form monogamous relationships have larger brains and smaller testicles.

Bat experts believe that there are a few monogamous bat species. These faithful males have a significantly larger brain. A monogamous bat's brain equals 2.6% of its overall body weight, while the polygamous bat's brain is only 1.9% of its total body mass.

Bat species believed to be monogamous include:

- Samoan Flying Fox
- Dayak Fruit Bat
- Painted Woolly Bat
- Linneaus's False Vampire Bat

It's worth noting that even though a species might be considered monogamous, scientists have discovered that one, and sometimes both, partners will sometimes go elsewhere for a little fun. In nearly all monogamous species, there have been cases of "cheating" observed.

As odd as some of these courtship rituals might seem, they pale in comparison to some other bat reproductive habits.

Location, Location, Location

As a rule, male bats separate themselves from the females, preferring to roost individually or in small bachelor colonies, while the females can congregate in colonies of more than a thousand bats.

There are a few possible reasons for this. First, by living apart from the lady bats, the males protect themselves from the pests, fungus, and disease that can ravage a large colony. Another advantage is that by distancing them from the females, who can consume their weight in insects each night while they're lactating, the males have a better chance of meeting their nutritional needs.

One study that took a hard look at the living conditions of males and female Daubenton's bats discovered that as a rule, the two genders don't just separate themselves by distance, but also altitude.

The research team studied the bats that live in the Yorkshire Dales National Park near the River Wharf. Most of the bats the team caught while working in lower altitudes were females who were still caring for their young. When the team moved to a higher altitude, they caught primarily males.

An interesting thing happened when the scientists set their nets at a middling altitude. Suddenly, they were catching representatives of both genders.

The researchers concluded that there are two possible reasons the bats chose to mingle at this middle of the altitude range. The most obvious is that limited food supplies forced some of the females to fly higher and some of the males to descend.

It's also possible, that by staying in the middle, the bat, especially the males, have the best shot of passing on their genetic material during breeding season since they're already close to the lady bats, giving them an edge on the higher flying males who have to make a long journey to the caves where this species likes to mate. Plus, the shorter trip means they have more energy to devote to both courtship and mating.

Male Bat Shows Displays His Genitals, a Courtship Routine Many Bat Species Have in Common

Figure 39 © panuruangjan
Acquired via Deposit Photos

Schira

Hammerhead Bat
(*Hypsignathus monstrosus*)

ZYGÆNOCEPHALUS   LABROSUS

Figure 40 © G H Ford

White-Throated Round-Eared Bat
(Lophostoma silvicolum)

Figure 41 © Desmodus
[CC BY-SA 3.0], via Wikimedia Commons

Greater Short-nosed Fruit Bat
(*Cynopterus sphinx*)

Figure 42 © Shantanu Kuveskar
[CC BY-SA 4.0], via Wikimedia Commons

Greater Sac-Winged Bat
(Saccopteryx bilineata)

Figure 43 ©Karin Schneeberger
[CC BY-SA 3.0], via Wikimedia Commons

Close up image of the wing-sac that a greater sac-winged bat fills with the stinky stuff that drives lady bats wild.

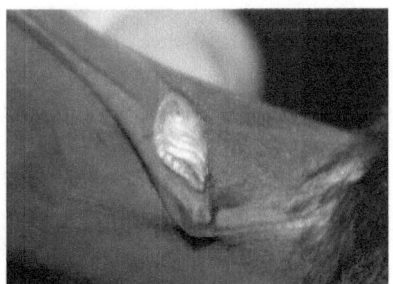

Figure 44 ©Karin Schneeberger [CC BY-SA 3.0], via Wikimedia Commons

Beautiful Bat Fact #34
Partner Swaps & Chasity Belts

Horseshoe bats are some of the most distinctive-looking bats you'll encounter. The unique mouth makes its face unforgettable in a so-ugly-it's-cute way. The more than seventy different species of horseshoe bats were named because of their horseshoe-shaped noses that have extra skin folds, which experts believe aids with the animal's echolocation while hunting insects.

The greater horseshoe bat is the largest of the seventy species, and ranges include Wales, Southwest England, Asia, and North Africa.

While hunting, greater horseshoe bats (*Rhinolophus ferrumequinum*) swoop close to the pasture land that they love, grabbing most of their prey directly off the ground before finding a comfy, safe branch or rock overhang where they dine. Cattle and sheep pastures make up their favorite hunting spots, probably because the livestock attract more insects than barren fields. They're particularly fond of grazing pastures that have some deciduous trees and southern slopes.

Species survival depends on them having a series of caves they can use for roosting, which allows them to choose from a variety of air flow temperatures, humidity levels, and temperatures, which is a necessary aspect of handling natural weather changes. Whenever possible, this shy species chooses quiet areas that are far away from humans for their roosts.

Conservationists are working overtime to learn as much as they can about the species so they can effectively halt the current decline in its population. They've uncovered some pretty interesting facts about the average greater horseshoes bat's sex life.

A Little Romantic Mood Music

The greater horseshoe bat is a vocal bat who enjoys singing, and never more so than during the mating season. The male sings to attract a mate. When a friendly female snuggles up to him, he changes up his song, using a series of short constant chirps as part of his foreplay routine. Once they're engaged in the actual sex act, the romantic song switches to long syllables.

Should the female decide that she's not made the right choice, she emits a series of broad-band vocalizations and other angry chirps in the moments leading up to penetration. Males don't argue with her angry tone; they fly away and search for a more willing partner. If pleased with her choice, the female remains silent during the copulation.

Sharing the Love

Most of the world's bats species are polygamous by nature, and at least some of the species, such as the greater horseshoe bats, happily share partners with their grandparents and parents. Don't let that lower your opinion of the bat. According to research conducted by a team led by Queen Mary, University of London's Stephen Rossiter, the ladies have developed a mysterious, but highly effective, method for avoiding incestual relationships, despite her current suitor being the father of her mother's pup.

The team believes the partner swap is more than the

ladies enjoying a wild and swinging life style. They think the partner swap tradition helps strengthen the colony's social ties, through related genes.

What the team can't figure out is how the bats know which guys they share DNA with and which aren't related. The researchers created family trees for 450 different bats within the species and discovered that while the genetics were confusing, there wasn't a single example of a female mating with her sire or grandsire. The best guess is that scent enables the bats to know who they can mate with and who they should avoid.

Before you form a low opinion of female horseshoe bats, know that they do have some sort of code when it comes to playing musical partners, the ladies have a strict understanding. While mothers and daughters are free to engage in carnal activities with the same guy, they don't mate with him at the same time. The daughter waits for her mother's relationship to run its course before she responds to the same fella's love song.

The study has the distinction of being one of the longest studies of wild animal populations ever conducted.

The Batty Version of a Chasity Belt

The ability to share partners with one another and identify which bats they're related to is just one of the things that makes the reproduction habits of the greater horseshoe bats interesting.

After mating, the male produces a natural vaginal plug, also referred to as a mating plug, which ensures that his sperm is used when the female chooses to fertilize her eggs. It's also possible that the plug keeps the sperm contained within the female while she waits for the conditions to be right and finally fertilizes her egg.

There has been some speculation that if the female encounters a male she prefers, she's able to expel the vaginal plug.

While the idea of a male bat using a plug to ensure his sperm creates a baby seems odd to you and me, the phenomenon has been observed before. Other animals that use a similar ploy include:

- Richardson's ground squirrel
- Acanthocephalan worms
- Rats
- Scorpions
- Mice
- Spiders
- Kangaroos
- Bees
- Chimpanzees

Threats to the Greater Horseshoe Bat

There are several different issues putting a strain on the greater horseshoe bat population including:
- Farmers getting away from using hedgerows
- Chemicals on vegetation that results in fewer bugs, making it harder for the bats to find sufficient food
- Loss of natural habitat.

Current protection efforts include working with farmers to discover ways they can continue to produce high yield crops and also provide good hunting grounds for the bats. Particular emphasis has been placed on keeping some hedgerows on the property.

Although the IUCN Red List admits that some regions have experienced a sharp decline in the greater horseshoe bat population, because the species has such a large range and manages to maintain a healthy population is other regions, the organization currently has the species listed as least concern.

Beautiful Bat Fact #35
Bringing up the Pups

Raising bat pups isn't for the faint of heart.

For most mammals, the rules are easy. Have sex, get pregnant, give birth a few months later. Bats break the rule.

The first rule they break? Conception takes place months after the actual mating act.

For example, in North America, most bat breeding seasons take place in the fall, but the actual gestating doesn't start until spring time. Bat mothers delay the gestation if environmental conditions aren't ideal. No one is sure why bats developed this trait or exactly how they're able to basically put everything in stasis for so long.

What does vary from one bat species to another is the length of time the bat remains pregnant.

Most microbats have a gestation period that's approximately three months long. Vampire bats' gestation period lasts for seven months, which ounce-for-ounce, makes them the longest gestating mammal in the world.

Most bats only have one pup per year, there are some exceptions. Hoary bats, Seminole bats, and Eastern red bats frequently have two and sometimes give birth to as many as four pups a year.

Bat Moms Are Tough

Bat moms are some of the toughest mammals around. Not only do they manage to carry and deliver a baby that weighs one third their weight (the equivalent of a 125-lb. female giving birth to a 41.6-lb. baby), since it can't fly, she must take it everywhere she goes.

The pups are born furless and defenseless. Like the offspring of all mammals, they depend on their mom for food, grooming, and shelter. For the first few weeks of its life, the pup goes everywhere its mom goes. Unlike kangaroos and other mammals that carry their young with them thanks to a special pouch, bats don't have anything to help them transport their child while they forage. While the mother flies thirty or more feet above the ground, her child clings to her body.

And the way the pups hang on to their mom is downright brutal. First, it winds its powerful hind legs around her torso. In addition to using muscles to cling to her, at birth, bat pups have a little hard spot that forms just beneath the hard toenail. The purpose of this hard sport is to allow the baby to secure its hold on Mom. That hard spot attaches to the mother a bit like Velcro. Once the baby is old enough to stay in the roost while their mother forages, the hard spot disappears.

Next, the pup bites down on one of her nipples and holds on for dear life. They do this thanks to tiny milk teeth that curve backwards and are specially designed for holding on tight. In addition to the milk teeth, the pup has tiny bumps where its canine teeth will eventually be that also improve the security of its hold. In most species, the milk teeth are replaced with permanent teeth when the baby bat turns about five weeks old.

No wonder most species only have one pup a year. Who'd want to put themselves through that kind of torture any more than necessary!

Even though female bats do take their pups on flights, there are also times when they leave them behind at the roost. This gives the mother an opportunity to do enough hunting so she can recover the energy she expends keeping her youngster fed.

Researchers have observed that many bat species have a system in place where other mothers watch over the pups while the pup's mom hunts. It's hard to know which is more remarkable. The fact that other mothers willingly step up to the plate and serve as babysitters, or that a female can identify her pup from the thousands of other pups that are in the cave. Scientists believe that the mothers rely on smell and echolocation to identify their pup.

Some extremely generous moms will even take over the care of orphaned pups.

The First Few Days

At birth, a baby bat is already one third its mother's size, but don't let the fact that's it's big fool you into thinking it's tough. Like human babies, baby bats are pretty vulnerable and delicate.

At birth the newborn bat's eyes are closed and it doesn't have any fur.

The good news is that baby bats grow quite quickly. While they're still nursing, they either hang on to their mom while she hunts, or they stay in the roost and wait for her return. It doesn't take long before the youngsters learn how to fly on their own, at which point they're ready to go on short flights and start learning how to use their echolocation and fend for themselves.

Most baby bats are ready for complete independence at about three months of age, though this can vary from one species to the next.

They're Chatty

Except for a small group of primates, it's always been assumed that baby babble was unique to human infants, but it's not. It turns out that newborn bat pups also like to babble.

A lucky research team from the University of Erlangen-Nuernberg got to spend a great deal of time hanging out with four-to-eight-week-old sac-winged bat pups and dedicated the time to learning as much as they could about the various sounds the young bats made.

One of the really interesting things the team noticed was that the female pups practiced a territorial song that had previously only been heard by adult males while they warned others off their territory. The team was flummoxed as to why the young females would practice something they've never been observed using as adults.

It's likely that the pups use the early babbling, barking, chirping, chattering, and singing to help strengthen their vocal chords, hone their echolocation, and to start identifying the sounds/songs of their species.

Bat Pups

Figure 45 © Benjaminboeckle
Acquired via Dreamstime.com

Figure 46 © Mickey Samuni-Blank
[CC BY-SA 3.0], via Wikimedia Commons

Beautiful Bat Fact #36
The Dayak Fruit Bat's Shocking Ability

The smell of ripe figs draws several small, greygreyish-brown dayak fruit bats away from the limestone cave where they've been roosting. The bats flit and flutter through the limbs, seeking out the ideal pieces of fruit, while maintaining a constant stream of chatter with one another. The bats select the piece of fruit they want and fly off with it to consume it in a safer location. When they're done, they drop seeds that are too big to swallow or defecate the seeds. Experts report that the seeds the species distribute throughout the forest have an extremely high germination rate.

If you're lucky, you'll get an opportunity to spend a little time exploring the old growth areas of Malaysia's rainforests. If you're incredibly lucky, you just might catch a glimpse of the rare dayak fruit bat (*Dyacopterus spadiceus*) that calls those parts of the forest home.

This is a small fruit bat, weighing in at under 150 grams. The tiny body is covered with short, soft greygrey fur. Its long tail adds an additional 10-20% of length to its body. It's most distinguishing feature is that its head appears too wide for its petite body.

The bat's primary function is eating native figs and distributing the seeds throughout the forest. When they're unable to find any figs, the bats will switch to other types of native fruit and will even chew on leaves.

Until recently, one of the dayak bat's most unique features was that experts believe it's one of just a handful of bat species that's monogamous. This was enough to catch the interest of researchers, but they never imagined just how unique dayak males really are.

After mist-netting several bats, they were surprised to discover that one of the male bats had noticeably enlarged nipples. For a moment, the researchers thought they'd made a mistake and actually captured a female, but a quick check showed that they'd been right the first time. The bat was male. When they squeezed the tiny nipple, the researchers were once again shocked when the bat produced a few droplets of milk.

It was all the inspiration needed to launch a detailed investigation of the male dayak bat's anatomy and physiology.

The investigation revealed that, for some reason, the males developed working mammary glands as well as additional physiological requirements they needed to produce milk. A comparison of the male and female Dayak bat shows that the males are only able to produce about 10% of the milk that their female partners produce while caring for their young. The nipples and mammary glands are also significantly smaller.

This is the first case of male lactation occurring in wild mammals.

There are two theories as to why the dayak fruit bats produce milk. The first is that the males are believed to help the females raise their offspring. It's possible that the ability to produce milk is nature's way of ensuring that the young are adequately cared for if something happens to the mother.

It's possible the bat's diet plays a role in the unexpected lactation.

In addition to locally grown fruit, the bats have also been observed feeding on leaves that contain phytoestrogens, estrogen-like compounds. It's possible that by introducing so much estrogen into their system, it triggered lactation. If the leaves are the reason the males lactate, it's unclear as to whether the bats eat the leaves to encourage lactation.

To date, males have not been observed nursing their young, but since little is known about the roosting/nesting habits or how this species cares for its young, it's possible that the male does use the milk to nourish the pup while his mate hunts.

Although rarely seen, it's believed that the dayak fruit bat has quite a large range that includes parts of Thailand, Malaysia, Indonesia, and the Philippines. Though it's difficult to get a handle on just how large the current dayak fruit bat population is, the IUCN Red List has decided to list them as near threatened, since the species is particularly sensitive to deforestation and human encroachment. The organization predicts that during the next ten years, the dayak fruit bat population will decrease by approximately thirty percent.

Beautiful Bat Facts #37
Plants and Bats: A Perfect Relationship

Nectar-feeding bats make up only a small portion of the estimated 1,300 bat species. They don't get the praise that the insect-feeding bats enjoy and they're not large enough to attract the attention that's lavished on the giant fruit bats, but nectar-feeding bats play an important role in the world's eco-system. Without them, many important plant species would go extinct.

It's only recently that researchers have started to fully grasp just how much plants have developed specific features that help them attract pollinating bats.

How Nectar-Feeding Bats Feed

One of the most important anatomical features of nectar-feeding bats is their tongue. If it's not in perfect working order, they're unable to draw the nectar away from the plant and into their own digestive tract.

The tongue of nectar-feeding bats is really long. The tongue of the tube-lipped nectar bat is more than one and a half times the bat's body length. That's way too long to merely retract towards the back of their mouth, so when the bat finishes eating, their tongue retracts all the way into their rib cage.

There are two classifications of nectar-feeding bats.

One group, glossophaginae bats, have a tongue that's covered in hundreds of tiny papillae, little bristles, that help move the nectar backwards towards the bat's throat. The other group, lonchophyllinae bats, has long grooves in their tongue, which allow their tongue to work as a kind of straw. Both systems are highly effective.

Researchers recently uncovered that in addition to grooves and little hairs, the bats also have a great deal of erectile tissue in their long tongues.

When some researchers decided to dissect the minute tongues of some nectar-feeding bats, they learned that large blood vessels deliver massive amounts of blood to the animal's mouth while it feeds. The researchers also found gaps, or sinuses, on each side of the tongue. The gaps could just be random, but the research team hypothesized that they were responsible for providing additional blood flow to the organ, and that the extra blood enabled the tiny papillae to move.

Observing how the tongues work while nectar-feeding bats eat isn't easy. The bats feed incredibly fast, often visiting the flower, drinking the nectar, and moving on to the next flower in the blink of an eye. Luckily, technology allows contemporary scientists to slow things down enough that they can really observe how the animals extract the nectar.

In order to determine whether the papillae moved during feeding, the research team set up feeding stations and pointed super high speed video cameras at each station. They enlisted the aid of the **Pallas's long-tongued bat** *(Glossophaga soricina) to help with the experiment.*

Seeing exactly how the papillae moved required that the footage be filed at a speed of five hundred frames per second and then slowed down so the researchers could observe the bat's feeding habits. They noted that when the bat approached a fresh bloom and started to stick its tongue out, the papillae laid flat against the tongue's surface.

However, just as the animal's tongue reached its maximum extension point, a full 50% longer than it was when the bat approached the bloom, the hairs leapt to attention at the same time the tongue turned bright red, indicating that all those little spaces and long blood vessels had become engorged with blood, triggering the erectile tissue in the organ.

Why is this research important? Obviously, it helps increase our understanding of bats and their influence on the eco-system, but there's another reason so many people have developed a keen interest in how nectar-feeding bats eat. There's hope that as more is learned about how the tongue works that the medical community will find a way to use the information to design gentler and more effective medical tools.

Another thing scientists noticed about the nectar-feeding bats is that they have long memories and will come back to the same spot night after night if plants continue to bloom. The same memory skills and behaviors have been observed in honey bees.

Hailing All Bats

If you're lucky enough to spend time in Cuba's stunning rainforests, you may come across a special flowering vine called *Marcgravia evenia.*

As the name indicates, the Marcgravia evenia is a night-blooming plant that relies exclusively on nectar-feeding bats for pollination. Instead of bright colors that sunlight-loving plants use to attract bees and daytime pollinators, the Marcgravia evenia has its own set of tricks for attracting bats.

First is the flowers themselves. They're pale in color, making them easy to see on even the darkest of nights, and the design enables the bat to easily access the life-giving nectar while also ensuring the flower is well and truly pollinated. The flower also has a peculiar, somewhat sulfur scent that doesn't appeal to most humans but drives bats wild.

Recent studies show that the Marcgravia evenia doesn't stop there. It also uses the bat's own echolocation to draw the tiny flying mammal to the blooms. The concave nature of the Marcgravia evenia's leaves creates a kind of echo beacon when it's hit with one of the bat's echolocation pulses. It works like a satellite dish that's designed to beam radio waves out and into the world, while the bat acts like a receiver. The echoing beam the plants produce is a two-point signal that the bats instantly recognize as coming from a food source.

The concave leaves stand perfectly upright and form circle around the bloom. Not only does this reduce the amount of time the bat spends looking for flowers, but also decreases the amount of energy the bat uses each night.

Research on how the Marcgravia evenia creates an echo beacon was conducted by a research fellow at the University of Ulm in Germany, Ralph Simon. Additional members of the research team included Marc Hodleried from the University of Bristol and the University of Erlangern-Nuremburg's Otto von Helversen and Corinna Koch.

IUCN has not yet assessed the status of Marcgravia evenia.

Nectar Feeding Bats Snatch a Quick
Snack at a Hummingbird Feeder

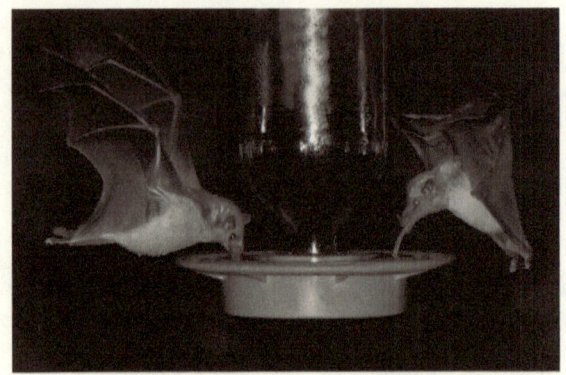

Figure 47 © Steve Byland
Acquired via Dreamstime.com

Beautiful Bat Fact #38
Pallas's Long-Tongued Bat: Master of Burning Fat and Consuming Nectar

With the full moon high in the sky, and the temperature too warm to really sleep, you decide it's the perfect time to take a stroll and enjoy the night time blooms few people ever have a chance to appreciate.

A flash of movement above your head catches your eye, and you pause for a better look.

There's … something hovering under one of the downward turned blooms, but before you can decide if it's a bit of dead leaf blowing in the hot summer breeze or an animal, it darts away, moving to a neighboring bloom.

Standing on tiptoes, you edge a little closer, curious as to exactly what this animal could possibly be. The only thing you've ever encountered that moves so quickly are hummingbirds, but they're not usually nocturnal and this creature moves differently, though its wings beat just as swiftly.

A split second later, the bat leaves the second bloom, darting just close enough for you to realize that what you're seeing definitely isn't a hummingbird, but is in fact a Pallas's long-tongued bat (*Glossophaga soricina*).

People who live in Central and South America will occasionally come into contact with a Pallas's long-tongued bat, though between the species' natural habitat and their super speed, encountering one is quite rare.

The nectar-feeding bat has the distinction of having the fastest metabolism of any mammal. The only animal that really comes to close to matching its metabolism is the hummingbird. Every single night, the bat burns approximately 50% of its fat stores, and that's just part of the story. In addition to going through its fat stores like they're rocket fuel, the bat gets approximately 80% of the energy it needs just to function from the simple sugars it sops up in the form of plant nectar.

The reason the bat burns so much energy is because while it feeds, it also hovers, a form of flying that takes an incredible amount of energy. If the bat isn't able to consume a great deal of nectar while it hovers over a bloom, it could actually starve to death.

Despite feeding in areas that get a great deal of moisture every single year, when it's time to go to sleep for the day, this particular species seeks out dry locations. For roosts, they favor dry, warm hollowed-out trees, rock crevices, and small caves.

When there aren't many flowers available, it's not unusual for members of the Pallas's long-tongued bat clan to visit hummingbird feeders. The hummingbird mixture is exactly the kind of food that the bats needs to thrive. Hummingbird feeders that are full in the early evening but dry the following morning indicate that a decent-sized population of Pallas's long-tonged bats are in the area, even though local residents may never spot one.

The long tongue isn't the only feature that makes the Pallas bat such a phenomenal nectar feeder/pollinator. The animal's hair is specially designed with divergent hair scales that grasp pollen particles and help transfer the pollen from one plant to the next.

It's believed that this particular species has a gestation period of 3.5 months. For the first eighteen or so days of their lives, the pups ride around with Mom while she looks for nectar. When they are a little under a month old, they're ready to learn how to fly.

Due to the fact that the Pallas long-tongued bat has such a wide range and appears to have some tolerance for human encroachment, the IUCN Red List currently has them classified as a species of least concern.

Pallas's Long-Tongued Bat
(Glossophaga soricina)

Figure 48 ©

Beautiful Bat Fact #39
Spix's Disc-Winged Bat: Calling All Roommates!

Deep in the rain forest, a small Spix's disk-winged bat circles around some tightly rolled leaves. Its ears twitch and wave as it sends out a shrill call that's too high for humans to hear without a special echolocation device. The bat falls silent, listening not for the return echo, which would tell it the coordinates of a tasty insect, but rather for a welcoming cry from its colony mates.

Undiscouraged, the little bat makes another turn and cries again, alerting all other Spix's disk-winged bats that it's in the area. This time, it not only gets a response, but also some coordinates.

The small bat banks its wings and makes a tight mid-air turn. With amazing precision, it flies headfirst into a tightly rolled leaf where it's greeted by its colony mates.

Tomorrow morning, the little bat and every other Spix's disk-winged bat will repeat the same process.

It's difficult to imagine a cuter bat than the Spix's disk-winged bat (*Thyroptera tricolor*). This particular insect-feeding bat looks more like a round fuzz ball than an actual bat. The bat lives in South America, where it consumes approximately 0.8 grams of insects every single night.

Physically, the most interesting thing about the Spix's disk-winged bat is the small disks located on both their hind feet and thumbs. It's these disks that allows the species to easily crawl all over the leaves they love roosting in.

The Spix's disk-winged bat has a few lifestyle choices that set it apart from other kinds of bats. Instead of roosting in caves or hollowed-out trees, they prefer to set up house in leaves that start out tightly furled and uncurl as the day goes on. The nature of the leaves forces the bats to find a new leaf to roost in every single day.

Another interesting thing about the Spix's disk-winged bat is that it likes to live in groups that consist of four to six bats. They form a close family unit and will stay together for several years, something that's rarely seen in other bat species.

Research indicates that while the bats are quite close and are very talkative, they have a difficult time determining when they're communicating with a long-term roost mate or a complete stranger. It turns out that the rolled-up leaf design is a key aspect of helping them determine who they're talking to and letting their friends know about the newest digs.

Proving the rolled leaves aid in bat communication required a team of scientists to record an array of bat calls. About eighty of the calls were the single-note calls the species uses while they're trying to connect with their roost mates. Another sixty-five calls were recorded. The response includes more than twenty different sounds.

The research team placed a recorded call both in and outside a leaf and used a microphone with an attached recorder to capture the response.

The results disproved their theory that the leaves served as a megaphone, making it easy for flying bats to identify their roost mates. It turned out that the recording that was played within the leaf was only a decibel higher than the one that was played outside the leaf.

However, just because the hypothesis was disproven, it doesn't mean the experiment didn't reveal some interesting information. Where the leaf made a big difference was how well the bats who were already tucked inside their new roost received the location call from their missing roost mate. The sound the leaf funneled into it was a full ten decibels louder.

The results also presented the team with a reason why the bats struggled to recognize the call of their friends. The response call is flattened and distorted by the leaf. In order to make up for this problem, the bats send a representative to hang out outside the leaf and establish that the owner of the response call is a bat they know.

Although the IUCN Red List currently has the Spix's disk-winged bats listed as a species of least concern, the organization has noted that further assessment is needed.

Beautiful Bat Fact #40
The Pallid Bat: A Bat with an Insatiable Appetite

Up and down, the bat's long wings beat a slow rhythm as the large bat flies just a few feet above the sandy desert ground. Moonlight reflects off its pale fur as its long ears swivel to and fro, picking up the different night sounds.

There! A soft patter of tiny feet against scratchy sand! The exact sound the bat has been seeking. It swoops, the tips of its toenails leaving faint tracks in the sand before they close around the body of an unsuspecting scorpion, the first meal this particular pallid bat (*Antrozous pallidus*) will feed on tonight.

The pallid bat is extremely attractive. Its soft cream-colored fur practically begs to be stroked, and yet its fur is rarely the first thing people comment on when they have a face-to-face encounter with this particular species. The characteristic that draws the most attention is its ears. They're enormous. And it's not an optical illusion. The length of the pallid bat's ears is half the combined length of his skull and spine. Looking at the bat, it's a little difficult to believe it can fly. It seems like the ears would make them front end heavy.

Despite the enormous ears, the pallid bat doesn't appear to have any trouble flying. They're frequently found flying low, just a meter or two off the ground, searching for their dinner.

Even in the world of bats, the pallid bat is considered highly social. Pups and mothers stay together for a full year before the pups go their separate ways and form their own colony.

The average roosting size colony consists of anywhere from twelve to one hundred bats, with the preferred colony size appearing to be twenty adults. One researcher observed a colony of 162 pallid bats, but it's the only recorded colony of that size.

In comparison to other types of bats, the pallid bat isn't a very good flier. It is both slow and lacks the maneuverability typically seen in bats of its small size. What it lacks in flying ability, it makes up for in climbing skills. Whether they're pushing themselves into a bloom or have been forced to the ground, this species is quite nimble while they crawl, an unusual trait for a bat.

In addition to sleeping the day away, the pallid bat will also take a nap during the night, which can last anywhere from two to five hours.

As a rule, pallid bats don't migrate other than a very short trip that takes them to their winter hibernacula, where they sleep and wait for the warm weather to return.

Because the day roosts location can vary from one day to the next, the pallid bat depends on a unique series of calls to identify its roost mates and new resting location.

Most bats have a pretty set diet. They either eat bugs, nectar, or fruit. Exceptions are bats that eat lizards/small rodents, blood, and fish. The pallid bat is another exception: this species eats just about anything that's smaller than itself. Strictly speaking, pallid bats are insectivores, but they will also eat small rodents and lizards. The bat is also capable of eating scorpions and has a natural tolerance for the scorpion's venom. One of the pallid bat's most unusual traits is that it rarely flies while hunting, but prefers stalking across the ground when it's seeking prey.

When the bat catches a bug, scorpion, or lizard, they will fly to a quiet place to eat. Pallid bats prefer to catch their prey on the ground, as opposed to snatching it out of mid-air. This is where the bat's enormous ears come into play. Their hearing is so sensitive, they're actually capable of hearing a bug strolling across the ground.

When they are sipping nectar, they land on the plant, rather than hovering near it like other nectar feeders. They land on the plant and basically crawl into the bloom and start dining.

The best place to spot a pallid bat is the United States' west coast. The species ranges the entire coastline, from Mexico all the way to Canada. They favor semi-arid areas as well as the mountains. When they're searching for a daytime roost, they look for a place that's in close proximity to water, has a horizontal entrance, and is quiet. They favor rock crevices and hollowed trees, and will sometimes settle in an attic.

For winter hibernation, they seek caves, deep rock cervices, and abandoned buildings.

Pallid Bat
(*Antrozous pallidus*)

Figure 49 © <u>Jerold Thompson</u>
Acquired via Dreamstime.com

Beautiful Bat Fact #41
Bats Hold the Key to Rainforest Conservation

Never before has the general population spent more time worrying about conservation, pollution, and deforestation. The future of the rainforests has been a particular concern. The fear is that if something isn't done to help rebuild them, there will be a significant depletion in air quality and oxygen levels.

Nectar Bats Make Fruit

Dense vegetation in the rainforest makes wind pollination impossible, so plants rely on animals, including bats, for reproduction, which explains why so many nectar-feeding bats have been found living in rainforests all over the world.

Like fruit bats, nectar-feeding bats use their eyes when foraging rather than relying completely on echolocation. The plants that attract these microbats are pale and easily visible, even in near total darkness. Many of the night blooming plants, such as Cuba's *Marcgravia evenia*, have also evolved in shapes that help aid with echolocation, increasing the odds of the bat quickly locating them. The flowers are sturdy and designed to withstand tiny bat claws. The nectar is generally sticky or gelatinous and the plants exude a musk scent.

Since most of these plants only bloom at night, their survival depends on the long-tongued bats every bit as much as the bats depend on them. If one goes extinct, the other will quickly follow.

Fruit Bats Deposit Seeds

Fruit bats, like the little golden mantled flying fox, don't know it, but they're playing a huge role in helping maintain vast tracks of rainforests. Their dietary needs prompt fruit bats to cover much longer distances than native birds, which means the seeds they deposit, either by spitting them out or in guano pellets are scattered over a greater distance, increasing the odds of at least some seeds landing in the ideal spot for optimal growth. Another feature that makes the bats such important seed scatterers is that they're willing to fly over open tracts of land, such as land that's been cut and needs to be recovered with plant growth before the top soil erodes. Birds often avoid these areas, preferring to stay where there's already plenty of vegetation.

The fact that bats defecate while flying is another advantage. Birds will defecate in flight, but the bulk of their droppings generally pile up beneath their perches so that all the seeds they consumed end up competing against one another.

Many of the seeds the bats deposit are considered "pioneer plants," fast-growing specimens whose roots hold the soil in place and that set the scene for additional plants to grow.

Encouraging fruit bats to spread seeds is faster and less expensive than tackling the reforestation problem by hand. The challenge is encouraging the fruit bats to frequent the areas that are in need of planting. While bats are willing to travel across the areas while foraging, they prefer roosting in the older sections of the forest where there are plenty of older trees that provide good roosts.

With financial assistance from a Bat Conservation International Student Research Scholarship, a group of bat lovers that included Detlev H. Kelm, Kerstin Wiesner, and Otto von Helversen worked together to create roosts that would encourage fruit bats to leave the deeper sections of the forest. The team made sure the artificial roosts were set up in places that provided enough vegetation for the fruit bats to stay cool and remain safe from natural predation.

The goal was to create affordable roosts that didn't require any maintenance and appealed to fruit bats. The solution came in the form of narrow bat houses. Instead of constructing the bat houses out of wood, these tropical bat houses were designed out of concrete slabs. Tough plastic netting was attached to the top and provided the bats with something to hang from.

The team was delighted when the bats found and moved into the brand-new bat houses just a few weeks after they'd been installed. An additional bonus was that having the bats roost in one place allowed the research team to easily gather guano and analyze the types of fruit the bats were eating and seed concentration.

The tropical bat houses prove that it's possible to use "housing" to manage the bat population and encourage specific migration patterns.

Insect-Eating Bats Protect New Growth Plants

While those of us who live in North America can't say enough nice things about the bats that eat hundreds of bugs every single night, things are different in the rainforests. There, people are less concerned about the fate of insectivorous bats and devote the bulk of their conservation concerns to the bats that they believed would be instrumental in rebuilding the forests, the pollinating bats and the fruit bats.

Ignoring the bug lovers is a mistake. Research indicates that they're just as crucial to the rainforests as the flying foxes and other fruit-eating and nectar-sipping bats. The research was completed with the help of a U.S. Forest Service International Program funded BCI Student Research Scholarship.

There have been two reasons the insect-feasting bats have been largely ignored during rainforest conservation efforts. The first is because no one really understood what type of insects the bats were consuming. The second reason is that so much focus is placed on planting and rebuilding clear cut areas, that the concept of working to save already existing vegetation sometimes slips people's minds.

The research took a long look at the common big-eared bat, a species that's commonly found in Panama's tropical forests. A detailed analysis of the bat guano indicated that approximately 70% of the bugs that make up this particular species' diets are insects that consume plants. Had it not been for the fecal analysis, it's likely that 50% of the insects the bats foraged on wouldn't have been noticed, and the bats would have been written off as not being helpful with rainforest conservation efforts.

An intense study that involved the use of nets birds couldn't penetrate revealed that the number of insects consumed at night significantly exceeded the number of insects consumed during the daylight hours by native bird species. One study indicated that when bats weren't allowed near a tree so that only birds could feed on the bugs that liked to hang out there, the insect activity went up sixty-five percent.

The wonderful thing the study illustrated is how well-balanced nature and bats are. One set of bats pollinates flowers that turn into fruit, the seeds of which the fruit bats scatter, and the insectivorous bats keep the young plants healthy and growing.

Beautiful Bat Fact #42
Bats of the Rainforest

Quick. What's the most abundant mammal found in the world's rainforests?

If you said bats, congratulations, you answered correctly, but be honest with yourself, would they have even crossed your mind if you weren't reading this book? I know I would have probably said squirrels, or some other type of rodents.

As it turns out, the different species of tropical, tree-loving bats that populate the rain forests adds up to an impressive 50% of all the mammals found in those unique conditions. They range from enormous flying foxes to the miniscule Kitti's hog-nosed bat. Under the dense canopies, you'll find insect-feeding bats, fruit-feeding bats, nectar-eating bats, and even a few carnivorous bats.

While the species you'd encounter in the rainforest depends which region you're in, here are examples of bats who happily dwell in the rainy, humid, tropical climates.

Commissaris's Long-tongued Bat

Most people know about insect eating bats, which make up approximately 70% of the world's bat population. A somewhat smaller group of people are familiar with fruit-eating megabats. What very few people realize is that that there's a third sub-species of bats, nectar-feeders. There are two types of nectar-feeding bats. One, called Glossophaginae, use papillae on their tongue to coax the nectar from the plant and into the bat's digestive tract. The Commissaris's long-tongued bat (*Glossophaga commissarisi*) is just such a nectar-feeding bat.

By nectar-feeding bat standards, the Commissaris's long-tongued bat is a mid-sized bat that ranges from 43 to 65 mm long and generally weighs about 9.5 g.

The head-to-toe fur is short and comes in a variety of shades that range from light to dark brown with some reddish-brown thrown into the mix.

The long tongue for which it gets its name is covered with several tiny bristles called papillae. The main food source for this little nectar-loving bat is plant nectar. Its feeding style bears a remarkable resemblance to how hummingbirds feed. In the span of a single night, a single Commissaris's long-tongued bat is capable of pollinating several hundred flowers. Depending on the flower's shape, the bat can drain its nectar in one-fifth of a second. The bat feeds on the nectar from five hundred different flowering species.

The Commissaris's long-tongued bat lives in rainforests as far north as Southern Mexico and as far south as Panama. It's frequently spotted in banana groves and evergreen forests. It tends to prefer wetter sections of the rainforest over the drier spots.

At this point, Commissaris's long-tongued bat populations appear stable, though there's concern about habitat destruction.

Dryadonycteris Capixaba Bat

Just when you start thinking we know everything there is to know about the animals we share this planet with, a new species is discovered. One such recently discovered species in the bat family is the dryadonycteris capixaba bat. This particular rain forest dwelling bat was discovered in the tableland Atlantic forest in southeastern Brazil. Other specimens of the same species have been collected in Espírito Santo and southern side of the Rio Doce.

The *dryadonycteris capixaba* bat has been placed in the *lonchophyllinae* genus of bats, a genus of nectar feeders that are categorized by the fact that their tongues have deep grooves on each side that allow the bat to draw the nectar from the plant in a manner that bears a remarkable resemblance to humans sipping sweet tea through a straw. It's unclear why some bats evolved with grooved tongues while others developed bristly tongues.

The *dryadonycteris capixaba* bat has only been captured a few times in the three regions in which it's known to exist, indicating that it's a very rare species. With an adult length of approximately 55 mm, it's on the small side. Its nose leaf helps it send echolocation pulses and identify which flowers are ripe for pollination.

Wagner's Mustached Bat

Don't be fooled by the Wagner's mustached bat's diminutive appearance. While adults are tiny, with a body length of 6 to 6.7 centimeters, this particular species has been fascinating scientists for years, mostly because even by bat standards, its echolocation skills are highly developed and complex. The Wagner's mustached bat is one of a very small group of bat species that's capable of Doppler-shift compensation. What this means is that when the bat detects prey, rather than emitting the exact same call frequency, they actually lower the frequency to compensate for the Doppler shift. The closer they get to the bug they're hunting, the lower the frequency becomes.

The bat lives in the rainforests near Central and South America. It prefers hunting in the wet sections of the forest, particularly rivers, where it feasts upon mosquitoes, scarab beetles, and moths. The bat flies low to the ground. During the day, it prefers to roost in caves and frequently shares its quarters with other bat species.

Painted Woolly Bat

If you're in a Malaysian rainforest or banana grove and are lucky enough to spot a painted bat, it will be an experience you'll never forget.

The most distinctive feature of the painted bat is their coloring. While most bats favor earth tones that allow them to blend into their surroundings, the painted bats are black with bright orange stripes on their wings. While this might seem garish at first, the coloring is actually the perfect camouflage for the sections of rainforest they thrive in.

Painted woolly bats are small. They weigh a paltry 5 grams and are 3 to 5.5 cm long.

Unlike other bats that live in large colonies, painted woolly bats prefer smaller groups of less than ten bats.

This particular insect-feeding bat is native to:

- Cambodia
- Malaysia
- Bangladesh
- Vietnam
- India
- Nepal
- China
- Sri Lanka
- Indonesia
- Thailand

In addition to their stunning coloring, one of the most fascinating things about the painted woolly bats is that their family lives break from tradition. In most bat species, the mother is charged with raising the pups, but the painted woolly bats appear to favor a nuclear family, with both parents staying together and taking an active interest in the pups. It's believed that this is one of perhaps five bat species that practices monogamy.

Madagascan Rousette

When people hear the word megabat, they expect an enormous bat with a six-foot wingspan, like the black flying fox. While megabats are bigger than their microbat cousins, that doesn't mean each species of megabat is a sky giant. The Madagascan rousette fruit bat is a perfect example of a megabat that isn't going to wow anybody with its epic proportions. Of the three-different species of fruit bats that call Madagascar home, the Madagascan rousette fruit bat is the smallest of the lot.

This particular fruit bat prefers the lowland rainforests and seldom ventures more than 800 meters above sea level. The fact that they've been found living near eucalyptus plantations suggests that they're adapting to the fragmentation of their preferred range and learning to live in closer proximity to humans. While this could be good for the overall survival of the species, it also makes them more susceptible to hunters who sell the fruit bats at local markets.

Whenever possible, the Madagascan rousette fruit bat prefers to eat native fruit rather than fruit that has been imported for commercial purposes. They are particularly fond of fruits with a high moisture content and that are loaded with calcium. Very few seeds have been detected in the bat guano, suggesting that the species spits out the seeds as they consume the fruit. This species prefers to gather their food and carry it well away from the fruit tree/vine before dining, making it a valuable seed dispenser.

Little Golden-Mantled Flying Foxes

Many who live in the Philippines Islands don't realize how much they owe the little golden-mantled flying foxes that inhabit the secondary lowland forest. The species, which is the smallest of the flying foxes, is one of the only animals that dispenses seeds beyond a primary habitat, making them a far more efficient seed distributor than any of the local birds. The little golden-mantled flying foxes are credited with dispensing more than 145 different types of fruit seeds and are the only animal that's known to disperse silk cotton tree seeds to different parts of the islands.

Unlike most flying foxes, the little golden-mantled flying fox is a solitary species and prefers to nest by itself in trees. The female is responsible for raising the pup, and generally weans the youngster when they're about eleven weeks old.

The little golden-mantled flying foxes are currently listed as a threatened species and many ecologists believe that they're at a high risk of becoming extinct if conservation efforts aren't implemented.

Commissaris's Long-Tongued Bat
(*Glossophaga commissarisi*)

Figure 50 © Karin Schneeberger
[CC BY-SA 3.0], via Wikimedia Commons

Wagner's Mustached Bat
(Pteronotus personatus)

Figure 51 © Bernard DUPONT
[CC BY-SA 2.0], via Wikimedia Commons

Beautiful Bat Fact #43
Guano Matters!

One of the few definitive facts in the bat world is: where there are bats, there's also guano. It's just the way things work.

It turns out, that bat guano has played an interesting role in the way the underworld has turned out.

Guano Shapes the Underworld

One of the more startling discoveries regarding bat guano is that it's changing the interior of the caves bats habitually use as roosting sites. As time passes, the bacteria, insects, and other organisms that feed on the guano change its composition, which results in an increase in the phosphoric acid and nitric acid. The acid is so strong it slowly eats away at the rock faces.

Other Species Depend on Guano

In limestone caves, near the Russian border, the shy, cave-loving Caucasian parsley frog's survival depends on the bats with whom it cohabitates.

Because the frogs prefer to stay in the caves, researching them hasn't been easy, which is why the link between the tiny amphibians and bats is only just now becoming clear. While observing the frogs, researchers from the University of Tennessee at Knoxville noticed that the frogs actively sought out the caves bats roosted in. A little more digging revealed that the reason for this was because the bat guano attracted insects that frogs fed upon, making this yet another example of how much the ecosystem relies on bats.

Make Your Garden Grow

One of the perks of having a bat house in your back yard is that in addition to getting to watch bats take flight every single night and having less mosquitos on the property, you also have your own supply of bat guano that you can use to fertilize your garden and flower beds.

Bat guano has an extremely high concentration of nutrients. While the exact amount of nutrients differs depending on the bat species, most bat guano is:

- 10% nitrogen
- 1% potassium
- 3% phosphorous

All you have to do is shovel up the guano and turn it into guano tea. It's not hard!

For every of cup of bat guano you collect, add one gallon of non-chlorinated water.

Leave the water and the guano alone overnight

Pour the mixture on your garden

If a soil test reveals that your soil is lacking key nutrients, you can add things like molasses, seaweed, coffee grounds, and other organic items to the guano tea.

The best time to apply the guano tea to your garden is either early in the morning or late in the evening.

You can use bat guano as a top dressing.

Rakang Cave and Khao Chong Pran Cave

There are two caves (technically a series of caves) in

Thailand that have served as homes to millions of bats for thousands of years. The bats who roost in and the locals who live near the Rakang Cave and Khao Chong Pran Cave have always enjoyed a perfect symbiotic relationship (humans benefited a bit more than the bats, but the bats didn't seem to mind). In addition to eating bugs, helping with pollination, and spreading fruit seeds throughout the surrounding forests, the bats also deposit enormous quantities of guano in the caves.

While enormous piles of guano might not seem like a good deal to you, to the villagers living near both caves, the guano represents a huge economic boon. To this day, villagers venture into the caves and gather up large baskets of the guano which they sell as fertilizer to local farmers. It's one of the most stable economic commodities the villages near both caves have at their disposal.

In the eighties, the future of the guano trade in both these villages looked grim. The number of bats roosting in the caves had dropped to an all-time low and the guano harvester wondered how long they could depend on a steady income.

A little investigation by bat conservationist Merlin Tuttle revealed that while limestone mining in the area was disrupting the bats, the main reason for the declining numbers was actually the high amount of poaching happening in the area.

It took some time, a lot of conversation, and some new laws, but eventually an understanding was created between everyone involved, and steps were taken to protect the bats that called the caves home. Once the poaching decreased, locals saw a noticeable increase in the bat population and reported that after a few years, the amount they earned from the guano they sold had doubled.

Guano War Draws Presidential Attention

People have developed a strong appreciation and understanding for the importance bats play in the world's overall ecosystem, but few stop and think about the importance of bat guano.

While using bat guano to feed a family (or entire village) might seem odd to you, but there's a historical precedent.

In the mid-1800's, several countries, including the United States, were engaged in what can only be described as a guano war.

A few barrels of bat guano were sent to Europe and analyzed in 1806, but no one really thought too much about the guano at the time.

Eighteen years later, the editor of the *American Farmer* magazine was given a few barrels of guano. He divided the contents into several sample packages and sent them to various people, including Maryland's former governor, who spread it on his corn. The results? Well, according to ex-governor who spread the guano on his corn, it was the most powerful manure he'd ever encountered. It didn't take long for his fellow farmers to start spreading bat guano on their own fields. They had no idea that it wouldn't be long before they'd be fighting for continued access to the guano.

In 1840, twenty guano-filled barrels made the trip across the Atlantic Ocean to England. Farmers spread it on their fields and were impressed with the results and demanded more Peruvian guano. Because of this demand, approximately 2 million barrels of guano were shipped to the UK between 1841 and 1857.

US farmers quickly demanded more guano for themselves. Their outcry was so intense that President Fillmore took note and tried to assuage concerns during his very first State of the Union address.

"Guano has become so desirable an article to the agricultural interest of the United States that it is the duty of the Government to employ all the means properly in its power for the purpose of causing that article to be imported into the country at a reasonable price," President Fillmore told the country. "Nothing will be omitted on my part toward accomplishing this desirable end."

Congress took drastic measures.

In 1856, when they passed the Guano Islands Act, enabling US citizens to lay claim to any uninhabited island that hadn't been previously claimed provided guano was found on the island. More than fifty different islands, including Midway, became a part of the United States as a direct result of the Guano Islands Act.

Demand for guano remained high. In 1865-1866, Spain engaged in the Guano War against both Chile and Peru, the leading exporters of guano. The US Navy entered into the fray and fought against Peru.

By the start of the twentieth century, guano supplies had been depleted and science had progressed to the point where farmers on both sides of the Atlantic gained access to chemical fertilizers.

Despite the Guano War and tense international relationships, Peru made out quite well. In the span of just forty years, they exported an estimated 20 million tons of guano and generated $2 billion in profit.

Several families in all countries turned an interest in guano into a sizeable fortune.

It's worth noting, that before all this, the Incas already knew about guano. They started using it as corn fertilizer long before Columbus sailed across the Atlantic Ocean. They considered guano such an important part of their survival, they created a system for when and how the guano was gathered. And if someone was caught disturbing the birds (and presumably the bats) the Incans relied on to produce guano, Incan law stated it was a crime punishable by death.

Bat Guano Aids Military Efforts

Some historians would argue that, had it not been for bat guano, the War of 1812 might have had a very different conclusion. Why? The high levels of phosphorus and nitrogen, the same things that make guano excellent fertilizer, happen to be key ingredients in gun powder. Had the US army not been able to retrieve the guano from bat caves and quickly make more gun powder, historians feel they would have lacked the fire power needed to defend themselves against the British troops.

The Confederate Army harvested enormous quantities of bat guano, which was used to replenish their dwindling supply of gun powder.

For the record, bat guano isn't the strangest way that bats have contributed to US war efforts.

Using Guano to Learn About Climate Change

The scientific community has found bat guano to be a highly useful research tool. It's an easy way to determine things like how many insects a bat eats, what types of insects they favor, migratory patterns, and can even help identify which bats are roosting in a certain location.

It turns out that bat guano can also help improve our knowledge about climate change.

Two researchers, Bogdan Onac and Daniel Cleary, did an extensive research project on bat guano. They found some 1,200-year-old bat guano located in an ancient Romanian cave and examined the isotopes.

The pair sifted through the several meters-deep pile of guano, collecting samples to be analyzed. When they compared the results of the isotope analysis to the winter precipitation levels and nitrogen cycling, the pair was able to not only create a model of how and when the climate experienced changes during the past 1,200 years, but they also used the results to create predicted changes for the future.

Roosting Bats

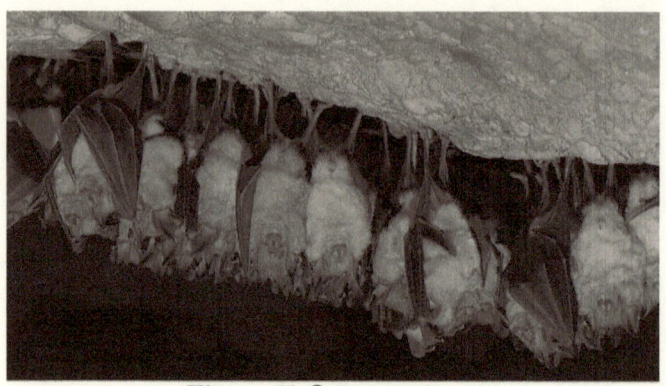

Figure 52 © Remus Cucu
Acquired via Dreamstime.com

Beautiful Bat Fact #44
Hardwicke's Woolly Bats and the Bornean Carnivorous Pitcher Plant: A Relationship Built on Guano

It's not a secret that, at some point, plants and animals evolved until they were perfectly suited for one another's needs. Bats and Bornean carnivorous pitcher plants (*Nepenthes hemsleyana*) are a perfect example of just such a symbiotic relationship.

Pitcher plants grow wild in Borneo's peat forests. The humans who also enjoy living in and near the same forests have always known that local bat species, including Hardwicke's woolly bats (*Kerivoula hardwickii)* call the pitcher plants home.

What no one realized was just how much the pitcher plants depended on their occupants.

The pitcher plant's distinctive curled up leaves provide the small bats with the ideal home. Not only does the shape of the leaves create the perfect micro-climate for the bats, but they also make it difficult for hungry predators to locate the animals.

Studies reveal that while the pitcher plants provide the bats with free living quarters, the bats are far from free-loaders. They have something the pitcher plants need in order to survive.

Bat poop.

Guano, especially the guano produced by insectivorous bats like the Hardwicke's woolly bat is extremally high in the nitrogen the plants need to survive. Testing shows that a minimum of one-third of the pitcher plants nitrogen intake is provided from its winged tenants.

Scientists believe that the pitcher plant developed its distinctive shape via evolution specifically to help attract bats. If they're right, it marks the only known time that a plant has evolved for an animal that wasn't responsible for pollinating/spreading the seeds of that same plant.

What interested the scientists involved in a recent study was why Hardwicke's woolly bats prefer dwelling in Bornean carnivorous pitcher plants as opposed to other, similar plants such as *Nepenthes ampullaria* and *Nepenthes bicalcarata*, two species that meet the Hardwicke's woolly bats requirements, but don't have the same high guano requirement as the Bornean pitcher plants.

When the research team looked at the lifestyle of the woolly bat, they noted that the species didn't seem all that reliable, especially considering how badly the Bornean pitcher plants need the guano. Considering what Hardwicke's woolly bats require to feel safe while they roost, there were plenty of other options available to the bats, some that were closer to ideal hunting grounds, water sources, and that provided better protection from the elements. So why do they keep making their homes in the Bornean carnivorous pitcher plants?

The first and most obvious reason is that even when the Bornean pitcher plants haven't grown in the ideal location, they still provide the bats with the ideal shelter. Not only are the interior curves of the leaves perfectly sized for the bats, but studies indicate that the way the leaves are shaped creates an echo-reflecting structure that allows the bats to locate the pitcher plant, no matter how dense the forest vegetation is.

A closer examination of a Bornean pitcher plant reveals that the plant also helps preserve their occupant's health. The waxy layer that coats the plant's inner wall makes it impossible for arthropods to lay their eggs within the plant. As a result, the bats who roost exclusively in the pitcher plants lack some of the ectoparasites that plaque the bats who roost in different types of pitcher plants. Not having to fight the effects of the ectoparasites leaves the bats in better physical condition.

Another advantage the Bornean pitcher plants have when it comes to attracting Hardwicke's woolly bats is that the leaves stay furled longer than other plants. The less frequently the bats have to look for a new home, the more energy they ultimately conserve.

A research team recently created a study to determine how loyal Hardwicke's woolly bats are to the Bornean pitcher plant.

The team caught several Hardwicke's woolly bats, making sure they had some that were found roosting in the Bornean pitcher plant and some that were found roosting in other types of plants. They recreated conditions in a lab where they were able to observe that the bats favored the type of plant they were originally found in.

During a different portion of the experiment when the bats were presented with a variety of furled leaves, not only did the bats who were originally roosting in the pitcher plants choose to do so again, the team noted that twenty-one percent of the bats that were found roosting elsewhere also chose the Bornean pitcher plant.

Genetic testing that was performed during the course of the study revealed a surprising fact about the woolly bat. The research team learned that the bats who favored the Bornean pitcher plant were more closely related than the bats found in different types of roosts.

Based on the results, the research team concluded that the reason bats preferred roosting in Bornean pitcher plants is a combination of familiarity, genetic preference, and the overall quality of the roost site. This information is of use to groups who are working to save the lives of bats by attempting to make up for loss of natural habitat via alternative roosting options.

Beautiful Bat Fact #45
Mexican Free-Tailed Bats Sail to the US
Military's Aid ... Almost

There was a period of time when the military was very interested in Texas's population of Mexican free-tailed bats. This wasn't the first time the caves where the massive colonies roosted attracted military attention; guano from the caves had been very useful to the American Army during the War of 1812 and the Confederate Army during the Civil War. However, this was the first time it was the bats, and not just their poop, that drew the attention of highly decorated military minds.

In 1941, Pennsylvania dental surgeon, Lytle "Doc" Adams was worried about how he was going to contribute to the war effort. Wanting to be useful kicked his imagination into overdrive and he came up with some pretty interesting concepts. Most never made it any further than his drawing board.

Things changed when Adams took a vacation at New Mexico's Carlsbad Caverns, which happened to be home to millions of Mexican free-tailed bats. Watching the tiny bats chase insects caused the synapses in Adams' brain to fire and he concocted a scheme. He was so excited about his latest and greatest idea, he sent President Roosevelt a letter detailing the idea. While the president recognized that the idea seemed pretty radical, he also saw the possibilities and composed an interagency memorandum urging certain people to further explore the Adams' plan.

Adams' idea will forevermore be remembered as Project X-Ray. The concept was surprisingly simple. All the military needed to do was catch a bunch of the Mexican free-tailed bats, attach tiny incendiary bombs to them, transport them to Japan, and turn them loose.

The military loved the idea and took the precaution of placing guards at many well-known bat caves, protecting the mammals, who had no idea that the fate of the free world could well rest on their tiny backs. At the time, the bats didn't care about the war; their biggest concern was chasing bugs.

Project X-Ray was passed on to the Air Force, who put Adams in charge of the program. The team he assembled was … interesting. It looked more like a ragtag group that should star in spaghetti westerns or early con-movies than an elite, secret military group. The team consisted of:

- A former gangster
- 2 high school assistants
- A mammologist
- Pilot/actor
- Marine/lobster fisherman
- A former hotel manager

He wasn't part of the original team, but eventually, Dr. Theodore Fieser became a part of Project X-Ray. Sound familiar? He should. He invented napalm.

One of the first things the team had to deal with was how to transport the bats from Texas to Japan. They wouldn't be able to feed the bats during the trip and once the animals were over Asia, it would take even more time to determine the best place to release them. In the end, it was decided that before leaving the United States, the bats would need to be coaxed into a state of hibernation.

The team caught a collection of Mexican free-tailed bats, and after some trial and error, determined that the bats could transport 15 to 18 grams of napalm when it was attached to their chest with some adhesive. The team also designed a container that allowed them to ship 1,040 fully armed bats across enemy lines.

Approximately six thousand bats were used in a trial run, which was conducted at Muroc Lake, California. The simulation was full of problems, which included bats failing to wake up out of their forced hibernation and some disappearing (luckily, only dummy bombs were loaded onto the bats at the time). Things went from bad to worse when six bats who were strapped with live bombs got loose on the base. Things got better when a fake village was created and the bats successfully destroyed it.

After a year, Project X-Ray was shifted from the Air Force to the Marines and was eventually picked up by the Navy (who was the group that actually dubbed it Project X-Ray). More than two years after Adams originally pitched his idea to President Roosevelt, it was ready to be launched. By this point, it had cost $2 million.

Despite all the time and money the military spent on Project X-Ray, in the end, the government chose to use the Manhattan Project's atom bomb rather than releasing thousands of bomb-bearing Mexican free-tailed bats on Japan.

Beautiful Bat Fact #46
Mexican/Brazilian Free-Tailed Bats: Fast, Useful, and Amazing

Mexican free-tailed bats, which are also called Brazilian free-tailed bats, depending on which part of North America you happen to be in, are the most abundant bat species in the Northern Hemisphere.

Free-tailed bats take their name from the fact that unlike most other groups of bats, their tail extends past their tail membrane and is clearly visible, even when the little animal is in flight. The tail is generally the fastest way of identifying the animal.

The second thing most people notice is that this is a fast bat, really fast. Until recently, it was believed that they were capable of attaining speed of up to sixty miles per hour, but a recent study revealed that the estimate was way too conservative. They actually move closer to one hundred miles per hour (actual recorded speed was 99.42 mph). They do more than fly fast. They've been observed flying at an altitude of 528 feet above the ground and it's estimated that on any given night, they may cover over fifty miles as they feed.

Mexican free-tailed bats are a migratory species. They prefer warm climates, which is why they're commonly found in Arizona, New Mexico, California, Utah, Nevada,

Oklahoma, and sometimes they're spotted in southern Kansas. The ones that live further north head south during the winter, while the ones that are already in warmer climates stay put. No one is sure why some of the bats venture north while others don't.

Most bat species are social, but even by bat standards, Mexican free-tails seem to enjoy a great deal of companionship. It's not unusual for roosting caves to contain colonies that include thousands of bats. In one nursery cave, researchers were stunned to learn that a single foot of space contained approximately four hundred young pups. Even more shocking was that despite the massive amounts of pups, each one looking exactly like all the others, each mother was able to quickly pick out her child. Experts believe that both the sound of the pup's voice and scent allow the mother to locate her child. It can take up to twelve minutes for the mother to locate her pup, which given the crowd and the fact that the pups mill around, is really impressive.

Bracken Cave in Texas is believed to contain the world's largest population of Mexican free-tailed bats. It's estimated that 20 million bats call the cave home at any given time, with that number swelling after the mothers birth their pups.

A single Mexican free-tailed bat consumes an amazing amount of bugs. It's estimated that mothers with young pups that are just about ready to fly are the most voracious eaters. In order to keep herself and her pup fed, the female must consume nearly her entire body weight, about 12 g, in insects every single night. Researchers estimate that when the mothers in Bracken Caves are caring for their pups, the colony consumes approximately 250 tons in flying insects every single night. Should the colony suddenly disappear for some reason, the immediate impact that increased insect population would have on the local agriculture industry would be devastating and reflected in grocery prices around the world.

Mexican free-tailed bats do more than simply keep the price of groceries affordable, they also contribute to the economy in another their way. Their poop (guano) is incredibly valuable and given their large colony sizes, it's also plentiful.

When the bats migrate, trained guano miners move into the newly abandoned caves and start excavating the enormous piles of guano, which is sold as a highly prized fertilizer.

Mexican Free-Tailed Bat
(Tadarida brasiliensis)

Figure 53 By NPS

PUBLIC DOMAIN

Beautiful Bat Fact #47
Drunk Bats

The life of a fruit bat seems pretty cushy. They get to hang around in trees, sleeping, swapping stories, grooming themselves, and doing all the other things bats like to do during their down time. Doesn't seem like a bad deal.

Flying While Drunk

It turns out that there's a dangerous problem that only fruit bats have. Sometimes, the very food they need to survive makes them so drunk, they struggle to make it back to their roost.

Fruit doesn't stay good for long. Once it starts to go bad, the pulp starts breaking down and ferments. The dates and figs that most fruit bats are attracted to produce high quantities of ethanol as they over ripen. When you're making wine, fermentation and ethanol is good, but when you're a bat, it means a drunken flight home.

Considering how small bats are, it wouldn't take much fermented fruit to boost their blood alcohol level to dangerous levels. Curious, a group of researchers delved into the topic.

It turns out that nature took steps to help prevent fruit bats from taking too many drunken flights. The bats use their sense of smell as well as taste to determine which fruits are heavily fermented and which are still good for eating. Unlike humans, who often consume things they shouldn't, the bats avoid the fermented fruit, preferring to stick to options that allow them to maintain a clear head. However, there are times when limited food options force the bats to eat fruit that sends their blood alcohol level soaring.

A Francisco Sanchez led study conducted in Israel indicated that after consuming alcohol, the bats were disoriented and crashed into obstacles, putting themselves at great risk while flying to roost after they consumed bad fruit.

These boozed-up bats have precious few options at their disposal. They can hang out near the fruit tree until they sober up, something that makes them vulnerable to predation, or they can attempt the flight back to the roost. The drunken flight means a high chance of colliding with other bats, trees, fences, and other things that the bat would avoid if sober.

A research team consisting of representatives from multiple schools decided to explore the effects of alcohol-rich fruits on bats. To do this, they created an obstacle course and gathered some fruit bats to fly through it. Six different fruit bat species participated in the study.

The bats were split into two groups. One group was the sober test group. The other group drank water that contained 1.5% alcohol. The team used each bat's body mass to determine how much spiked drink each bat needed to drink to reach a 0.11 blood alcohol level. At this level, if caught behind the wheel, the bat would have been arrested for drunk driving. In most states, the legal limit is 0.08.

When the team released the bats into the flight cage obstacle course, they were surprised by how well the bats performed, indicating that they're designed to handle their alcohol better than humans, probably because they're naturally more exposed to it. Despite the high blood alcohol level, the bats were willing to take flight, didn't seem to have any trouble with their echolocation, and were willing to maneuver through the obstacle course.

The results of the experiment contradicted the earlier study, causing the researchers to determine that because the bats they were testing lived in Belize, where the warm, humid weather conditions causes fruit to ferment a great deal faster, the bats developed a natural tolerance.

Sobering Up After a Wild Night Out

Many rainforest fruit bats are particularly fond of eating over ripe figs and other fruits.. While the figs are a good source of nutrition, they're also high in ethanol (alcohol), and the riper they are, the more alcohol the bat consumes. There have been two different research projects that explored how bats handle high levels of ethanol.

The first study was conducted by a biologist at Ben-Gurion University of the Negev in Israel, Francisco Sanchez, developed an experiment to see if the bats had somehow devised a natural hangover cure.

During the course of the study, Sanchez and his colleagues fed some Egyptian fruit bats two different liquid meals that included minute levels of drinking alcohol that was mixed with either glucose or sucrose.

The team then gave the bats a breathalyzer test. Not only did the breathalyzer test prove that the bats did in fact become drunk after consuming the ethanol rich fruit, but that when the bats were fed fruits that are high in fructose, they sobered up a great deal faster than the bats that weren't granted access to the sugary fruits. The fructose serves as an almost instantaneous hang-over cure for the bats.

Knowing how to instantly reverse the negative impact of the ethanol is important to bats. It doesn't take much for them to start feeling tipsy. A one percent ethanol concentration is all it takes for a bat's blood alcohol level to reach a toxic level, and researchers noticed that after consuming a much smaller amount, the Egyptian fruit bats showed signs of the sluggishness that intoxicated humans experience. And being intoxicated puts the bat's life in jeopardy. Not only did the inebriated Egyptian fruit bats crash into objects, the way they behaved would have also made them attractive to any nearby predators.

After learning about how the Egyptian fruit bats responded to blood alcohol levels, another research team decided they wanted to see how ethanol impacted fruit bat species in Central and South America responded.

The team caught 106 bats which represented six local fruit bat species. The bats happily consumed either the sugar water or ethanol the researchers offered them. The team made sure that each of the bats was given ethanol/sugar water in amounts that were proportional for each bat's body mass.

After the bats had consumed the substance, the team took a saliva sample from each animal which indicated that at least some of the participating bats had a blood alcohol level of 0.3 percent. Convinced that the bats were intoxicated enough to feel the effects of the ethanol, the team released them into an obstacle course. The team anticipated that not only would the intoxicated bats not be able to fly as well as their sober counterparts, but that the echolocating calls would be "slurred." The bats surprised the research team.

Not only did the bats manage to successfully navigate obstacle course, thier echolocating calls remained clear.

Based on the information gathered during both of these experiments, it's obvious that different bat species have a different tolerance for ethanol, a tolerance that was most likely developed as a direct result of the types of fruit the bat routinely has access to.

Saving Bats, One Bottle of Tequila at a Time

Some of the best tequila in the world is made from the blue agave plant. Blue agave is not a cactus, but like cactus, it thrives in the hot climates that don't experience a great deal of rainfall. The blue agave flowers only once during its lifetime. When it's ready to bloom, a long stem appears in the center of the plant's rosette and several tubular blooms adorn the stem. After pollination, these blooms turn into fruit. The plant dies after bearing the fruit, though suckers will grow out of the original stem. Each of these suckers can develop into a brand-new plant, allowing the cycle to begin all over again.

The part of the plant that's important to tequila connoisseurs is the blue agave's piña, or heart. At harvest time, the piña weighs anywhere from 80-300 pounds. The size of the piña isn't nearly as important as how much sugar it contains. Older piñas have a higher sugar level than young ones, which is why only older plants are harvested. It can take anywhere from six to ten years before the plant's ready for harvesting. Contemporary farming practices have had farmers harvesting the blue agave before it blooms, since that's when the sugar content is at the highest concentration. After harvesting the blue agave, they plant entirely new plants that were started elsewhere.

One liter of blue agave tequila requires 15 pounds of piña.

Fertilizing the blue agave plant is complicated. The plant's spine is deadly to some species and the shape of the tuber flowers makes it difficult for most pollinating animals to get to the nectar found deep within the blossom. Enter the long-nosed bat.

The long-nosed bat is perfectly adapted to retrieve the plants nectar and pollinate the blue agave at the same time, a process that's vital for the continued production of blue agave. The problem is that the long-nosed bat population is declining.

When he learned about the falling long-nosed bat

population, conservationist Rodrigo Medellín stepped in and started working with local farmers and exploring ways of saving the bat so they could continue to produce the tequila that's so important to their region.

Prior to Medellin's involvement, most blue agave farmers harvested the plants prior to the plant blooming. The reason for this was because blooming decreased the plant's sugar content. For years, this system worked, but then crops were hit by a disease that made it difficult for farmers to find replacement plants. This, as well as Medillin's urging, was enough to convince the farmers to set aside a portion of their crop to flower, allowing the bats to feed and creating a sustainable farming situation.

In addition to convincing the farmers to let some of the plants fully mature, Medillin also took steps to preserve some of the caves that the long-nosed bats roost in.

Medellin worked with others to create the Tequila Interchange Project, a nonprofit organization that's made up of blue agave farmers, tequila makers, scientists, distributers, and anyone else concerned with the fate of the long-nosed bats that explores how they can continue to create a bat-friendly environment while also producing great-tasting tequila. Their efforts have led to the production of "bat-friendly" tequila. The bat-friendly tequila is distributed by La Alteña, Don Mateo, Tequila Cascahuin, and Siete Leguas.

Beautiful Bat Fact #48
The Lesser Long-Nosed Bat: Long Distance Fliers

The lesser long-nosed bat is a moderately-sized North American bat that with an impressive travel history.

When it decides it's time to migrate, this species covers a lot of miles. During the warm summer months, they like to hang out in the south eastern section of Arizona, southern California, and most of New Mexico, where they enjoy sipping all the nectar local cacti provides. As the days grow shorter, they head south, winging their way into Mexico. They've been observed in Honduras, Guatemala, and El Salvador. Some banded members of the species have traveled as far as one thousand miles each during a single migratory season.

Their preferred habitat is grasslands and some scrub forests. They're able to thrive on a minimal amount of water and do well in temperatures that reach as high as 106 °F. but will die if they're exposed to anything much below 50°F. Since they migrate, the lesser long-nosed bat doesn't hibernate and must find a way to feed year-round. During the day, the bats like to roost in caves and abandoned mines where they can keep cool.

The lesser long-nosed bat's distinguishing features include a ten-inch wingspan, a small "noseleaf" that protrudes from bridge of their nose, and a three-inch-long body. The fur ranges from a yellowish-brown color to a light brownish-grey mixture.

One of their most fascinating features is one you won't see when you look at the bat: its tongue, which happens to be the same length as its body. The tongue is covered in both long ridges and bristle-like papillae, both of which help the bat draw nectar from plants. Scientists also feel that it's possible that the bat's rough tongue also gets used to scrape plaque from the animal's teeth, decreasing the risk of developing periodontal disease.

The wings of the lesser long-nosed bat are uniquely suited for its lifestyle. They're designed in such a way that the bat can fly long distances easily without burning a great deal of energy; however, in order to make the long trips, the bat sacrificed the incredible mobility and speed that insect-feeding bats enjoy.

The exact type of nectar the lesser long-nosed bat consumes depends on the time of year and where the bat happens to be located. They prefer dining on blooming cactus but will visit other types of plants as the need arises. They frequently feed on the nectar from:

- Organ Pipe Cactus
- Century Plants
- Agaves
- Saguaro

While the bat feeds on the plant's nectar, it aids in the plant's pollination. In the case of most species of night-blooming cactus, the bats are the only reliable source of natural pollination. If the lesser long-nosed bat and other nectar-feeding desert bats go extinct, the night-blooming cacti would quickly follow.

When left to its own devices, a healthy lesser long-nosed bat can live approximately twelve years. They usually give birth during May and June following a six-month

gestation period. Mothers care for their pups for
approximately eight weeks.

Beautiful Bat Fact #49
The Great Alliance Between Bats and Farmers

For years, bat experts have touted ecological value of bats, and some people listened; however, it's a hard fact of life that the best way to get people really interested in something is to break out the calculators and start talking economics.

When you start adding up the dollars and cents, you start to fully grasp how valuable each and every bat really is. The most recent economic estimate revealed that worldwide, bats are worth about $1 billion.

Coming up with this number required a unique and very clever experiment.

A cornfield was selected and covered with a net that prevented bats from getting to the field, but allowed the insects to get in. During the day time, the net was opened so that daytime-loving birds such as swallows could gain access to the field, and the net was reclosed each night. At the end of the harvest, the field was compared to another that wasn't closed off to bats.

The results were surprising.

- When the ears were examined, the netted field revealed an 50% increase in earworm

damage
- 60% more earworm larvae was found in the netted field
- The netted field had significantly more fungal growth and toxins than the unnetted field

Based on these results, it was concluded that bats were responsible for saving the global corn industry $1 billion every single year. That's a lot of bushels of corn!

It's important to note that this economic value was assigned to bats based purely on how much corn they save. Now imagine how it works with the rest of the crops and think about how much higher your monthly grocery bill would be if bats suddenly disappeared.

Bet the idea of building a bat house and providing a colony of bats with a safe roost suddenly seems a lot more appealing, doesn't it!

The Exploration of Bats in Macadamia Orchards

Macadamia nuts are important, not just to those of us who love eating them, but also to South Africa's economy. In 2013, approximately 21,696 tons of macadamia nuts had been produced in South Africa, which accounted for 95% of the international market.

Needless to say, no one wants to see anything bad happen that would cause a decrease in the country's macadamia production, which is why South African macadamia producers and scientists from all over the world have dedicated a great deal of time and resources to exploring the best way to control stinkbugs, which represent the biggest threat to the industry. Every single year, the damage done by stinkbugs costs producers millions in lost revenue. An estimated 60-80% of the macadamia kernels rejected during processing are rejected as a result of stinkbug damage. After exploring various pesticides, many now feel that bats (and some birds) may provide the most efficient and effective stinkbug control.

A report published on ResearchGate in 2013 effectively proved that the bat species frequently observed foraging in macadamia orchards feed on stinkbugs. The research team involved in that particular study used second generation sequencing of a 157 bp fragment of the COI-barcoding region on fecal samples from multiple bat species which indicated that the amount of stinkbugs the bats in the macadamia orchards fed on was 20-50% higher in stinkbug remains than fecal samples of the same species that were collected in the wild. What that particular research project didn't show was how big an impact the bats had on the macadamia crop.

The fecal samples the research team analyzed came from:

- Slit-faced bats (Nycteris thebaica)
- African pipistrelles (Pipistrellus hesperidus)
- Angolan free-tailed bats (Mops condylurus)
- Yellow house bats (Scotophilus dinganii)

Based on the analysis of the bat guano in macadamia orchards, Green Farms Nut Company, the SA Macadamia Growers' Association, and the University of Venda have joined forces to learn just how effective bats and birds are in the ongoing war against stinkbugs. A series of three field studies was devised with the intention of determining the economic impact bats and birds have on the macadamia industry.

The research projects were designed to measure the stinkbug and bat/bird activity at six different macadamia farms over a two-season period, with the projects wrapping up after the 2017 season.

The University of Venda arranged for two of their researchers, Valerie Linden and Sina Weier, to go to all six of the participating farms and set up cages that completely encompassed the trees. Half of the cages were designed to prevent bats and birds from accessing the trees, allowing the stinkbugs to feed in peace. The second set of cages was designed in a way that both bats and birds could feed at will. A total of forty-eight trees were covered.

The pair then erected a third batch of cages; these were designed to allow birds to gain access to the covered trees during the day, but then were closed at night, which would prevent bats from removing any stinkbugs. This particular aspect of the experiment should help the research team determine how big an economic impact that bats have on the stinkbug population in comparison to birds, since most of the birds that patrol the macadamia orchards aren't nocturnal.

During the course of the two-season field study, the pair took samples from the forty-eight trees and analyzed them for signs of stinkbug infestation. In addition to comparing the nuts collected from the different trees to help determine just how big an impact the bats and birds have on the stinkbug population, fecal samples would also be analyzed, which would help the team identify exactly which species are the most beneficial.

The final results of this particular study haven't been published yet. Once they are, the plan is to use the results and explore what South African macadamia producers can do to help attract the most beneficial bat or bird species to their orchard, which will help decrease the amount of expensive pesticides they use while increasing their profit margin.

Bats and Livestock Production

I'll admit it. I haven't been able to track down any scientific studies that explore the relationship between bats and livestock, but there's no doubt in my mind that having one or two bat colonies on the property benefits livestock producers every bit as much as it benefits farmers who focus their attention on crops.

Insects, even a small population, can drive livestock crazy. Biting, scratching, and stomping at flies (as well as running from larger insects) not only means that the animals are burning a surplus of calories, it is also stressing the animals, which in turn leads to decrease in productivity. Plus, there's a risk of an insect that's carrying a harmful disease biting a cow, pig, or horse, infecting the animal, which in turn can lead to major veterinarian bills and possibly even cause the farmer to lose the animal.

While things like making sure stagnant water is emptied out of tubs/buckets before it has a chance to become a mosquito breeding ground, good manure management, and the use of fly sprays goes a long way to reducing the local insect population that has a negative impact on livestock, a colony of bats will lead to an even greater reduction.

I hypothesize that not long after livestock producers and stable owners take the steps needed to attract a colony of bats to their farm, it wouldn't take long before they'd see a reduction in the number of insect bites they're forced to treat, and notice that their livestock is noticeably less stressed during the insect season.

By the Numbers

One of the hardest parts about gauging just how important bats are to the farmers is that there are so many different variables in play. Location, type of crop, general farming practices, and more have a huge impact on the final results. The one thing that all the scientists do agree upon is that bats are a huge help to farmers.

A 2011 article published in *Science* called the "Economic Importance of Bats in Agriculture," did its best to provide a financial analysis of the situation. Here are the numbers provided.

- The value of bats to farmers across the United States ranges from $12 to $173 per acre.
- In Texas, the value of bats to the state's agriculture industry ranges from $3.7 to $53 billion every year.
- Texas cotton farmers can thank bats for saving/generating $6.4 million each cotton harvest by decreasing the amount of pesticides the cotton farmer uses and helping increase the overall yield and quality of the crop.
- In Texas, farmers and ranchers saved more than $724,000 every single year, thanks to local Mexican free-tailed bat colonies.

Any way you look at it, turning their farm into a bat-friendly environment greatly benefits farmers. Best of all, encouraging bats to move onto the property isn't difficult. All it takes is a few minor tweaks.

Farmers interested in attracting bats should:

- Create a water source
- Try to use bat-friendly lighting wherever possible (bats don't appear bothered by red light)
- Plant one or two hedgerows and place a couple of bat houses nearby

Contacting the local Cooperative Extension office or DNR office to learn about the needs of native bat species is also a good idea.

Beautiful Bat Fact #50
Bats May Hold the Key to Keeping Your Chocolate Stash Full

Chocolate residue found on the inside of an ancient Mayan teapot indicates that as far back as 2,600 years ago, the culture consumed the same thing we still turn to whenever we're happy, sad, hungry, cold, or simply want a sweet treat.

Mayans made a paste out of the cacao fruit and added chili peppers, water, cornmeal, and additional spices into a drink that was believed to have been consumed following meals, with the wealthy sipping it on a regular basis and the commoners enjoying it on special occasions.

Many museums display bits of Mayan pottery decorated with images depicting both the drinking of the chocolate and how the mixture was prepared.

And they didn't just drink the chocolate.

Mayans called chocolate "God Food." They incorporated it into their religious ceremonies and sometimes used chocolate rather than blood during some rituals. During marital ceremonies, the bride and groom sipped the drink. Chocolate was also used during baptismal ceremonies.

Archeologists have found cacao beans and brewing pots for chocolate entombed with ancient Mayan rulers.

Mayans used cacao as currency. It became such a valuable commodity to the culture that Mayan farmers learned how to cultivate the trees. They became quite adept at the practice. Even in the Yucatan, where cacao trees didn't grow naturally, local farmers discovered how to breed and grow cacao trees. Their efforts were rewarded by an elevation in wealth and status.

As cacao became increasingly popular, trade networks developed, ensuring Mayans who lived in areas where the cacao trees couldn't be cultivated had access to the valuable fruit.

Chocolate is an important part of our lifestyles. In the United States, it's estimated that the average person consumes ten pounds of chocolate during a single year. And humans aren't alone in our love of all things chocolaty. Fruit bats can't get enough cacao.

Looming Chocolate Disaster

It's estimated that the average American consumes about ten pounds of chocolate during a single year. What some of us don't realize is that two of our biggest suppliers are concerned about the future. Based on current conditions in the areas where cocoa is produced, they're worried that soon they won't be able to meet current demands.

Approximately 70% of the chocolate we consume is crafted from cocoa beans that are produced in either the Ivory Coast or Ghana. West African chocolate producers have done an excellent job of keeping up with the rising demand for affordable chocolate, but now companies such as Mars, Inc. are concerned.

The issue West African producers face is that during the past few years, the cocoa farmers have been slammed with two problems.

The first issue is a drought that made it difficult to keep the water-loving trees happy and healthy, which in turn led to a significant drop in production. The second problem they're battling is frosty pod, a fungal disease that's triggered a 30-40% decrease in production. Unable to cope with such a significant loss in income and knowing how long it will take to restore their orchards to full strength, many producers have opted to cut down their trees and replace them with high yield cash crops such as corn.

It's predicted that the world may experience a chocolate shortage as soon as 2020.

What does this mean to the world's chocolate lovers?

If the year 2020 rolls around and Ivory Coast producers are no longer able to meet the public's demands, it's likely that producers in South America will have to fill the void. And, while it's good to know that there's a backup system in place, the producers in South America face some problems of their own.

The Beloved Cacao Tree

Wild cacao trees grow in the rainforests, where they are one of the understory trees and are frequently found alongside rivers. In order to thrive, the trees need shade and a great deal of moisture. The trees grow a taproot that sinks about 2 meters (6.56 ft.) deep, while the tree itself grows approximately 15 meters tall. It takes four to six years for the tree to reach the fruit-bearing stage. Healthy wild cacao trees can live for one hundred years.

Most of the chocolate used in the candy bars and baked goods we love has been grown on a commercial plantation. To provide the trees with the shade they need, farmers generally plant the cacao trees amongst banana trees, which provide a nice canopy.

. The producers start the young trees from cuttings. These commercially cultivated cacao trees don't grow as tall as the wild versions and don't develop a deep taproot. Farmers replace the trees every sixty years when the production of the commercially cultivated trees starts decreasing.

While most trees bear flowers during one season and fruit during a different one, the cacao tree is unique in that it bears fruit and flowers simultaneously, a trait that likely developed because the fruit takes five to eight months to mature. A healthy tree produces approximately seventy cacao fruits each year. Each fruit contains twenty to sixty 2.5 cm (1 in.) cocoa beans.

One of the challenges commercial cacao producers face is low levels of pollination. One of my sources indicated that out of one thousand flowers, only three develop into the fruit that produces the cocoa beans we love. That's remarkable inefficiency.

Studies indicate that the reason the cacao producers face such an uphill struggle with pollination has to do with the types of trees they use. Traditionally, small midge flies (appropriately called chocolate midges) are responsible for pollinating the flowers, but due to the large size of the plantations and the fact that the midges aren't really designed to travel long distances, there simply aren't enough midges on each plantation to handle the pollination needs. As a result, smaller plantations that grow cacao trees in a manner that bears a stronger resemblance to how wild cacao trees grow experience higher pollination rates. The problem is that these smaller plantations can't meet the global demand for chocolate.

Bats, particularly the Underwood's long-tongued bat (*Hyloncyteris underwoodi*), may prove to be the chocolate industry's salvation.

The Underwood's long-tongued bat is a little bat that ranges from the western section of Panama to Vera Cruz, Mexico. The species favors heavily forested areas that with an elevation that is between 50 and 2640 meters. They tend to stick to heavily forested areas that have a full canopy. While they will occasionally roost in a hollowed-out tree, they prefer the protection provided by caves and tunnels.

One of the few things we know about this particular species is that they are remarkably efficient pollinators and that they specialize in difficult-to-pollinate blooms. According to the Bat Eco-Interactions, in 1977, A.L. Gardner observed the species sipping nectar from wild cacao blossoms. Considering how effective bats are as pollinators and how far they're willing to travel, it's reasonable to believe that if the plantation owners can attract colonies to their plantation, they stand to experience a huge increase in their overall yield.

Bats Lay the Groundwork for Future Generations to Enjoy Chocolate

Potentially improving farm-cultivated cacao yields is just one of the ways bats can keep the chocolate industry booming.

Fruit-eating species also play a key role in ensuring that the world always has enough chocolate.

One such species is the Jamaican fruit bat.

Although the bat will occasionally feed on nectar, their primary food source is fruit, including cacao fruit. When the Jamaican fruit bat eats a piece of fruit, it drains the fruit of what it wants and spits out a pellet of chewed up fibrous material, which includes the cocao seeds, which eventually germinate and grow into a tree.

Not only does this help replant the rainforest, but it also spreads out the genetic material, making each generation of wild grown cacao trees healthier than the generation before.

Producers can then choose to collect some of these wild grown trees and use them to cross pollinate the cultivated cacao trees, a practice that not only introduces some new genetic material to the plantation, but can also result in the development of a brand-new variety of cacao that produces a cocao bean that tastes even chocolatier than current varieties.

Beautiful Bat Fact #51
Jamaican Fruit Bats

Several thick-bodied bats flutter around a cluster of wild grown cacao trees. They chatter amongst themselves while they seek out pieces of the heavy fruit, favoring the pieces that are under-ripe. Once a bat has selected the perfect piece of fruit, it sinks its sharp teeth into the flesh and starts pulling until the stem breaks. Keeping the fruit clenched tightly between its teeth, the bat wheels away from the small stand of trees and finds a quiet, safe branch a short distance away from which it hangs while consuming its sweet, sticky treat.

Don't let the fact that it's called the Jamaican fruit bat (*Artibeus jamaicensis*) fool you into assuming that the only place you'll find representatives of this particular species is in Jamaica. The island merely happens to be the spot where the first member of the species was captured. If you want to catch a glimpse of one of these bats, there's no shortage of places where you can go. They've been identified in the southern Bahama islands, the Caribbean, Argentina, Brazil, and even as far north as the Florida Keys.

As a rule, Jamaican fruit bats stick to lowland rainforests, but some members of the species are exceptions to this rule and will not only forage for fruit in forests that experience seasonal rains, but will also venture into cultivated plantations.

When it comes to roosts, Jamaican fruit bats aren't picky and will make do with whatever they find. Roosting sites have been found in dead, hollowed-out trees, caves, and occasionally, a group settles into a quiet building. There have even been instances when the bats have gotten to work converting large leaves into tents that serve as a temporary roost, which is unusual for bats of this size.

Like many other types of fruit bats, Jamaican fruit bats don't eat at the same trees where they find fruit, preferring to fly away with it. The feeding roost is typically between 25 and 200 meters (82 and 656 feet) from the food supply. For the bat, this is a great way to avoid predators, and ecologically speaking, it's good for the rainforest since it means the seeds the bat dispenses are well away from the parent tree, which is a good way to spread out genetic material and reforest the land. While fruit like figs and cacao pods make up the bulk of the Jamaican fruit bat's diet, on occasion, they'll sip nectar.

While some fruit bats consume the entire piece of fruit, the only thing that interests the Jamaican fruit bat is the juice. They grind up the under-ripe piece of fruit with their powerful molars, pulverizing it until they've drained every drop of juice before spitting out the pulp and seeds. The species has a remarkably fast digestive system. The bats completely digest their meal in less than twenty minutes. Since the food remains in the gut for such a very short time, experts believe that digestive bacteria aids with the breakdown of nutrients.

Jamaican fruit bats prefer harem-style living. The harems generally include about fourteen bats, plus any young the females are caring for. Researchers have observed Jamaican fruit bat harems with both one and two adult males who were responsible for protecting the females and the pups. The males don't venture far from the roost and will vigorously defend it against any male rivals who start sniffing around.

One of the things that sets Jamaican fruit bats apart from most other bat species is their breeding habits. Researchers believe that some females give birth twice a year, generally bearing one pup at a time. There is also evidence to suggest that in some parts of the world, Jamaican fruit bats breed year-round, rather than limiting themselves to one or two months, but even in these areas, the female holds off on conception until she's confident she'll give birth when food is plentiful. The gestation period is about four months long. The pups start flying between one and two months of age and are full size by the time they're eighty days old. They become sexually active between eight and twelve months.

The IUCN Red List currently has the Jamaican fruit bat listed as least concern.

Jamaican Fruit Bat
(*Artibeus jamaicensis*)

Figure 54 ©Karin Schneeberger alias Felineora
[CC BY-SA 3.0], via Wikimedia Commons

Beautiful Bat Facts #52
White-Nose Syndrome Kills Bats

White-nose syndrome (WNS) is a term that refers to a fungus found in bat caves that has led to the highest bat mortality rates North America has ever experienced. Bats suffering from WNS are easily identified by the buildup of white fungal spores on their noses. While there have long been reports of WNS in Europe, the fungus wasn't officially documented in North America until 2007, when it was found in a New York State cave. Once the fungus was officially documented, researchers went back and looked at older photos and detected signs of the fungus on hibernating bats in New York during 2006. Since 2006, approximately 6.5 million bats in the Northern United States and Canada have perished from WNS. The condition wipes out entire hibernating colonies in a shockingly short period of time. Since most bats species have just one pup a year, it will take a long, long time for the population to recover.

What Causes White-Nose Syndrome

White-nose syndrome is caused by *Pseudogymnoascus destructans*, a fungus that thrives in cold, humid areas, like bat caves. As the bats hibernate, the fungal spores gather on the tiny bodies. The presence of the spores causes the bats to burn through their energy stores long before their hibernation period ends. Since it's too cold for the bats to go outside and hunt, the only thing that would allow them to replenish the energy and moisture they've lost, the bat dies.

Many compare the staggering impact WNS has on bats to Colony Collapse Disorder that devastated the honey bee community.

Signs that Bats/the Hibernacula Have White-Nose Syndrome:

- Hibernating bats have white dots on their noses (the visible white are mold spores). The spores have also been seen on the wings, tail, and ears
- Instead of being inside the hibernacula, sleeping and conserving energy stores, bats are clustered near the entrances
- Multiple dead bats on the ground
- Bats spotted outside during cold temperatures

How White-Nose Syndrome Kills Bats

Even though white-nose syndrome was observed in the United States more than ten years ago, scientists are still trying to figure out exactly why it takes such a toll on North American bats.

Scientists representing the U.S. Geological Survey (USGS) and the University of Wisconsin created an experiment that allowed them to observe exactly what happens to bats once the fungal spores settle on their bodies. At the end of the experiment, they reported that bats fighting WNS used more than twice the amount of energy as bats who managed to avoid the spores.

Despite the name, white-nose syndrome does more damage to the wings than to the noses of bats. Bats store a great deal of moisture in their wings, moisture that's supposed to keep them hydrated while they hibernate.

The current working theory is that *Pseudogymnoascus destructans* attacks bat wings in much the same way fungi attack invertebrates. The most likely reason for the wing damage and extreme dehydration is that the fungus is wicking water from the wing's membrane, though some researches have hypothesized that the spores cause the wing's evaporative surface to increase. Researchers observed that in aggressive cases, the bat's hair follicles, apocrine glands, and sebaceous glands were destroyed.

The degree of wing damage doesn't have to be severe to have a negative impact on a bat's health. As soon as the fungus attacks the cells, the bats become severely dehydrated and are unable to do anything to hydrate themselves.

The way the fungus attacks the wings goes a long way towards explaining the why some species are more susceptible than others. Species who require more moisture while hibernating always select hibernacula with a high humidity, where *Pseudogymnoascus destructans* thrives. These same bats are most likely more susceptible to the dehydrating effects the fungus has on their wings.

One of the things USGS noticed while studying bats with WNS was that even the animals who had a relatively minor amount of wing damage had a significantly higher carbon dioxide to oxygen ratio in their blood. This leads to both pH imbalances and acidification. Bats with WNS also have increased potassium levels, which suggests an increased risk of heart problems.

Bats are the only known animals to experience negative effects from contact *with Pseudogmnoascus*, but if something isn't done to save the lives of bats, the ecological impact will be staggering and difficult to recover from.

How Does White-Nose Syndrome Spread from One Bat Cave to Another

The general consensus is that WNS most likely made the trek across the Atlantic Ocean from Europe to North America on the clothing of people who'd visited a bat cave while in Europe and then wore the same clothing while in New York bat caves. Now that it's here, it's quickly spreading from one bat colony to another and has already spanned the distance between the east and west coasts.

Researchers believe that the main way the fungus travels is via bat-to-bat contact. Since bats cuddle while they hibernate, the fungus quickly moves through the entire colony, killing it.

In a desperate attempt to slow the progression of WNS, cavers and bat experts alike are strongly urged to completely decontaminate themselves and their clothing after exploring a cave. Many caves and mine shafts have now been closed in a desperate attempt to keep them safe for hibernating bats.

Bad News for the Little Guys

Many believe that bat behavior, particularly while bats are preparing to hibernate, influences which colonies survive the winter and which are ravished by WNS. There's also evidence to suggest size plays a role in how well species fight the fungal infection.

A University of New Zealand group led by David Hayman of Massey compared big brown bats and little brown bats and explored why the larger bats are more likely to survive WNS. The early results indicate that, in this case, size matters. The larger bats simply have more fat stores, which allows them to live a bit longer even if WNS disturbs them.

It's worth noting that the smaller bats also prefer a

more humid hibernaculum, as does the fungus that causes WNS and are most likely more susceptible to dehydration than larger bats.

How Do European Bats Survive?

WNS disease is believed to have originated in Europe and doesn't wipe out entire colonies. The general consensus is that the bats have simply evolved and developed better coping mechanisms. It's likely that when the fungus first appeared in Europe, many bat colonies were destroyed, but since few people paid attention to local bat populations, no one really knew that anything was wrong.

Bats in Europe, where the fungus that causes white-nose syndrome likely originated, also have high survival rates. Over time, they developed behaviors and physical traits that made them less susceptible to the disease, the researchers suggest.

As with so many things, WNS does have a silver lining. It's providing scientists with a unique opportunity to learn how animals that live in colonies respond to illness.

Boston University graduate student Kate Langwig started observing the roosting and hibernation patterns of the little brown bats and noticed that instead of thousands of bats bunching up together during hibernation, many of the remaining bats have taken to resting in smaller groups. Even more importantly, they stopped cuddling together as tightly during the hibernation period.

This isn't a new pattern. Throughout history, there's documentation of groups of humans separating themselves from others in an effort to stop a disease from spreading, but this is one of the first times researchers have noticed such behavior in the animal kingdom. It shows that bats identified the reason so many in their colonies were dying and were willing to change their social behavior to preserve their species.

If, and that's a big if, a solution is found to WNS or if bats are able mirror what it appears their European cousins did and develop an immunity to the fungus, it will be interesting to see if they resume their previous group cuddling if they continue putting a little space between themselves.

While spacing themselves out seems to be helping the little brown bat, other bats haven't been so lucky. The northern long-eared bat has always hibernated by itself, yet the population hasn't been spared from WNS.

Fighting White-Nose Syndrome

Fighting back against WNS is a Herculean task, but bat conservationist believe bats are more than worth the effort.

One of the challenges they face in fighting WNS is how quickly the fungus spreads, not just from bat to bat, but from one hibernaculum to the next. The inability to stop the fungus from spreading means that bat colonies are dying faster than the conservationists work.

The way that bats hibernate, in large huddles, makes it nearly impossible to use traditional methods of damage control.

Conservationists and scientists alike hope that the secret to licking WNS will be found in microbes, particularly natural anti-fungal compounds. The hope is that the scientific community will find an organic compound that destroys Pseudogmnoascus and that by spreading the compound in the caves where bats hibernate, the fungus can be eradicated. The science community is looking for organic compounds that either use the same resources as the Pseudogmnoascus and will out-compete the fungus for those resources, or that actually attack the fungus itself.

So far, the VOCs that show the most promise are a

bacterium, *Rhodococcus rhodochrous*, which in lab studies reduced the impact of WNS on bats, even when the bacteria didn't come into direct contact with the *Pseudogmnoascus*.

Researchers are also taking a close look at fungistatic soils. In clinical trials, these soils had a negative impact on the fungus, which hopefully means a brighter future for bats.

A bacterium found on some bats may prove to be an important factor in preventing more bats from losing their lives to WNS. A team of University of California, Santa Cruz scientists conducted a lab study that indicates that a specific type of bacteria they removed from the hide of four different bat species inhibited the growth of *Pseudogymnoascus destructans*. The lab-managed bacterium was particularly effective when the fungus passed the thirty-five-day stage.

Based on what the team saw in the laboratory, they believe that the bacterium has the ability to inhibit the growth of the fungal spores, hopefully before they do much damage to the bat's wings. They believe that the current problem is that the levels of the bacteria that occurs naturally is too small to effectively overcome WNS. If the team can create a spray that covers the bats with a higher concentration of the bacteria, they're optimistic they can start saving the lives of thousands of North American bats. Even if the bacteria just slow the progression of the fungus, it may be enough to get the bats through the winter, at which point they can replenish themselves and heal during their active season.

Researchers representing the U.S. Geological Survey (USGS) and Massey University in New Zealand joined forces to study something that has always been of great interest to science: the tendency for some bat species to wake up and have a short burst of time when they essentially warm up their little bodies before resuming deep hibernation. The team used thermal imaging surveillance cameras to view the hibernating bats without disturbing them and published their results in *Methods in Ecology and Evolution*.

On its own, the data they gathered would be fascinating, but what the images revealed about WNS and how some bats are able to survive through an outbreak of the fungus makes it doubly so.

The team chose two different hibernacula to observe. WNS was known to be present in both of these caves. Reports indicated that the fungus was responsible for a 30-40% drop in the colony population in one of the caves, while the second had experienced a 90% mortality rate. The first cave was a preferred hibernaculum of Indiana bats and a large colony of little brown bats utilized the second hibernaculum.

The group was stunned when they realized that the Indiana bats weren't rousing themselves once or twice every few weeks, but rather went through a group warm-up period every single night. Meanwhile, the little brown bats sleep through the entire winter without the wake-up, warm-up periods.

While the researchers still don't know why the Indiana bat goes through so many group warm-up periods during the winter, based on the lower mortality rate, they're confident that these group warm-ups make them somehow less susceptible to WNS, possibly because the species has a higher amount of reserved energy going into their hibernation, which is just enough to let them survive the dehydrating effects of the fungus. Another hypothesis the team had about why the Indiana bat colony hasn't experienced the same high mortality rate as the little brown bat is because as the bats raise their temperature, fungal growth slows.

What does this mean in terms of preventing WNS from continuing to kill massive amounts of bats? It's possible that this new information will pave the way for scientists to determine how specific bat species will respond to WNS as the fungus continues to spread from one region to another and explore steps that will aid the bats' ability to withstand the fungus based on that specific species' hibernating patterns.

There has been one bright spot connected to WNS. It has shined a spotlight on bats. Never before have so many people been aware of bats, and scientists and bat-friendly groups are rushing to make the most of this newfound interest by doing everything in their power to educate the general populace about the important ecological role bats play. This includes everything from visiting schools, to publishing articles, to even organizing bat walks.

It's strange to think that a flesh-eating fungus managed to do what no one else has been able to accomplish. It made bats desirable.

Beautiful Bat Facts #53
Species Impacted by White-Nose Syndrome

North American Bats that Have Been Diagnosed with WNS:

- Big brown bat
- Eastern small-footed bat
- Grey bat *endangered*
- Indiana bat *endangered*
- Little brown bat
- Northern long-eared bat *threatened*
- Tricolored bat
- Yuma bat

Additional North American bat species where WNS has been detected in the colonies, though no actual signs of the condition have been diagnosed:

- Eastern red bat
- Southeastern bat
- Silver-haired bat
- Rafinesque's big-eared bat
- Virginia Big-Eared Bat *endangered*
- Cave bat
- Townsend's big-eared bat

European/Asian Bats that Have Been Diagnosed with WNS:

- Common bent-wing bat
- Greater mouse-eared bat
- Daubenton's bat
- Bechstein's bat
- Natterer's bat
- Brandt's bat
- Geoffroy's bat
- Pond bat
- Northern bat
- Barbastelle
- Brown long-eared bat
- Mediterranean horseshoe bat
- Lesser horseshoe bat
- Eastern water bat

Additional European/Asian bat species where WNS has been detected in the colonies, though no actual signs of the condition have been diagnosed:

- Whiskered bat
- Lesser mouse-eared bat
- Big-footed bat
- Large bat
- Ussuri tube-nosed bat
- Greater tube-nosed bat
- Greater horseshoe bat

This information was obtained via the White-Nose Syndrome.org

Beautiful Bat Facts #54
The Little Brown Bat

Prior to white-nose syndrome making its way to North America, the little brown bat populated just about the entire continent. The only places it didn't live was Mexico, Texas, and Florida. New Hampshire was the state that had the highest population of little brown bats who like to live and hunt in swampy, humid areas.

They're Bug Eating Machines!

Even though the little brown bat weighs a mere half ounce, it plays a significant role in the ecosystem. A single little brown bat consumes half of its body weight every single night, and while a quarter-ounce worth of bugs might not seem like much to you, anyone who lives in swampy areas will tell you they've noticed a huge increase in the insect population since WNS started decimating little brown bat colonies. In a single hour, a little brown bat can eat six hundred flying insects.

You do not want to get into an eating contest with a little brown bat. Once it catches a bug, it doesn't waste any time eating it; it goes straight into its mouth. While it chews, its jaw moves a complete seven cycles a second. The food doesn't stay in its system long. In less than an hour, it exits the alimentary canal. When it closes in on the insect it wants to turn into dinner, the little brown bat closes in on the bug it wants to turn into dinner, it uses a variety of methods for capturing the insect. Sometimes it uses its tail as a net, sometimes it bats the bug with its wing and shoves it into its tail membrane and than sweeps its tail membrane forward, lifting the insect to its mouth. At other times, it'll just use its teeth and pluck the unsuspecting bug right out of the night sky.

Once a little brown bat spots an insect, the bug doesn't stand much of a chance. The bat's wings are a thing of beauty and allows the animal to perform complicated maneuvers the bug can't hope to duplicate. Beating their wings as fast as fifteen strokes a second, the species can attain a flying speed of up to 21mph.

The bats drink while in flight. Occasionally, a little brown bat will be knocked into the water. When this happens, it uses its powerful wings to swim and can travel several hundred feet before wearing out.

If the population continues to decline, it will become difficult to control the insect growth in the swampy areas the little brown bat prefers. As the insect populations, especially mosquitos, increases, so does the risk of the humans who call those areas home contracting mosquito-borne diseases such as malaria, Eastern Equine Encephalitis, Malaria, West Nile Virus, Yellow Fever, Zika Virus, and more.

Home Sweet Home

Its diminutive size makes it impossible for the little brown bat to handle any type of freezing weather, which is why it hibernates for up to six months. Despite the inability to handle chilly conditions, little brown bats have been spotted as far north as Alaska.

Little brown bats enjoy active social lives; they're frequently found living in colonies that can number in the hundreds of thousands, which is how WNS managed to destroy such a high number of bats in a brief period of time. The bats show no sign of being territorial or aggressive to one another. For roosting, they prefer bat houses, wood piles, buildings, trees, and even rock crevices. It's not unusual for a little brown bat to fly several hundred miles in search of a hibernaculum.

They're a Promiscuous Bunch

Little brown bats have pretty specific criteria that they use when searching for a good day roost. They prefer roosts that open to the southwest, which makes it easy for them to keep their bodies in tune with the sun. The roost must be dry, dark, and warm. Females join forces and form maternity colonies and generally return to the same colony year after year.

One of the interesting things about the little brown bat is how they mate. It appears that they have two mating phases, which have been dubbed the active phase and the passive phase. The mating appears to be random and the girls like to take multiple partners. Researchers have observed that the nasal glands do expand during the autumn mating season, and that some bats will do some limited singing and honking.

The mating season takes place during the autumn before the weather forces the bats into their hibernacula.

Little Brown Bat
(Myotis lucifugus)

Figure 55 ©U.S. Fish and Wildlife Service Headquarters
Public domain

Beautiful Bat Fact #55
Bats Face Many Threats

While White-Nose Syndrome poses the most immediate threat to North American bats, by no means is it the only challenge modern bats face. There are multiple things that make their lives more challenging than it once was.

Fear

For a long, long time, the biggest threat bats faced was human fear. Not only did people kill any bat they found in their house, they also went out of their way to destroy natural habitats. It's impossible to calculate the number of bats who've lost their lives because humans didn't bother to take the time to learn just how useful and marvelous these tiny creatures really are.

The good news is that as we continue to learn more about bats, the fear decreases and we look for ways to establish harmony and become involved in conservation efforts. This is why bat-related education is so important.

Destruction of Habitat

Habitat destruction is a huge problem for bats. Mines

and caves that previously served as a hibernacula for several large bat colonies have been blocked off or destroyed. Urban development, forestry, and changes in the way farmers operate is another problem.

Luckily, most professional farmers and foresters recognize the value of bats and actively search for ways they can continue to do their jobs, use modern technology, and still provide bat-friendly habitats and hunting grounds.

Pesticides

Pesticide use is a tricky issue to deal with. It's easy to say that farmers should stop using the pesticides that kill the insects that the bats feed on, while they're also facing a demanding and hungry population. The good news is that some companies are looking for ways to create bat-friendly pesticides while farmers take steps to set aside bat-friendly hunting areas.

The real secret to making sure that bats thrive in the modern world is education and communication. If all sides understand the important role bats play in the ecosystem, they'll remain willing to take the steps needed to protect these precious mammals.

Wind Energy

Wind energy seems like a really good idea. Wind is free and converting the wind to electricity is relatively inexpensive.

The downside to wind energy is the toll it's taking on bats. While a bat can use echolocation to detect the smallest wire stretched across their flight path, they don't have any natural system in place to help them avoid giant oscillating propellers. Ongoing efforts are currently happening in order to make wind farms safer for bats that fly through them.

Hunting

In North America, most people's stomachs turn at the thought of eating a bat. They simply don't seem like much of a delicacy, but in areas with large fruit bat populations, fruit bat meat is in high demand. Not only is it a popular ingredient for local dishes, but many countries export it, making fruit bat hunting a thriving business.

This is fine when the populations are too high and the numbers need to be thinned, but right now, most fruit bat species populations are strained, the numbers decreasing to the point where they've been placed on either the threatened or endangered species lists.

In some locations, the government has gotten involved and banned the exportation of fruit bat meat, while still allowing hunting for domestic purposes.

In other places, such as a small island off the coast of Sulawesi, hunters have ravaged the local population of native Sulawesi flying foxes in a span of just eighteen months, that the flock, which had consisted of ten thousand bats, has fled the island, leaving many to wonder if they'll ever return.

Beautiful Bat Facts #56
Bat Habitats

The first thing you need to know about bats is that they have two homes. In the summer, they look for roosts where they hang out during the day. During the winter, they need a hibernaculum that provides them with a very specific environment.

Choosing the Best Hibernacula

Not only are bats not designed to withstand the cold, the food they rely on can't be found during the winter, which is why many species hibernate once the weather turns chilly.

Bats are very particular when looking for a hibernaculum, which is why they generally use the same one for as long as possible.

The place they choose to spend the winter needs:

- To have a regular internal temp that stays between 0° and 15°C (32° and 59°F)
- Fairly humid
- Free of predators

Favorite bat hibernacula include:

- Mine shafts
- Caves
- Large hollow trees
- Deep crevices in stone walls or rock faces

Once the bats choose their winter hibernaculum and settle in for the winter, they bunch up at the top of the space, cuddling as close to one another as they can and sharing body heat. At this point, their core temperature lowers, their heart and respiration rate slow to an almost undetectable rate, their immune system shuts down, and they enter a state of torpor.

Sometimes, if the conditions are just right, bats will hibernate in a house. If you locate a bat hibernaculum, it's vital you leave it alone. There are two reasons for this.

Disturbing the colony while they hibernate causes the bats to use up their precious energy stores, decreasing the odds of them surviving the winter, and if they do survive, it's unlikely they'll return to the same place

White-nose syndrome is a huge problem and it's believed that people walking through the caves bats hibernate in is one of the main reasons it's spreading so quickly. You don't want to be the reason the fungus gets introduced to what had been an unaffected hibernaculum.

Choosing the Best Roost

Different species of bats have different roosting requirements. The checklists bats have when looking for a good roost includes:

- Large enough to hold the desired colony size
- Close to good feeding grounds
- Protection from the elements
- Easy access and exit

- Lack of predators
- Someplace they won't be disturbed by humans

Places that bats like to roost include:

- Trees
- Caves
- Abandoned mine shafts
- Under bridges /overpasses
- Buildings

Most bats seem to like returning to the same roost year after year. In the United Kingdom, bat roosts are protected by law.

Many bats have learned how to incorporate human structures into their roosts. This doesn't always make the humans living in or near those structures happy, but with just a little effort, a peaceful co-existence can be arranged.

Beautiful Bat Fact #57
You Have the Power to Provide Bats with a Happy Home!

There are many reasons so many bat species are considered threatened or endangered, including loss of habitat. The good news is that this particular problem has an easy solution. Attracting bats to your backyard and providing them with a safe place to live helps preserve their lives.

Best of all, the bats will reward your generosity with an assortment of benefits that improve the overall quality of your life.

Create a Watering Hole

Bats prefer roosting somewhere close to a reliable water source. This is reasonable since records indicate that in a span of just twenty-four hours, they can lose up to fifty percent of their body weight in water. They need to constantly rehydrate. In a perfect world, you have a pond or small, slow-moving creek on your property, but lacking this, a simple water feature or even a bird bath suffices.

Don't worry about the standing water attracting even more mosquitoes to your property; the bats happily resolve that problem.

Set up a Roost

Bat houses have become a vital part of bat conservation. They're making up for a great deal of lost natural roosts and encourage bats to move into urban areas. A well-designed single-chamber bat house provides a roosting place for up to fifty bats.

When it comes to acquiring a bat house, you have two choices: you can purchase one or you can build your own.

If you decide to take the pre-made option, I politely request that you turn to one of the bat conservation groups for the purchase. Not only do these groups sell beautifully made bat houses, but the proceeds go towards additional conservation efforts.

Bat conservation groups in the United States that sell bat houses include:

- Organization for Bat Conservation
- Bat Conservation International
- Bat World

If You Build it, Bats Will Come

The great thing about building bat houses is that they're easy to construct. There are even several 4-H organizations that have annual Build-a-Bat-House events. In Norway, a large scale bat-house project was implemented in an effort to provide bats with roosts while simultaneously preventing them from taking up residence in local attics where they weren't exactly given a warm welcome.

I used the guidelines the Bat Conservation International organization provided on how to build an economy bat house. This is a single-chamber bat house that will provide your local bats with several years' worth of happy roosting.

Stuff you need to get together before the construction process begins includes:

- 1/4 sheet (2' x 4') 1/2" AC, BC, or T1-11 plywood. It needs to be outdoor grade and not pressure treated.
- 1" x 3" x 28" board that will serve as the roof.
- Black asphalt shingles (galvanized metal also works)
- 1" x 2" (3/4" x 1 1/2" finished) x 8' piece of pine
- 20-30 1 1/4" exterior-grade Phillips screws
- 7/8" roofing nails
- 1 pint of exterior grade, water based, wood stain
- 1 pint exterior-grade, water-based primer
- 1 quart of exterior-grade water-based paint
- Latex caulk
- Table saw/handsaw
- Caulking gun
- Reversing drill with a Phillips bit
- Paintbrushes
- Tape measure

Step One

Cut the wood. You can choose to do this yourself or order it pre-cut. Your plywood should be cut into three pieces. According to Bat Conservation International, the measurements for each piece is

- 2 61/2" x 24"
- 161/2" x 24"
- 5" x 24"

Add Some Grooves

To roost in the bat house, the bats need something to hold on to. The simplest way to do this is use your circular saw and gouge some grooves into the longer piece of plywood that will make the back of the bat house. Each of the grooves should be approximately ½" apart and extend down the entire length of the piece of plywood. Another option is stapling a piece of heavy-duty plastic mesh to the board. The advantage of the grooves is that they're sturdier and more natural.

A circular saw is the best way to create the grooves; just be careful you don't cut through the board.

Use a dark color to stain the interior of the bat house. The darker color keeps the bat house warmer.

Putting it all Together

Cut three side strips. One should be 24" and the other two should be 20 ½" pieces. Attach these strips to the piece of plywood that will make up the back of the bat house. Line the side pieces with caulk which not only helps keep the bats warm, but also prevents moisture from seeping into the house. Make sure you leave a ½" vent between the top and bottom front pieces, this vents the bat house.

Run some more caulk along the outside of all joints.

At the top of the bat house, attach a 1" x 4" x 28" board strip.

Cover the exterior with a few coats of exterior grade paint.

Use the shingles to form a roost.

Getting the Environment Just Right

The bat house doesn't do you or the bats any good if it sits in your garage for years and years. The sooner you get it installed, the sooner everyone benefits.

The way your property is set up impacts exactly where you'll be able to install the bat house. Ideally, it should be mounted on either the side of a building or a pole (trees work in a pinch, but they do make the bats more vulnerable to predators) and be fifteen feet off the ground.

There are two reasons that the bat house should be a minimum of fifteen feet above the ground.

- The height discourages most predators
- Bats have a tough time obtaining lift. They fall before they soar. Fifteen feet gives them the time and distance needed to build up the necessary pressure beneath their wings.

Bats hate to be cold, so place the house you've built them in a location that allows it to face south/southeast. The sunlight striking the box throughout the day will keep the colony warm and happy all day long.

The bat house must be secure. Remember, it not only has to put up with lots of tiny bodies entering and exiting it, but must also withstand wind and rain.

Once you've mounted the bat house, keep an eye on it and make sure that it doesn't become a haven to wasps and other insects prior to the bats moving in. Once they do, they'll keep the house free of pests.

During the spring and summer, leave the house alone. If you spend too much time hanging around it, the bats will feel threatened and move out.

Piles of bat droppings on the ground will tell you if you've attracted a colony.

Add a Pup Catcher

One of the things people don't think about when they build a bat house is the youngsters who will share the roost with their moms. On very hot days, the inside of the bat house grows too warm and the overheating babies fall out. If there's not a pup catcher, which stops their descent and allows them to climb back into the house, they'll die.

Making a pup catcher and installing it on your bat house doesn't take much time or effort.

The supplies you need so a pup catcher can be added to your bat house include:

- 24" of plastic bat house mesh (lacking this, you can use an equal amount of nylon window screen)
- 2 pieces of scrap wood. Make sure they're sanded
- Some staples
- A staple gun
- Screws
- A few zip ties

Cut the mesh so that the width matches the width of your bat house.

Create a pouch to catch the pups on one end of the mesh. Don't worry; it's easy. Simply fold up four inches of the bottom section. Use the zip ties to close of the sides, creating a pouch that catches fallen pups. Staple both ends of the mesh to your scrap wood. Screw the wood scraps on to the same pole that you've mounted the bat house to.

Now if a pup falls out of the bat house, the pouch catches them, and they can climb up the screen and return to their mother.

The only downside to the pup catcher is that it also catches guano. You can work around this by adding a few holes to the mesh that allows it to drop to the ground. The holes built into the bat house mesh are designed for just this purpose.

Change Your Lights

Now that you're trying to attract bats to your home, it's time to think about your outdoor lighting. Some bat species are sensitive to some types of artificial lights, including the light you use to illuminate your backyard. This doesn't mean you have to decide between being able to see what's happening outside of your house and providing bats with a place to stay. It just means you should seriously consider switching your current bulb with a red one.

A study managed by the Netherlands Institute of Ecology indicates that even bat species that are typically light shy treat red light the same way they would total darkness, and even species such as the pipistrelle, who don't shy away from artificial light sources, appeared happier when they were exposed to red light.

The red light vs. artificial light study represents a five-year research project during which time a team of researchers led by Kamiel Spoelstra explored how bats and other nocturnal animals responded to green, white, and red LED-lighting.

Human Made Bat Hibernacula

As a rule, bats are on their own when it comes to finding a place to spend the long, cold winter. They usually look for caves or old mine shafts that are both warm enough and quiet enough for them to enjoy a long, uninterrupted hibernation.

There's one exception.

In an attempt to stop the decline of the local barbastelle bat, which have been declining at a rate of approximately 2% a year, the British environmental conservation group WREN teamed up with the Forestry Commission. The two groups managed to obtain the funding needed to construct a large underground cave to serve as a hibernaculum for local bats.

The "cave" was constructed at the High Lodge Forest Centre. It's called the Thetford High Lodge.

With North American bats continually losing more and more of their natural hibernacula combined with the rising problem of white-nose syndrome, it won't be surprising if local bat conservation groups start exploring similar projects.

One example of this would be the efforts being made to make abandoned mines in Copper Mountain a better home for the 40,000+ colony of endangered desert bats, including the Lesser long-nosed bats, that call it home.

With the help of Bat Conservation International, ongoing efforts are in place to not only keep the current bat population safe, but to also create an environment that encourages the bat population to continue to grow and thrive.

Bat House

Figure 56 © Daniela Pelazza
Acquired via Dreamstime.com

Beautiful Bat Fact #58
Bats and Pets Can Co-Exist

One of the reasons so many people work hard to keep bats out of their backyards is because they're worried the bats pose a direct threat to their pets. Their worries are unfounded.

Bats and Dogs

Dogs and bats are able to co-exist quite nicely. Bats are gentle creatures who generally ignore dogs, even the ones that like to chase birds and bats. Their echolocation makes it easy for the bats to detect your dog and remain out of its reach.

While a very small number of bats, less than 5%, of bats have rabies, it's reasonable to worry about the possibility of them biting your dog and passing the disease on. However, not only are the odds of your dog meeting a rabid bat long: legally, the dog must be vaccinated against the disease, so even if bitten, they're safe.

If your dog does receive a bat bite, you should bring them to the vet and have the wound treated for a bacterial infection.

The biggest risk to your dog isn't the bats, but rather bat guano. The guano contains elevated levels of ammonia gas, which can have a detrimental impact on your dog's respiratory health.

Bats and Cats

Cats are a much bigger threat to the bats living in your backyard than the bats are to your cat. The aerial antics the bats perform each evening fascinates cats. Many cats quickly become obsessed with the idea of catching one. If the cat can get up high enough to reach the bats, it will attack the smaller animals and play with them the same way they would a mouse. Even if the bat manages to live through this scenario, the combination of internal injuries and infections triggered by cat saliva generally causes the animal to pass away.

It's your responsibly to make sure your backyard bat colony doesn't experience genocide at the paws of your kitty.

The best way to prevent cat-induced genocide on your bat colony is keeping your cat indoors during the time the bats leave and return to their roost (it doesn't take long). If you have a bat house, set it up in a location where your cat can't reach it.

If your cat does catch a bat, make sure its rabies vaccination is current and if it sustained a bite, have your veterinarian clean the wound.

With just a little forethought, pets and bats can easily co-exist in the same backyard.

Beautiful Bat Fact #59
Leave Bat Wrangling to the Experts

Far too many people panic when they discover that a bat has invited itself indoors. If the bat is one of the lucky ones, it quickly realizes that it's not welcome to stay and leaves the same way it came. Other bats are captured in a handy butterfly net and set free. While they might not agree, these are also very lucky bats.

Far too many bats who accidentally make their way into houses are killed.

It's possible to remove bats from your home without having to resort to bat homicide.

How Bats Make Their Way into Your Home

People who are diligent about keeping their doors closed and window screens in good repair are often baffled by how a bat managed to find its way into the house. Remember, bats aren't nearly as big as they look. Most of what you're seeing is their wing span. Their actual bodies are quite small, usually weighing less than two ounces. Those same tiny bodies have been designed to let bats wiggle into some pretty tiny openings. Companies tasked with removing bats from houses report that the animals frequently entered the building through a small hole that wasn't much bigger than the circumference of a finger.

Rather than fretting about how the bat got into your home, your main priority is getting them out. Once you've done that, you can work on blocking their entrance.

First Create a Quiet Environment

The bat really doesn't want to be in your home any more than you want it to be there. This is good news. It means you're working towards a common goal.

When you discover you're temporarily sharing your living quarters with a bat, you need to send your pets and any humans who can't contain their excitement to another section of the house. The only thing screaming and hysterics does is cause the bat to panic. The quieter the house, the less stressful the removal process will be for both you and the bat.

The Correct way to Remove a Bat from Your Home

The traditional way to remove a bat was by capturing it with a butterfly net and releasing it. While you can do this, there's another way that decreases the odds of the bat getting hurt, or your accidentally swinging the net and breaking a window, vase, or knickknack.

The far better method is to select a room with a door or window that leads outdoors. Open the door/window. Turn off the lights in the room. Gradually guide the bat to the empty room. The best way to guide the bat is to have two people holding up sheets who walk towards the bat. The sheet might not seem like much of a barrier to you, but the bat's echolocation tells it that it's a solid wall. Once the bat is in the room with an exit, block the interior entrance. If there's not a door, use push pins and a sheet. Now all you have to do is use your previous guidance system to urge the bat through the exit.

When Lots of Bats Stop By

Sometimes a bat discovers a small crack or crevice in your home's exterior and after exploring the situation, they decide it's a great place and they invite all their friends over to roost. This isn't a good situation. It's also one that's easily corrected.

The best people to call when you discover a colony of bats roosting in your attic is animal control or nuisance control. Even if they don't have someone on staff who's trained to safely remove the colony without harming a single bat hair, they'll have a list of recommendations of removal companies who will handle the problem in no time at all.

It's extremely important to make sure that you work with people who understand the nature of bats and who understand the importance of keeping each animal alive and healthy. With so many Canadian and American bats falling victim to white-nose syndrome, it's more important than ever before to spare the lives of as many bats as possible.

Beautiful Bat Fact #60
Bat Conservation is Happening All Over the World!

As our understanding of bats continues to grow, so does our realization that if steps aren't taken to protect bats and make sure they're around for future generations, the very ecology of the world will change. The challenge is working out a way to protect bats while also allowing current farming/forestry/energy conservation/lifestyle to continue.

Another challenge facing people involved in bat conservation is the fact that each region and each bat species presents unique conservation issues. For example, in the rainforests, one of the biggest challenges that any fruit bats, particularly the magnificent flying foxes, face is overhunting, while in North America, white-nose syndrome is killing one colony of little brown bats after another.

In order to preserve as many species as possible and still allow current lifestyles to continue, conservation efforts are adapted to suit specific needs and requirements. In tropical areas where flying foxes and other fruit bats are actively hunted, steps are underway to control hunting (many countries do allow domestic hunting of flying foxes but no longer allow the meat to be sold on the international market) as well as looking into how to use nets to protect cultivated fruit from the bats. Many sections of the various rain forests have been set up as national parks so the bats continue to have a place to live.

In North America, some of the greatest biologists and bat experts are hard at work looking for a way to stop the spread of the fungus that causes white-nose syndrome. Hopefully, if once it stops spreading from one bat cave to another, those same scientific minds will come up with a way to eradicate it once and for all and then help the decimated bat populations to regrow.

In addition to working on the WNS problem, steps are also underway to preserve the abandoned mines and caves that serve as a hibernaculum to various bat species.

In England, bats are highly prized and laws are in place that prevent people from killing innocent bats that accidentally make their way into residences. **Bat Conservation Trust** has spent the past twenty-five years not only aiding in the study of bats, but also helping people learn how to safely remove bats from their homes, and providing a great deal of information about local bat habits and species.

Studies and experiments are currently underway to learn how things like wind energy can be adapted and made safe for bats.

Hands down, education is the most effective form of conservation. The better people understand bats, the more likely they become to look for ways that they can preserve the species. This is why organizations like **Bat Conservation International** in Texas and the **Organization for Bat Conservation** in Michigan work so hard to provide detailed, up-to-date information about all bat species. Both organizations have a reputation for providing detailed information, working with local groups and farmers, and taking part in various studies. Both have websites that are virtual treasure troves of bat-related information.

Bonus Section

There are a few species I wanted to include in this book, but for one reason or another, I wasn't able to find a home for them. So, after a great deal of pondering, I decided to create a bonus section just for these special bat species. I hope you enjoy.

Ghost Bat

Tourist exploring the Mount Etna Caves Park hold their breath and tremble in terror as a pale, ghost of a bat bears down on them. In the moonlight, they can see every feature perfectly, the large forward-facing ears, the intelligence in its bright eyes, and the pale fur that is so different from the dark brown bats they've removed from their home, they know that this bat can't possibly be real. They must be ghost bats, possibly even the reincarnation of the evil souls so many cultures believed bats represented.

These long-eared, pale bats actually are called ghost bats (*Macroderma gigas*); they're members of the false vampire bat club. Native to Australia, at one time, they were found in both arid areas as well as rainforests, but today only a few colonies remain, with one of the largest being the colony that lives in Mount Etna Caves Park.

Although not white like Honduran tent-making bats, ghost bats, who have long, soft fur that ranges from a kind of dirty white to a pale greyish brown are one of the palest bat species. Their wings are a kind of whitish color, which seems to reflect moonlight. Their long ears are connected at the base and a nose leaf stands tall and proud above their tiny nostrils. They're typically 10 - 14 cm long with a wingspan of 60 cm. Adult male ghost bats are a slightly larger than the females.

While ghost bats don't harm humans, they are a carnivorous species that basically eats anything that's smaller than itself. They've been observed feeding on lizards, small rodents, birds, large insects, and even other bats. When hunting they, use both their eyes and echolocation to locate prey. Once they find something, they fly directly above it, hovering silently until the moment is just right, when they swoop down and sink their teeth into the unsuspecting animal's neck, instantly killing it. The ghost bat than hauls their prize to a feeding roost. In most cases, the prey the ghost bat has selected is quite large in comparison to the bat. Researchers have noted that the bats are easily able to kill, transport, and consume lizards and small mammals that weigh up to eighty percent of the bat's weight.

Guano analysis indicates that bats eat basically everything they kill. The samples revealed evidence that the ghost bats consumed the bones, feathers, and even teeth of their prey. When captive ghost bats were fed nothing but straight meat, they quickly became distressed, but when the roughage was reintroduced to their diet, their health improved.

The breeding season may vary from one region to the next, but for the most part, the bats get together in April and May with the female finally giving birth between July and November, depending on how plentiful the food supply is. After giving birth to her pup, she'll carry it with her on hunting trips for the first four weeks of its life. The pup starts flying at approximately seven weeks, and once it's strong enough will start following its mother on hunting expeditions. She'll wean the pup when it's about three months old. It takes about two years for the pups to become sexually mature. Captive ghost bats have lived up to sixteen years, but no one has determined the natural life span for wild ghost bats.

Ghost bats prefer to live in small colonies and the two sexes don't roost together. The bats favor caves and mines for roost sites and are very sensitive to the presence of humans. They're so elusive, that miners who work in the areas where guano indicates a colony of ghost bats resides, frequently tell researchers that while they are familiar with other species of bats that use the caves, they never saw any ghost bats. Roost destruction and disruption has had a devastating impact on the ghost bat population.

The IUCN Red List has ghost bats listed as a vulnerable species. It's believed that the current population consists of 10,000 adult bats, and that the population has decreased by more than ten percent over the past three generations. Given that the ghost bats have been identified as an important aspect of mouse control, this isn't good news.

Ghost Bat
(Macroderma gigas)

Figure 57 © Perth Zoo
[Copyrighted free use], via Wikimedia Commons

Greater False Vampire Bat

You're sitting on a rock in Sri Lanka, trying to capture the perfect photo of a small frog, when all of a sudden, there's a high-pitched clicking sound, a flash of soft grey, and the startled croak of the toad as it attempts to jump, and then … nothing. The toad and whatever that grey thing was are gone without a single trace. It's as if they never existed.

A glance at your phone reveals a blurry image of the toad, and just above it, the grey thing you saw. Zooming in reveals the fuzzy image of … a long-eared, big-winged bat.

Congratulations, you've just experienced a close encounter with a greater false vampire bat.

Don't let the fact that the greater false vampire bat (*Megaderma lyra*) has the word "vampire" in its name or that it's a carnivorous species fool you. No matter how hungry the species gets, it doesn't actively seek out blood. If there's any human blood in its system, it came from eating an insect that recently finished feeding on a person.

If you hear the words "carnivorous" and "false vampire bat" and assume that the animal must be ugly, you're in for a surprise. With their short, greygreyish-colored back fur and white underside, large oval ears, and warm, expressive eyes, this is a very attractive species.

Adults weigh anywhere from 40-60 g with a body length of 65-95 mm. The species doesn't have an external tail and a rostrum connects the bat's ears.

When kept in captivity, this species can live up to fourteen years.

The species has a large range that includes:

- Sri Lanka
- Eastern Pakistan
- Southeastern China
- The northern part of the Malay Peninsula

When it comes to day roosts, they prefer settling into quiet buildings, caves, and hollow trees. The general rule of thumb is that day roosts contain a moderately-sized colony of no more than thirty bats, but in India, there's at least one seasonal colony that contains approximately two thousand greater false vampire bats. Researchers have also observed small contact cluster colonies that consist of about five different bats, which are made up of a mother and her offspring. While roosting, this species likes to maintain about 9 cm between one another. The males and females of the species happily share the same roosts.

Greater false vampire bats prefer to use the same day roost for years and years, indicating that the loss of the roost through habitat destruction would have a devastating psychological impact on the animals, though it's unclear how they'd handle the stress and deal with relocating.

What makes the greater false vampire bat stand out is that insects only make up a portion of its diet. The bat is strong enough and clever enough to also take on small song birds, the occasional fish, small lizards, and even, if the opportunity presents itself, other bat species.

If you love bat watching, you'll have a great time observing the greater false vampire bat in action. While they're hunting, these bats skim along the ground and the surface of quiet lakes and ponds. When they spot a tasty morsel, they snatch it directly off the ground. This hunting style is dubbed "gleaning" and bats such as the greater false vampire bat and the pallid bat are often referred to as "gleaning bats."

This particular bat is up all night long, and they're not afraid to travel. There have been multiple reports of the adults flying approximately 4 kilometers from their roosting site in search of food.

The greater false vampire bat uses a combination of hunting practices. The bulk of its meals are obtained while the bat flies low, about a meter above the ground, and scans the landscape it's flying over. When the bat spots a large bug or a small lizard, it swoops down and grabs it right off the ground!

About 15% of the time, the greater false vampire bat changes its approach. Instead of actively hunting for prey, it finds a place to rest and stays very still, waiting for something edible to come along.

There are times when the bats rely on echolocation to help locate prey, and at other times, they've been observed using a passive listening technique. So far, no one knows why or how the bat switches from one hunting method to another.

Once the bat makes a capture, it carries its food to a safe location where it settles in and starts dining.

Males and females get together during the breeding season, which generally runs from November to January. Following a 150-160-day gestation period, the females give birth to one (occasionally two) pup. She spends several weeks flying with the pup clinging to her chest before it's finally old enough to be left alone while she forages. She'll continue to nurse her pup until it's two or three months old. The male pups become sexually mature at about 15 months of age, while the females generally reach sexual maturity at 19 months old.

In 2006, a group of researchers collected genetic samples of greater false vampire bats from different colonies with the intent of discovering if there was any sign that the population could be in trouble as a result of not enough genetic diversity.

Based on the results the team collected, that while family members do live in the same colonies, there's nothing to indicate that any inbreeding has taken place. It's assumed that the males visit different colonies during the breeding season, allowing them to spread their DNA around. It also might explain why so many young females stay close to their mothers. By living in the same colony with both their mothers and their fathers, the youngsters actually decrease the odds of a genetic slip-up happening. The species still has a diverse gene pool, which will help ensure their survival, provided they don't start to suffer from habitat loss.

This brings up another concern. As more of the colonies are uprooted and the distance between each colony grows, will the male bats continue to be able to find enough non-related females in order to maintain a diverse genetic make-up or will the increased distance increase the likelihood of inbreeding?

The team also noted that while all greater false vampire bats are one and the same species no matter where they're geographically located, the bats in, say Sri Lanka, do have some minor genetic quirks that set them apart from those that inhabit the Malay Peninsula. It's possible, that after a few hundred years, these small changes could alter the bats so much, they evolve into a separate species of bat.

The ICUN currently has the Greater False Vampire Bat listed as least concern.

New Zealand's Walking Bats

New Zealand is home to some pretty unusual animals, including the world's only walking bats: the greater short-tailed bat (*Mystacina robusta*) and the lesser short-tailed bat (*Mystacina tuberculate.*)

The Lesser Short-Tailed Bat

As the sun slips beneath the horizon, blanketing New Zealand in darkness, a small head pokes out from a narrow rock crevice. The lesser short-tailed bat's bright, tiny eyes peer into the deeper shadows, looking for signs of danger before the small winged creature slips out of the roost. Dried leaves crackle beneath its folded up wings as it ambles across the forest floor. Long, pointed ears swivel from side to side as it sends and receives echolocation signals that not only help it navigate the dark forest, but also identify food sources.

The forest-dwelling lesser short-tailed bat can only be found in New Zealand and the surrounding islands. While this is the only remaining mammal that's native to New Zealand, that's far from the only thing that makes the species unique. It has several traits that make it stand out from all other bat species.

To begin with, the lesser short-tailed bat walks. When it emerges from its roost for a night of hunting, it walks on its back legs and uses its folded-up wings for support, with the result being an odd-looking shuffle that serves the bat well. While the bat is capable of flight, it truly seems to prefer walking across the forest floor. Although no one knows exactly why New Zealand's bats started walking, most feel that it's in response to the lack of native mammal predators, which is why many believe that so many of the native birds are also flightless.

The lesser short-tailed bat has developed a unique anatomy in response to its terrestrial lifestyle. The thick 6-8 cm (2.3-3.14 in.) long body is covered with greyish-brown short, thick fur. (The fur is considerably thicker than that of most other bat species, including the ones that live in cold northern climates.) The underside is covered in a paler colored fur that's just as thick. When the bat is walking, it doesn't just fold its wings, but actually rolls them up, rather like an umbrella. This allows the bat the freedom to use its forearms as braces. The wing membranes are a bit thicker than other bat species' and the bat's fingers are designed in such a way that when the wing is rolled, the first phalanx folds to the outside. The species is the only microbat that has a small talon on its thumb, which is attached to the bat's claw. Stiff bristle-like whiskers sprout from the bat's nose. The bat's short, thick feet are covered with small grooves that also adorn the animal's powerful legs. Although it's not as long or as mobile as nectar-feeding bats, the lesser short-tailed bat's tongue does have extendable tissue and there are small papillae on the end of it that allow the bat to sip nectar.

Those who are lucky enough to spot this extremely rare bat will marvel at how smoothly it navigates the debris-strewn ground and how quickly it races, squirrel-like, up tree trunks before scurrying across branches.

Research indicates that the walking bats evolved to fulfil the role of mice and rats, which until recently weren't found in New Zealand and which now represent invasive species that are taking a huge toll on the native ecology.

Fulfilling the role of rodent certainly explains the lesser short-tailed bat's diet. It is one of the only known bat species that's an omnivore. It eats pretty much anything it encounters and doesn't seem to have a preference if the food is an insect, nectar, or piece of fruit. The bat is credited with being the primary pollinator of New Zealand's woodrose (*Dactylanthus* spp.)

While the lesser short-tailed bat prefers walking when it's foraging for food, it's not flightless. The bats do fly, though they tend to stay close to the ground and don't enjoy the same amount of speed or agility as other types of microbats.

Like most bats, the lesser short-tailed bat bears just one pup a year. The pups mature quickly. They're ready to start learning how to fly when they're about a month old and are fully grown between eight and twelve weeks. The species uses a lek (singing) courtship routine. Between the months of February and April, males select a nice tree branch and sing about their love. Researchers have noticed that an interested female will travel as far as 10 km (6.2 mi.) while she's searching for a mate.

The Greater Short-Tailed Bat

Little is known about the greater short-tailed bat. They were primarily spotted on New Zealand's Solomon Islands and Big South Cape, though fossils suggest that there was a time when they were also present on both North and South Islands.

Like its lesser short-tailed cousin, the greater short-tailed bat was believed to have dined on a wide assortment of food options and hunted primarily by stalking along the ground. The last time anyone had laid eyes on any representative of the species was in 1965. While it's believed that the laughing owls took a huge toll on this bat population, experts believe that what finally drove the greater short-tailed bat into extinction was the accidental infestation of ship rats to Big South Cape Island. The introduction of the rats had a massive impact on the island's ecology. Shortly after the infestation, the greater short-tailed bat disappeared, as did many of the flightless birds that called the island home. The ship rat invasion has the distinction of being the first recorded time in history when rats were pinpointed as the cause of the extinction of another species. In addition to the greater short-tailed bat, rats also led to the extinction of both the Stead's bush wren and the Stewart Island Snipe. The rats continue to have a devastating impact on the region's ecology, leading conservationists to discuss some extremely drastic options, including gene editing as an eradication method.

The greater short-tailed bat is believed to be extinct. The New Zealand Department of Conservation considers the lesser short-tailed bat to be a Species of Highest Conservation Priority and they're committed to doing everything they can to preserve the species. In addition to exploring ways to manage the rat problem and preserve the bat's preferred habitat, research programs designed to learn as much about the species, including its social behavior, are currently underway.

Lesser Short-Tailed Bat
(*Mystacina tuberculate*)

Figure 58 © Colin O'Donnell
http://www.doc.govt.nz/nature/native-animals/bats-pekapeka/short-tailed-bat/

Figure 59 © Colin O'Donnell
http://www.doc.govt.nz/nature/native-animals/bats-pekapeka/short-tailed-bat/

Whiskered Bat

While enjoying a late evening walk along the edge of a pond in Ireland, you stop to watch several small brown bats zip to and fro over the water. One of the bats veers off course, flying rapidly towards you, and snatches a moth that looks nearly as big as the bat's head right in front of your nose. As you're marveling at the bats speed and agility, it disappears into the nearby tree line, the moth clutched between its tiny jaws.

You've just been lucky enough to see a whiskered bat (*Myotis mystacinus*) in action.

The whiskered bat has the distinction of being the smallest of Europe's native myotis bat species. The long brown fur that covers their back and shoulders gives them a shaggy appearance. Their underbelly is covered in somewhat shorter hair that's greyish-white. Their wings, face, and triangular ears are darker than their fur and show a bit of pink. While they hibernate, the adults drop to about 4-5 grams, which blooms to 8 grams after they wake and have fed for a few weeks.

The average wing span for the whiskered bats is about 25 cm. The wings are shaped in such a way to allow the whiskered bat to fly quite quickly in long straight lines, but also to use a rapid fluttering motion when they're maneuvering through trees or chasing a wily gnat. Whiskered bats are often observed gliding for long distances at a time.

Like most European bats, the whiskered bat is active in the summer and goes dormant during the winter months. In the summer time, they seek out small crevices in trees and behind cladding that they use as a roost. Females form maternity colonies that range from twenty to sixty bats, though in some special cases, maternity colonies that approach a hundred bats have been found. No one is sure exactly why the bats occasionally form such large colonies, though its food supply and space are considered to be factors. Little is known about the roosting habits of the males, other than they're more solitary and likely roost by themselves.

Whiskered bats have been observed sharing a roost with other species, including:

- Natterer's bats
- Various Pipistrelles
- Brown long-eared bats

Because whiskered bats are a bit hardier than other species and do a better job withstanding cooler periods, they tend to gather near the front of both roosting sites and hibernacula. They also emerge from the hibernaculum a few weeks earlier than the others.

It's not uncommon for whiskered bats to set up a roost in older abandoned buildings, and if they can find a building that's near the ideal hunting ground, the species will move in, happily settling into crevices, under eaves, or moving into the attics.

Unlike other types of bats that stay loyal to a single roost site, the whiskered bat likes to move around. As a rule, they change their location every fortnight or so. There are two suspected reasons for the location change. One, the bats may be following a food supply. Two, it's possible that the species moves in an attempt to avoid predators that might use large piles of guano to help locate the roost and destroy a colony. In the case of large colonies, chiropterologists have noticed that while the colony itself might stay in one place, it's not unusual for different mothers to abandon one maternity colony and start roosting with another colony. Again, no one is sure why this happens.

When winter approaches, whiskered bats seek out caves and old mine shafts with a winter internal temp of between 2-8 degrees Celsius.

Female whiskered bats reach sexual maturity at about fifteen months old. The mating season takes place in the autumn, just before the bats enter the winter hibernaculum. The sperm is stored within the female while she hibernates and used to fertilize her egg when she wakes up the following spring. The females generally give birth sometime during June or July, indicating that the gestation period is two or three months. Although twins occasionally happen, as a rule, the mother only births a single pup, which is weaned at about six weeks of age, the point that it's able to both fly and forage on its own.

The single best way to spot a colony of whiskered bats is by locating a nice spot that's damp, such as a shallow pond, and close to a wooded area. The combination of the trees and the water not only provides the perfect breeding ground for the soft-bodied insects that make up the whiskered bat's diet, including moths, mayflies, and gnats. Find a nice spot to sit and settle in. If there's a nearby colony of whiskered bats, they'll start to appear as the sun sets and remain active for about the next thirty minutes as they eat their fill of available insects. When the whiskered bat first emerges, their flight pattern keeps them low to the ground, where they exhibit a nice level style of flying. Later in the night, they'll take to the tree canopy to hunt.

While whiskered bats capture most of their prey in mid-flight, if they spot a spider or moth sitting on a leaf or branch, the bat will swoop over and snatch the bug right off the plant.

Whiskered bats don't like traveling long distances, so they seek out roosts that are right on top of their hunting grounds.

A recent study suggested that Derwent Valley is favored by whiskered bats.

Remember, if you're going out bat watching, you must sit quietly and do nothing to disturb the bats. Human disruption can have a devastating impact on the colony and even the overall bat population.

The life span of the whiskered bat is considerably shorter than that of the Brandt's bat. While Brandt's bats (which are frequently mistaken for whiskered bats and vice versa) can reach their forty-first birthday, making them the oldest living mammal, ounce-per-ounce, in the world, whiskered bats only live until their mid-twenties. That being said, the average life span of the whiskered bat is about four years.

The biggest threat the whiskered bat population faces is roost destruction, via dismantlement, renovation, or the use of chemical repellants. Pesticides used for agriculture is another problem. At this point, getting a fix on this bat, which has a range that extends across most of Europe, isn't easy, but it's believed that their status is vulnerable. As such, International and European legislation is in place to help provide the whiskered bats with some protection.

The IUCN Red List has the whiskered bat labeled as least concern.

Whiskered Bat
(*Myotis mystacinus*)

Figure 60 © Manuel Ruedi
[CC BY 3.0], via Wikimedia Commons

Beautiful Bat Facts
References

"7 Steps of Tequila Making, The." IZKALI Tequila,
http://izkalitequila.com/blog/the-7-steps-of-tequila-making/

Aizpurua, Ostaizka. Alberdi, Antton. Aihartza, Joxerra. Garin, Inazio.
"Fishing Technique of Long-Fingered Bats Was Developed from a
Primary Reaction to Disappearing Target Stimuli." PLOS. 14 December
2016. Web.
http://journals.plos.org/plosone/article?id=10.1371/journal.pone.0167
164

Allen, Glover M. "Bats: Biology, Behavior, and Folklore." Dover
Publications, 2004.

Amelon, Sybill K. Hooper, Sarah E. Womack, Kathryn M. "Bat Wing
Biometrics: Using Collagen–Elastin Bundles in Bat Wings as a Unique
Individual Identifier". *Journal of Mammalogy*, 2017; 98 (3): 744 DOI:
10.1093/jmammal/gyx018

Andrei, Mihai. "The Myths and Folklore behind Halloween's Most
Popular Characters." ZME Science, 30 Oct. 2010,
www.zmescience.com/other/halloween-monsters-witches-vampires-
30102010/.

Andrei, Mihai. "The Myths and Folklore behind Halloween's Most
Popular Characters." ZME Science, 30 Oct. 2010,
www.zmescience.com/other/halloween-monsters-witches-vampires-
30102010/.

Archipelago Bat Guano, http://archipelagobatguano.com/6.shtml

Arita, Hector T, and Don E Wilson. "Long-Nosed Bats and Agaves:
The Tequila Connection." BATS Magazine, Bat Conservation
International, 1987, www.batcon.org/resources/media-education/bats-
magazine/bat_article/299.

"Baby Bats Babble Too." New Scientist. 26 July 2006.
https://www.newscientist.com/article/mg19125625-000-baby-bats-babble-too/

"Baby Bats." The Surprising World of Bats. 2010. http://www.the-surprising-world-of-bats.org/baby-bats.html

Balter, Michael. "Early Dinosaur May Have Flown like a Bat." Science | AAAS, Science, 26 July 2017,
www.sciencemag.org/news/2015/04/early-dinosaur-may-have-flown-bat

"Barbastelle Bat Photos and Facts." Arkive,
www.arkive.org/barbastelle-bat/barbastella-barbastellus/.

"Bats and Agriculture." Bat Conservation International.

"Bats Are Worth One Billion Dollars, So Why Are We Destroying Them?" The Rainforest Site. http://blog.therainforestsite.com/cs-bat-billionaires-worth/

"Bat Festivals." About Bat Festivals, BSCJ,
www.2r.biglobe.ne.jp/~fruitbat/bscj/festa/festivals.htm.

"Bat in Chinese Culture Meaning and Symbolism." Game Frog. 2009.
http://chinesehoroscop-e.com/astrology/feng-shui-bats.php

"Bat Myths of Japan: Separating Scientific Fact from Cultural Fiction in the Island Nation." BATS, vol. 34, no. 4,
www.batcon.org/resources/media-education/bats-magazine/bat_article/1542

"Bats Affected by WNS." Bats Affected by WNS | White-Nose Syndrome, www.whitenosesyndrome.org/about/bats-affected-wns.

"Bats Are Everywhere." BATS Magazine, Bat Conservation International, www.batcon.org/why-bats/bats-are/bats-are-everywhere.

"Bats Best Birds at Slow Flight." Science | AAAS, 26 July 2017,
www.sciencemag.org/news/2007/05/bats-best-birds-slow-flight

"Bats in Chinese Culture." Occult World, Occult World, http://occult-world.com/bats-chinese-culture/

BATS Magazine Article: Long-Nosed Bats and Agaves: The Tequila
Connection, www.batcon.org/resources/media-education/bats-
magazine/bat_article/299.

Bats May Use Bidirectional Echolocation to Detect Prey, Orient
Themselves: Bidirectional Sound Emission Facilitates 'Stealth
Echolocation' in Barbastelle Bats. 9 Sept. 2015,
www.sciencedaily.com/releases/2015/09/150909145146.htm.

"Bats Use Second Sense to Hunt Prey in Noisy Environments."
ScienceDaily, The University of Texas at Austin,
www.sciencedaily.com/releases/2016/09/160915154232.htm.

Becker. "Why Do Bats Live Long and Healthy Lives?" Mercola.com,
Healthy Pets, 25 Feb. 2013,
https://healthypets.mercola.com/sites/healthypets/archive/2013/02/2
5/bats-live-longer.aspx#!

Bakalar, Nicholas "Vampire Bats Hunt by Sound of Victims' Breath,
Study Says." National Geographic News. 19 June 2006.
https://news.nationalgeographic.com/news/2006/06/060619-vampire-
bats.html

"The Benefit of Bats." Doctors Foster and Smith,
www.drsfostersmith.com/pic/article.cfm?articleid=1816.
"Billion-Dollar Bats." BATS Magazine , Bat Conservation International,
2015, www.batcon.org/component/batmag/bat_article/1543.

"Billion-Dollar Bats: BCI-Funded Research Reveals Bats' Key Role in
the Agricultural Production of Corn." BATS Magazine , Bat
Conservation International, 2015,
www.batcon.org/component/batmag/bat_article/1543.
Biology For Kids - KidsBiology.com, www.kidsbiology.com/animals-
for-children.php?animal=Greater%2Bhorseshoe%2Bbat.

Birkett, K.; K. Weidman and Y. Woo 2014. "Vespertilionidae" Animal
Diversity Web. http://animaldiversity.org/accounts/Vespertilionidae/

"Brandt's bat." Bat Conservation Trust.
http://www.bats.org.uk/data/files/Species_Info_sheets/brandts_bat.p
df

"Brandt's Bat." Gwent Wildlife Trust..

https://www.gwentwildlife.org/species/brandts-bat

"Brandt's Bat." University of Bristol School of Biological Sciences. 24 February 2005. Web
http://www.bio.bris.ac.uk/research/bats/britishbats/batpages/brandts.htm

"Brandt's Bat." Wildscreen Arkive. http://www.arkive.org/brandts-bat/myotis-brandtii/image-A14655.html

"Brown long-eared bat trends for Great Britain." Bat Conservation Trust. http://www.bats.org.uk/pages/-brown_long-eared_bat-829.html

"Brown long-eared bat (Plecotus auritus)" Arkive.
http://www.arkive.org/brown-long-eared-bat/plecotus-auritus/

Bryner, Jeanna. "Sticky Science: Why Some Bats Sleep Head-Up." LiveScience, Purch, 14 Dec. 2009, www.livescience.com/9764-sticky-science-bats-sleep-head.html.

Bumblebee Bat. The Animal Files, 2014,
www.theanimalfiles.com/mammals/bats/bumblebee_bat.html.

Butler, Rhett. "Rainforest Bats." Mongabay.com, Mongabat, 9 June 1999, rainforests.mongabay.com/0409.htm.

"Camazotz the Death Bat." Bad Ass of the Week. 3 January 2013.
http://www.badassoftheweek.com/index.cgi?id=537935724254

"Carolus Linnaeus." Famous Scientists, Famous Scientists,
www.famousscientists.org/carolus-linnaeus/.
Carter, Gerald G., and Gerald S. Wilkinson. "Food Sharing in Vampire Bats: Reciprocal Help Predicts Donations More than Relatedness or Harassment." Proc. R. Soc. B, The Royal Society, 22 Feb. 2013,
www.rspb.royalsocietypublishing.org/content/280/1753/20122573
"Cat Attacks." The Bat Conservation Trust.
http://www.bats.org.uk/pages/cat_attacks_on_bats_and_other_predators.html

Chatterjee, Rhitu. "This Bat Knows How To Drink." NPR, NPR, 7 May 2013, www.npr.org/2013/05/07/181634051/this-bat-knows-how-to-drink

Choi, Charles Q. "Hidden Similarity Found Between Bats & Dolphins." LiveScience, 4 September 2013. https://www.livescience.com/39414-what-bats-dolphins-share.html

Choi, Charles Q. "Study Reveals How Drunken Bats Sober Up." LiveScience, Purch, 10 Apr. 2007, www.livescience.com/4411-study-reveals-drunken-bats-sober.html.

Chronister, Nathan. "Bird Flight." The Ornithopter Zone - Discover Flapping Wing Flight, www.ornithopter.org/birdflight/bats.shtml. "Control Your Startle Response." Effective Mind Control, www.effective-mind-control.com/startle-response.html.

Cooper, J. 2002. "Macroderma gigas." Animal Diversity Web. Accessed January 01, 2018 at http://animaldiversity.org/accounts/Macroderma_gigas/

Couffer, Jack. Bat Bomb: World War II's Other Secret Weapon. Univ. of Texas Press, 1992.

Cox, Dr. Paul A. "Flying Fox Nearly Extinct in Samoa." BATS Magazine, Bat Conservation International, 1984, www.batcon.org/resources/media-education/bats-magazine/bat_article/205.

Cryan, Paul M. Uphoff Meteyer, Carol. Boyles, Justin G. Blehert, David S. "Wing Pathology of White-Nose Syndrome in Bats Suggests Life-Threatening Disruption of Physiology." BMC Biology. 11 November 2010. https://bmcbiol.biomedcentral.com/articles/10.1186/1741-7007-8-135

"Cytokine Storm Natural Immune System Boosters." Sites.google.com/Site/Naturalimmunesystemboosters/Cytokine-Storm, www.bing.com/cr?IG=C955AA12C8FA444D919C5BB051AF5BB7&CID=04EFC11E666D64933689CA3C676B65FA&rd=1&h=d-zkTAoXodVuoTMXgf3vtAorgWC7Yimn0-FpdwLTa3I&v=1&r=http%3a%2f%2fsites.google.com%2fsite%2fnaturalimmunesystemboosters%2fcytokine-storm&p=DevEx,5066.1.

Dell'Amore, Christine. "Drunk Bats Fly Right--Discovery Surprises

Scientists." National Geographic News. 9 Febuary 2010.

https://news.nationalgeographic.com/news/2010/02/100209-drunk-

bats-fly/

De Pastino, Blake. "Ancient 'Clawed Bat' Reveals Clues to Flying
Mammal's Evolution." Western Digs. 31 October 2013.
http://westerndigs.org/ancient-giant-clawed-bat-reveals-clues-to-flying-
mammals-evolution/

"Disc-Winged Bat." Encyclopedia Britannica. Web.
https://www.britannica.com/animal/disk-winged-bat

"Fun Facts for Kids on Animals, Earth, History and More!" DK Find
Out!, www.dkfindout.com/us/animals-and-nature/bats/megabats/.

"Garden for Wildlife." Home, The National Wildlife Federation,
www.nwf.org/~/media/Content/Specialty%20Programs/Garden%20f
or%20Wildlife/SingleChamberBHPlans.ashx.

"Ghost bat (Macroderma gigas)." Arkive.
http://www.arkive.org/ghost-bat/macroderma-gigas/

Greif, Stefan. Siemers, Björn M. "**Innate Recognition of Water
Bodies in Echolocating Bats.**" *Nature Communications*, 2010; 1 (8): 107
DOI: 10.1038/ncomms1110

Håkansson, Jonas. Jakobsen, Lasse. Hedenström, Anders, Johansson, L.
Christoffer. "Body Lift, Drag and Power Are Relatively Higher in
Large-Eared than in Small-Eared Bat Species." *Journal of the Royal Society
Interface*, 25 Oct. 2017,
http://rsif.royalsocietypublishing.org/content/14/135/20170455

"Greater False Vampire Bat." Infogalatic. 12 November 2015. Web.
Accessed 1 November 2017.
https://infogalactic.com/info/Greater_false_vampire_bat

Hayman, T.S. Cryan, Paul M. Dannemiller, Nicholas G. "Long-Term
Video Surveillance and Automated Analyses Reveal Arousal Patterns in
Groups of Hibernating Bats." Methods in Ecology and Evolution. 29

June 2017. http://onlinelibrary.wiley.com/doi/10.1111/2041-210X.12823/abstract;jsessionid=59976B3F35AB42E1FED9085D819225EA.f02t03

Hester, L. and P. Myers 2001. "Emballonuridae" Animal Diversity Web. http://animaldiversity.org/accounts/Emballonuridae/

"The History of Chocolate." How Stuff Works. https://www.howstuffworks.com/history-of-chocolate1.htm

"How Does White-Nose Syndrome Kill Bats." U.S. Geological Survey. 5 January 2015. https://www.usgs.gov/news/how-does-white-nose-syndrome-kill-bats

Hoyt, Richard. "Facts on the Cacao Tree." GardenGuides.com. 21 September 2017. http://www.gardenguides.com/119132-cacao-trees.html

"Icaronycteris." Prehistoric Wildlife. Web. Accessed 13 November 2017. http://www.prehistoric-wildlife.com/species/i/icaronycteris.html

"The Incredible Milk-Producing Male Bat." BATS Magazine Article, 1995, www.batcon.org/resources/media-education/bats-magazine/bat_article/684?tmpl=component.

"Insect-Eating Bat May Be Origin of Ebola Outbreak, New Study Suggests." National Geographic, National Geographic Society, 2 May 2016, https://news.nationalgeographic.com/news/2014/12/141230-ebola-virus-origin-insect-bats-meliandou-reservoir-host/

Ivaldi, F. 1999. "Mystacina tuberculata" (On-line), Animal Diversity Web. http://animaldiversity.org/accounts/Mystacina_tuberculata/

Johansson, L. Christoffer. Håkansson, Jonas. Jakobsen, Lasse. Hedenström, Anders. "Ear-body lift and a novel thrust generating mechanism revealed by the complex wake of brown long-eared bats (Plecotus auritus)." Scientific Reports. 27 April 2016. http://www.nature.com/articles/srep24886

Junchang Lü, Qingjin Meng, Baopeng Wang, Di Liu, Caizhi Shen, Yuguang Zhang. "Short note on a new anurognathid pterosaur with

evidence of perching behavior from Jianchang of Liaoning Province, China." Geological Society London Special Publications. 8, September, 2017.
http://sp.lyellcollection.org/content/early/2017/09/08/SP455.16

Kalka, Margareta. "New Respect for Tropical Bats: Demonstrating the Value of Insect-Eating Bats." BATS, vol. 26, no. 2, 2008,
www.batcon.org/resources/media-education/bats-magazine/bat_article/1026.

Kelm , Detlev H. "Restoring Lost Rainforests: Artificial Bat Roosts Attract Seed-Dispersing Bats." BATS, vol. 26, no. 2, 2008,
www.batcon.org/resources/media-education/bats-magazine/bat_article/1025.

"Large or Malayan Flying Fox." Lubee Bbat Conservancy.
http://www.lubee.org/bats/our-bats/large-flying-fox-or-malayan-flying-fox/

"Lesser short-tailed bat (Mystacina tuberculata)." Wildscreen Arkive.
http://www.arkive.org/lesser-short-tailed-bat/mystacina-tuberculata/

Lund University. "Bats' flight technique could lead to better drones." ScienceDaily. ScienceDaily, 4 May 2016.
www.sciencedaily.com/releases/2016/05/160504121446.htm

Lund University. "The Pros and Cons of Large Ears." ScienceDaily. ScienceDaily, 10 November 2017. Accessed 13 December 2017.
www.sciencedaily.com/releases/2017/11/171110084634.ht

"Macadamia Nuts Processing Industry in South Africa."
Shellingmachine.com

"Malayan Flying Fox." Organization for Bat Conservation. Accessed 13 December 2017. Web.
http://cms.batconservation.org/drupal/malayan-flying-fox

Malburg, Sarah. "Facts and Information About the Fishing Bat." 19 January 2011. http://www.brighthub.com/environment/science-environmental/articles/103670.aspx

Malory, Marcia. "Pollination." Earth Facts,
www.earthfacts.com/rainforests/pollination/.

Max Planck Institute for Ornithology. "For Bats, All Smooth,
Horizontal Surfaces are Water -- Even When They Look, Smell and
Feel Differently." ScienceDaily. ScienceDaily, 4 November 2010.
www.sciencedaily.com/releases/2010/11/101102124419.htm

McCracken, Gary F. "Bats in Magic, Potions, and Medicinal
Preparations: The Multiple Uses of Bats in Magic and Folk Medicine
Are Clear Testament to the Fertility of the Human Imagination." BATS,
Bat Conservation International, 1992,
www.batcon.org/resources/media-education/bats-
magazine/bat_article/546?tmpl=component.

McNeil, Cameron L. "Tales from the Underworld: Cacao in Ancient
Maya Religion." Mexicolore.
http://www.mexicolore.co.uk/maya/chocolate/cacao-in-ancient-maya-
religion

Melnick, Meredith. "Vampire Bat Saliva Could Lead to Stroke
Treatment." Time Inc. 9 May 2011.
Moskowitz, Clara. "Early Bats Flew Without Navigation." Live Science.
13 February 2008. https://www.livescience.com/2297-early-bats-flew-
navigation.html

"Microbats: About Bats." Bat Conservation & Rescue QLD Inc., Bat
Conservation and Rescue QLD Inc., www.bats.org.au/about-
bats/microbats.php.
Moskowitz, Clara. "Early Bats Flew Without Navigation." LiveScience,
Purch, 13 Feb. 2008, www.livescience.com/2297-early-bats-flew-
navigation.html.

Munoz, Gabriella. "Vampire Bat Venom Could Lead to New Drugs For
Stroke And High Blood Pressure." ScienceAlert,
www.sciencealert.com/vampire-bat-venom-could-lead-to-new-drugs-
for-stroke-and-high-blood-pressure.

Newton, Steven. "5 Reasons Evolution is Important." Huffington Post.
13 April 2010. https://www.huffingtonpost.com/steven-newton/five-
reasons-why-evolutio_b_459636.html

Netherlands Institute of Ecology (NIOO-KNAW). "Red light has no effect on bat activity: Less disruption by changing artificial color." ScienceDaily. ScienceDaily, 2 June 2017.
www.sciencedaily.com/releases/2017/06/170602112814.htm

Norton, K. 2011. "Pteropus vampyrus" (On-line), Animal Diversity
http://animaldiversity.org/accounts/Pteropus_vampyrus/

Norwegian University of Science and Technology (NTNU). "How bats actually fly to find their prey." ScienceDaily. ScienceDaily, 19 June 2015.
www.sciencedaily.com/releases/2015/06/150619084612.htm

O'Brien, Emily. "5 Ways To Attract Bats To Your Yard." Rodale's Organic Life, Rodale's Organic Life, 20 Oct. 2016,
www.rodalesorganiclife.com/garden/5-ways-to-attract-bats-to-your-yard/slide/4.

Oh, Y.K. Mōri, T. Uchida, T.A. "Studies on the vaginal plug of the Japanese greater horseshoe bat, *Rhinolophus ferrumequinum nippon.*" The Journal of the Society for Reproduction and Fertility. 1 July 1983.
http://www.reproduction-online.org/content/68/2/365.abstract

"*Onychonycteris.*" Prehistoric Wildlife. http://www.prehistoric-wildlife.com/species/o/onychonycteris.html

Orbach, Dara. "Flying Under the Influence." BATS Magazine , Bat Conservation International, 2010, www.batcon.org/resources/media-education/bats-magazine/bat_article/1070.

Parsons, Brandon L. "Camazotz." MrPsMythopedia - Camazotz, 2015,
http://mrpsmythopedia.wikispaces.com/Camazotz

PLOS. "Insectivorous long-fingered bats may also be capable of catching fish, should the opportunity arise." ScienceDaily. ScienceDaily, 14 December 2016.
www.sciencedaily.com/releases/2016/12/161214145606.htm

"Pteropus vampyrus ." The IUCN Red List of Threatened Species.
http://www.iucnredlist.org/details/18766/0

Rajan, K. Emmanuvel. Marimuthu G. "A preliminary examination of genetic diversity in the Indian false vampire bat Megaderma lyra." 2006. http://abc.museucienciesjournals.cat/files/ABC-29-2-pp-109-115.pdf

Randerson, James. "Fossils Solve Mystery of Bat Evolution." The Guardian, Guardian News and Media, 13 Feb. 2008, www.theguardian.com/science/2008/feb/13/bat.evolution.

Reagan, Helen. "The World Could be Heading Toward a Global Shortage of Chocolate." Time Magazine. 17, November 2014. http://time.com/3588463/chocolate-cocoa-global-shortage/

"Saurischian." Encyclopedia Britannica. https://www.britannica.com/animal/saurischian

Shaffer, Leigh. "Blood Sisters: What Vampire Bats can Teach us About Friendship." Scientific America. 25 August 2016. https://www.scientificamerican.com/article/blood-sisters-what-vampire-bats-can-teach-us-about-friendship/

"Sheath-Tailed Bats." Encyclopedia Britannica. https://www.britannica.com/animal/sheath-tailed-bat

"Short-Tailed Bat." TerraNature. http://www.terranature.org/batShort-tailed.htm

Simmons, Nancy B. Seymour, Kevin L. Habersetzer, Jorg, Gunnell, Gregg F. "Primitive Early Eocene Bat from Wyoming and the Evolution of Flight and Echolocation." Research Gate. March 2008. https://www.researchgate.net/publication/5580657_Primitive_Early_Eocene_bat_from_Wyoming_and_the_evolution_of_flight_and_echolocation

Sishuba, Siyanda "Using Bats and Birds to Control Macadamia Crop Pests." Farmers Weekly. 16 August 2017. https://www.farmersweekly.co.za/agri-technology/farming-for-tomorrow/using-bats-birds-control-macadamia-crop-pests/

Strauss, Gary. "The Bat Man of Mexico; Tequila's Super Hero?" National Geographic, National Geographic Society, 21 Sept. 2016, https://www.news.nationalgeographic.com/2016/09/rodrigoa-medellin-explorer-moments-bat-agave/

Stumpf, J. 2002. "Megaderma lyra" (On-line), Animal Diversity Web. http://animaldiversity.org/accounts/Megaderma_lyra/

Taylor, P.J. Bohmann, P.J. Steyn, J.N. Schoeman, M.C. Matamba, E. Zepeda-Mendoza, M.L. Nangammbi, T. Gilbert, M.T.P. "Bats Eat Pest Green Vegetable Stink Bugs (Nezara viridula): Diet Analyses of Seven Insectivorous Species of Bats Roosting and Foraging in Macadamia Orchards."

Than, Ker. "Baby Bats Babble Like Human Infants." LiveScience, Purch, 8 Aug. 2006, www.livescience.com/949-baby-bats-babble-human-infants.html.

Trivedi, Bijal P. "Ancient Chocolate Found in Maya Teapot." National Geographic News. 17 July 2002. https://news.nationalgeographic.com/news/2002/07/0717_020717_T Vchocolate.html

"Thetford High Lodge - Bat Hibernaculum." Thetford High Lodge - Bat Hibernaculum - WREN, WREN, www.wren.org.uk/projects/bat-hibernaculum-the-bat-cave.

University of California - Santa Cruz. "Bacteria inhibit bat-killing fungus, could combat white-nose syndrome." ScienceDaily. ScienceDaily, 8 April 2015. www.sciencedaily.com/releases/2015/04/150408145246.htm

US Geological Survey. "Hot imagery of wintering bats suggests group behavior for battling white-nose syndrome." ScienceDaily. ScienceDaily, 5 July 2017. www.sciencedaily.com/releases/2017/07/170705164504.htm

"Vampire Bat." A Moment of Science. 17 September 2007. http://indianapublicmedia.org/amomentofscience/vampire-bat/

"Vesper Bat." Encyclopædia Britannica. https://www.britannica.com/animal/vesper-bat

Weinstein, B. and P. Myers 2001. "Myzopodidae" Animal Diversity Web. http://animaldiversity.org/accounts/Myzopodidae/

Weinstein, B. and P. Myers 2001. "Thyropteridae." Animal Diversity Web. http://animaldiversity.org/accounts/Thyropteridae/

"White-Winged Vampire Bat." Wikipedia, Wikimedia Foundation, 11 Oct. 2017, en.wikipedia.org/wiki/White-winged_vampire_bat.

Wiffen, Tina. "Brandt's Bat." The Natural History Society of Northumbria. http://www.nhsn.ncl.ac.uk/interests/mammals/mammals-north-east/brandts-bat/

Wiffen, Tina. "Whiskered Bat." Natural History Society of Northumbria. http://www.nhsn.ncl.ac.uk/interests/mammals/mammals-north-east/whiskered-bat/

"Whiskered Bat." Conserve Ireland. http://conserveireland.com/mammals/whiskered_bat.php

"Whiskered Bat: Pictures and Facts." The Website of Everything. http://thewebsiteofeverything.com/animals/mammals/Chiroptera/Vespertilionidae/Myotis

"Yi qi: Bat-Winged Dinosaur Discovered in China." Sci News. 30 April 2015. http://www.sci-news.com/paleontology/science-yi-qi-bat-winged-dinosaur-china-02750.html

Yong, Ed. "Chinese Dinosaur Had Bat-Like Wings and Feathers." National Geographic. 29 April 2015. http://phenomena.nationalgeographic.com/2015/04/29/chinese-dinosaur-had-bat-like-wings-and-feathers/

GNU Free Documentation License

Some of the pictures used in this book require a GNU
Free Documentation License, which is posted right here.

GNU Free Documentation License

Version 1.2, November 2002

> Copyright (C) 2000,2001,2002 Free Software Foundation,
> Inc.
>
> 51 Franklin St, Fifth Floor, Boston, MA 02110-1301 USA
>
> Everyone is permitted to copy and distribute verbatim copies
>
> of this license document, but changing it is not allowed.

0. PREAMBLE

The purpose of this License is to make a manual, textbook, or other
functional and useful document "free" in the sense of freedom: to
assure everyone the effective freedom to copy and redistribute it, with
or without modifying it, either commercially or noncommercially.
Secondarily, this License preserves for the author and publisher a way to
get credit for their work, while not being considered responsible for
modifications made by others.

This License is a kind of "copyleft", which means that derivative works
of the document must themselves be free in the same sense. It
complements the GNU General Public License, which is a copyleft
license designed for free software.

We have designed this License in order to use it for manuals for free
software, because free software needs free documentation: a free

program should come with manuals providing the same freedoms that the software does. But this License is not limited to software manuals; it can be used for any textual work, regardless of subject matter or whether it is published as a printed book. We recommend this License principally for works whose purpose is instruction or reference.

1. APPLICABILITY AND DEFINITIONS

This License applies to any manual or other work, in any medium, that contains a notice placed by the copyright holder saying it can be distributed under the terms of this License. Such a notice grants a world-wide, royalty-free license, unlimited in duration, to use that work under the conditions stated herein. The "Document", below, refers to any such manual or work. Any member of the public is a licensee, and is addressed as "you". You accept the license if you copy, modify or distribute the work in a way requiring permission under copyright law.

A "Modified Version" of the Document means any work containing the Document or a portion of it, either copied verbatim, or with modifications and/or translated into another language.

A "Secondary Section" is a named appendix or a front-matter section of the Document that deals exclusively with the relationship of the publishers or authors of the Document to the Document's overall subject (or to related matters) and contains nothing that could fall directly within that overall subject. (Thus, if the Document is in part a textbook of mathematics, a Secondary Section may not explain any mathematics.) The relationship could be a matter of historical connection with the subject or with related matters, or of legal, commercial, philosophical, ethical or political position regarding them.

The "Invariant Sections" are certain Secondary Sections whose titles are designated, as being those of Invariant Sections, in the notice that says that the Document is released under this License. If a section does not fit the above definition of Secondary then it is not allowed to be designated as Invariant. The Document may contain zero Invariant Sections. If the Document does not identify any Invariant Sections then there are none.

The "Cover Texts" are certain short passages of text that are listed, as Front-Cover Texts or Back-Cover Texts, in the notice that says that the Document is released under this License. A Front-Cover Text may be at most 5 words, and a Back-Cover Text may be at most 25 words.

A "Transparent" copy of the Document means a machine-readable copy, represented in a format whose specification is available to the general public, that is suitable for revising the document straightforwardly with generic text editors or (for images composed of pixels) generic paint programs or (for drawings) some widely available drawing editor, and that is suitable for input to text formatters or for automatic translation to a variety of formats suitable for input to text formatters. A copy made in an otherwise Transparent file format whose markup, or absence of markup, has been arranged to thwart or discourage subsequent modification by readers is not Transparent. An image format is not Transparent if used for any substantial amount of text. A copy that is not "Transparent" is called "Opaque".

Examples of suitable formats for Transparent copies include plain ASCII without markup, Texinfo input format, LaTeX input format, SGML or XML using a publicly available DTD, and standard-conforming simple HTML, PostScript or PDF designed for human modification. Examples of transparent image formats include PNG, XCF and JPG. Opaque formats include proprietary formats that can be read and edited only by proprietary word processors, SGML or XML for which the DTD and/or processing tools are not generally available, and the machine-generated HTML, PostScript or PDF produced by some word processors for output purposes only.

The "Title Page" means, for a printed book, the title page itself, plus such following pages as are needed to hold, legibly, the material this License requires to appear in the title page. For works in formats which do not have any title page as such, "Title Page" means the text near the most prominent appearance of the work's title, preceding the beginning of the body of the text.

A section "Entitled XYZ" means a named subunit of the Document whose title either is precisely XYZ or contains XYZ in parentheses following text that translates XYZ in another language. (Here XYZ stands for a specific section name mentioned below, such as "Acknowledgements", "Dedications", "Endorsements", or "History".) To "Preserve the Title" of such a section when you modify the Document means that it remains a section "Entitled XYZ" according to this definition.

The Document may include Warranty Disclaimers next to the notice which states that this License applies to the Document. These Warranty Disclaimers are considered to be included by reference in this License, but only as regards disclaiming warranties: any other implication that these Warranty Disclaimers may have is void and has no effect on the meaning of this License.

2. VERBATIM COPYING

You may copy and distribute the Document in any medium, either commercially or noncommercially, provided that this License, the copyright notices, and the license notice saying this License applies to the Document are reproduced in all copies, and that you add no other conditions whatsoever to those of this License. You may not use technical measures to obstruct or control the reading or further copying of the copies you make or distribute. However, you may accept compensation in exchange for copies. If you distribute a large enough number of copies you must also follow the conditions in section 3.

You may also lend copies, under the same conditions stated above, and you may publicly display copies.

3. COPYING IN QUANTITY

If you publish printed copies (or copies in media that commonly have printed covers) of the Document, numbering more than 100, and the Document's license notice requires Cover Texts, you must enclose the copies in covers that carry, clearly and legibly, all these Cover Texts: Front-Cover Texts on the front cover, and Back-Cover Texts on the back cover. Both covers must also clearly and legibly identify you as the publisher of these copies. The front cover must present the full title with all words of the title equally prominent and visible. You may add other material on the covers in addition. Copying with changes limited to the covers, as long as they preserve the title of the Document and satisfy these conditions, can be treated as verbatim copying in other respects.

If the required texts for either cover are too voluminous to fit legibly, you should put the first ones listed (as many as fit reasonably) on the actual cover, and continue the rest onto adjacent pages.

If you publish or distribute Opaque copies of the Document numbering more than 100, you must either include a machine-readable Transparent copy along with each Opaque copy, or state in or with each Opaque copy a computer-network location from which the general network-using public has access to download using public-standard network protocols a complete Transparent copy of the Document, free of added material. If you use the latter option, you must take reasonably prudent steps, when you begin distribution of Opaque copies in quantity, to ensure that this Transparent copy will remain thus accessible at the stated location until at least one year after the last time you distribute an Opaque copy (directly or through your agents or retailers) of that edition to the public.

It is requested, but not required, that you contact the authors of the Document well before redistributing any large number of copies, to give them a chance to provide you with an updated version of the Document.

4. MODIFICATIONS

You may copy and distribute a Modified Version of the Document under the conditions of sections 2 and 3 above, provided that you release the Modified Version under precisely this License, with the Modified Version filling the role of the Document, thus licensing distribution and modification of the Modified Version to whoever possesses a copy of it. In addition, you must do these things in the Modified Version:

- **A.** Use in the Title Page (and on the covers, if any) a title distinct from that of the Document, and from those of previous versions (which should, if there were any, be listed in the History section of the Document). You may use the same title as a previous version if the original publisher of that version gives permission.
- **B.** List on the Title Page, as authors, one or more persons or entities responsible for authorship of the modifications in the Modified Version, together with at least five of the principal authors of the Document (all of its principal authors, if it has fewer than five), unless they release you from this requirement.
- **C.** State on the Title page the name of the publisher of the Modified Version, as the publisher.
- **D.** Preserve all the copyright notices of the Document.
- **E.** Add an appropriate copyright notice for your modifications adjacent to the other copyright notices.
- **F.** Include, immediately after the copyright notices, a license notice giving the public permission to use the Modified

Version under the terms of this License, in the form shown in the Addendum below.

- **G.** Preserve in that license notice the full lists of Invariant Sections and required Cover Texts given in the Document's license notice.

- **H.** Include an unaltered copy of this License.

- **I.** Preserve the section Entitled "History", Preserve its Title, and add to it an item stating at least the title, year, new authors, and publisher of the Modified Version as given on the Title Page. If there is no section Entitled "History" in the Document, create one stating the title, year, authors, and publisher of the Document as given on its Title Page, then add an item describing the Modified Version as stated in the previous sentence.

- **J.** Preserve the network location, if any, given in the Document for public access to a Transparent copy of the Document, and likewise the network locations given in the Document for previous versions it was based on. These may be placed in the "History" section. You may omit a network location for a work that was published at least four years before the Document itself, or if the original publisher of the version it refers to gives permission.

- **K.** For any section Entitled "Acknowledgements" or "Dedications", Preserve the Title of the section, and preserve in the section all the substance and tone of each of the contributor acknowledgements and/or dedications given therein.

- **L.** Preserve all the Invariant Sections of the Document, unaltered in their text and in their titles. Section numbers or the equivalent are not considered part of the section titles.

- **M.** Delete any section Entitled "Endorsements". Such a section may not be included in the Modified Version.

- **N.** Do not retitle any existing section to be Entitled "Endorsements" or to conflict in title with any Invariant Section.

- **O.** Preserve any Warranty Disclaimers.

If the Modified Version includes new front-matter sections or appendices that qualify as Secondary Sections and contain no material copied from the Document, you may at your option designate some or all of these sections as invariant. To do this, add their titles to the list of Invariant Sections in the Modified Version's license notice. These titles must be distinct from any other section titles.

You may add a section Entitled "Endorsements", provided it contains nothing but endorsements of your Modified Version by various parties--for example, statements of peer review or that the text has been approved by an organization as the authoritative definition of a standard.

You may add a passage of up to five words as a Front-Cover Text, and a passage of up to 25 words as a Back-Cover Text, to the end of the list of Cover Texts in the Modified Version. Only one passage of Front-Cover Text and one of Back-Cover Text may be added by (or through arrangements made by) any one entity. If the Document already includes a cover text for the same cover, previously added by you or by arrangement made by the same entity you are acting on behalf of, you may not add another; but you may replace the old one, on explicit permission from the previous publisher that added the old one.

The author(s) and publisher(s) of the Document do not by this License give permission to use their names for publicity for or to assert or imply endorsement of any Modified Version.

5. COMBINING DOCUMENTS

You may combine the Document with other documents released under this License, under the terms defined in section 4 above for modified versions, provided that you include in the combination all of the Invariant Sections of all of the original documents, unmodified, and list them all as Invariant Sections of your combined work in its license notice, and that you preserve all their Warranty Disclaimers.

The combined work need only contain one copy of this License, and multiple identical Invariant Sections may be replaced with a single copy. If there are multiple Invariant Sections with the same name but different contents, make the title of each such section unique by adding at the end of it, in parentheses, the name of the original author or publisher of that section if known, or else a unique number. Make the same adjustment to the section titles in the list of Invariant Sections in the license notice of the combined work.

In the combination, you must combine any sections Entitled "History" in the various original documents, forming one section Entitled "History"; likewise combine any sections Entitled "Acknowledgements", and any sections Entitled "Dedications". You must delete all sections Entitled "Endorsements".

6. COLLECTIONS OF DOCUMENTS

You may make a collection consisting of the Document and other documents released under this License, and replace the individual copies of this License in the various documents with a single copy that is included in the collection, provided that you follow the rules of this License for verbatim copying of each of the documents in all other respects.

You may extract a single document from such a collection, and distribute it individually under this License, provided you insert a copy of this License into the extracted document, and follow this License in all other respects regarding verbatim copying of that document.

7. AGGREGATION WITH INDEPENDENT WORKS

A compilation of the Document or its derivatives with other separate and independent documents or works, in or on a volume of a storage or distribution medium, is called an "aggregate" if the copyright resulting from the compilation is not used to limit the legal rights of the compilation's users beyond what the individual works permit. When the Document is included in an aggregate, this License does not apply to the other works in the aggregate which are not themselves derivative works of the Document.

If the Cover Text requirement of section 3 is applicable to these copies of the Document, then if the Document is less than one half of the entire aggregate, the Document's Cover Texts may be placed on covers that bracket the Document within the aggregate, or the electronic equivalent of covers if the Document is in electronic form. Otherwise they must appear on printed covers that bracket the whole aggregate.

8. TRANSLATION

Translation is considered a kind of modification, so you may distribute translations of the Document under the terms of section 4. Replacing Invariant Sections with translations requires special permission from their copyright holders, but you may include translations of some or all Invariant Sections in addition to the original versions of these Invariant Sections. You may include a translation of this License, and all the license notices in the Document, and any Warranty Disclaimers, provided that you also include the original English version of this

License and the original versions of those notices and disclaimers. In case of a disagreement between the translation and the original version of this License or a notice or disclaimer, the original version will prevail.

If a section in the Document is Entitled "Acknowledgements", "Dedications", or "History", the requirement (section 4) to Preserve its Title (section 1) will typically require changing the actual title.

9. TERMINATION

You may not copy, modify, sublicense, or distribute the Document except as expressly provided for under this License. Any other attempt to copy, modify, sublicense or distribute the Document is void, and will automatically terminate your rights under this License. However, parties who have received copies, or rights, from you under this License will not have their licenses terminated so long as such parties remain in full compliance.

10. FUTURE REVISIONS OF THIS LICENSE

The Free Software Foundation may publish new, revised versions of the GNU Free Documentation License from time to time. Such new versions will be similar in spirit to the present version, but may differ in detail to address new problems or concerns. See http://www.gnu.org/copyleft/.

Each version of the License is given a distinguishing version number. If the Document specifies that a particular numbered version of this License "or any later version" applies to it, you have the option of following the terms and conditions either of that specified version or of any later version that has been published (not as a draft) by the Free Software Foundation. If the Document does not specify a version number of this License, you may choose any version ever published (not as a draft) by the Free Software Foundation.

ADDENDUM: How to use this License for your documents

To use this License in a document you have written, include a copy of the License in the document and put the following copyright and license notices just after the title page:

ABOUT THE AUTHOR

Jess Schira is a writer who has spent the past ten years writing about a wide assortment of topics that range from bats, to appliance repair, to cotton production, to fiction. When she's not writing, she's usually hanging out with one of her two horses, volunteering at the local 4-H therapeutic riding program or reading.

While *60 Beautiful Bat Facts* represents Jess's first foray into non-fiction publishing, but she seriously doubts it will be her last. She already has a few ideas about upcoming projects. To stay up-to-date on Jess's latest writing projects, check out https://jessschira.com/home/ or follew heron Twitter at @J_Schira or on Facebook.

www.ingramcontent.com/pod-product-compliance
Lightning Source LLC
Chambersburg PA
CBHW030417290526
45786CB00001B/20